IS PUBLIC EDUCATION NECESSARY?

Books by Samuel L. Blumenfeld

HOW TO START YOUR OWN PRIVATE SCHOOL—
AND WHY YOU NEED ONE

THE NEW ILLITERATES

HOW TO TUTOR

THE RETREAT FROM MOTHERHOOD

IS PUBLIC EDUCATION NECESSARY?

ALPHA-PHONICS: A PRIMER FOR BEGINNING
READERS

NEA: TROJAN HORSE IN AMERICAN
EDUCATION

For Ordering Information See Last Four Pages
of Book

IS PUBLIC EDUCATION NECESSARY?

Samuel L. Blumenfeld

THE PARADIGM COMPANY

Boise, Idaho

Library of Congress Cataloging-in-Publication Data

Blumenfeld, Samuel L.
   Is public education necessary?

   Reprint. Originally published: Old Greenwich,
Conn. : Devin-Adair, c1981.
   Bibliography: p.
   Includes index
   1. Public schools—United States—History. I. Title.
LA212.B58   1985   371'.01'0973   85-16721

ISBN 0-941995-04-6

Contents

To
Madeline Gilbert
for
spirit, faith, and wisdom

Preface to the Second Edition

It has been four years since the first publication of this book and everything that has happened in public education since then has proven my thesis to be correct: that not only is public education not necessary, but its continued existence makes true education for the vast majority of American children an impossibility, and it poses a threat to this country's future freedom and security.

The decline in academic and literacy standards has become so scandalous that in April 1983 the National Commission on Excellence in Education wrote in its now historic report: "If an unfriendly foreign power had attempted to impose on America the mediocre educational performance that exists today, we might well have viewed it as an act of war. As it stands, we have allowed this to happen to ourselves."

In addition, the education establishment—notably the National Education Association and its state and local affiliates — works continuously to prevent the American people from exercising freedom of choice in education. In Nebraska, a church school was padlocked by the state and its minister and parents jailed because they refused to bow down to state regulations requiring the hiring of certified teachers and a state-approved curriculum.

The unprecedented decline in academic quality has precipitated a veritable exodus of children from the government schools. More and more parents are choosing private, church and home schools. The phenomenal rise of home-schooling in recent years not only indicates a disenchantment with government schools but with formal schooling in general. The demand for greater educational freedom by parents is causing alarm within the educational establishment which has, for the last one hundred years, depended on the compulsory school attendance laws to supply it with a captive clientele no matter how poor the quality of their education.

Although these laws were enacted to get truants into the schools, they are now being used to deprive parents of their unalienable right to educate their children at home without interference from the state. The most flagrant example of state tyranny carried out in the name of education took place in New Plymouth, Idaho, in November 1984 when the three Shippy brothers and their wives were jailed for home-schooling their 16 children (all *three* mothers were separated from nursing infants by the jailing action).

"All the time we sent our children to public school, we never wanted to," explains Sam Shippy, leader of the clan. "We did it because we had to." What the Shippys objected to most was that the public schools were undermining the religious faith of their children. So in the fall of 1982 they created a home school. But the local school officials charged that the home school did not meet the State's arbitrary education requirements and they took the Shippys to court. The judge agreed with the bureaucrats and the Shippys were ordered to send their children back to school or go to jail. The children were returned to school.

In the fall of 1984, the Shippys once more decided to remove their children from the public schools. Again, the school officials went to court. This time the six parents were jailed and the 16 children placed under foster care. After three weeks in jail, the parents were released since the school age children were again attending public schools. The children were allowed to come home for Christmas.

The parents took another look at the government's home-schooling requirements. They included demands for a "full description of the proposed home school," including names and qualifications of teachers; samples of all instructional materials; "the schedule of instruction by hour, day, and week;" the methods and standards for measuring academic achievement; and "the methods by which normal social growth and peer interaction will be provided." Also, the Shippys' homes would have had to meet state safety regulations for public buildings.

It was clear to the Shippys that they would not be able to meet the government's home-schooling requirements which had obviously been written to discourage home-schooling. Nor would they voluntarily return their children to the public schools. So the court ordered the foster parents to take the children. But the foster parents never showed up. That set the stage for the violence of Thursday, January 10, 1985.

On that day, sheriff's deputies came to the home of Sam and Marquita Shippy and informed them that they had come for their children.

Unwilling and unable to resist, Sam and Marquita helplessly watched as armed authorities seized four boys and two girls, ages 7 to 15. Kicking and screaming, the frightened, crying children were stuffed into cars and driven off. It wasn't until the next day that the distraught parents were informed of their whereabouts.

The judge ordered the children placed indefinitely in foster homes. The four boys were put in a county detention home. The parents' visiting rights were limited to two hours each Sunday.

"God will get them back," Sam said. "The children are ours and are God-given for us to raise. When God wants an end to this, no man will stop it."

"The whole thing is about control," he explained. "They

want to rule over children. That's what's wrong. It isn't education. What good is education if you go around hurting people?"

There are thousands of home-schooling parents all across America who live in fear of the government taking their children away for the crime of educating them at home. The judges seem to have forgotten that most of our founding fathers, including Washington, Jefferson and Franklin, were educated at home. The question then becomes: Do parents have the unalienable right to educate their children at home without interference from the state, or don't they? If they don't, then the state owns the children, and America can no longer be considered a free country.

It should be remembered that before the compulsory school attendance laws were enacted, parents did indeed have that right. Did they lose it, did they willingly and knowingly give it up somewhere along the line?

Educational tyranny is the natural and inevitable result of a government school system controlled by monopoly-minded bureaucrats and educrats. The people of this country must soon decide what is more important to them: parents' rights or compulsory schooling; educational freedom or educational tyranny. Clearly we are reaching the point where these questions will have to be decided one way or another. And that is why this book was written: to help Americans make the right choice — to reject tyranny.

Meanwhile, the very problems described here have generated a host of encouraging responses: new private schools, new textbooks, parents reasserting their rights, the growth of home schooling. But the struggle between parents and educrats will continue as long as the education establishment persists in its' drive for monopoly power. What parents will need most in that struggle, besides courage and fortitude, is knowledge. My colleagues and I have founded a new publication to supply that information and guidance, *The Blumenfeld Education Letter*. I invite you to subscribe. Its motto is taken from HOSEA 4:6: "My people perish for lack of knowledge." Be assured, we shall not lack knowledge.

Boston, June 1985   S.L.B

Preface

SAMUEL BUTLER IS reputed to have said, "God cannot alter the past, but historians can." This book, in a sense, demonstrates how greatly the past has been altered or simply ignored by historians when they have written about public education. My original purpose, however, was not to demonstrate this at all. I had wanted to write a critique of contemporary public education, giving some historical background as a means of explaining the origin of some of our present dilemmas. But one question particularly intrigued me. Knowing that our country began its remarkable history without public education—except for some local common schools in New England—and that the federal Constitution did not even mention education, I was curious as to why Americans had given up educational freedom for educational statism so early in their history, adopting the notion that the government should assume the responsibility of educating our children.

I thought I could find the answer quickly and put it in an opening chapter. Instead, it took me four years and twelve chapters to get the answer. The result is a book in its own right—telling a history that has, until now, not really been told.

Out of this labor came some fascinating discoveries: that American intellectual history is inseparable from its religious history; that public education was never needed, and that literacy in America was higher *before* compulsory public education than it is today; that socialists, who were very active in the public school movement, began operating covertly in secret cells in America as early as 1829, before the word socialism was even invented; that philosophy is more powerful than economics; and that religion, in the long run, is more powerful than philosophy—which implies a great deal about human nature and human destiny.

These things could not have been learned without this intensive venture into the past. There is, understandably, a great deal of interest in the future these days as attested to by the growing fascination with science-fiction. But the time machine that goes backward can be far more rewarding and interesting, for in that world the people are real, their lives completed, the returns in. The past is an incomparable treasure, for it contains the true lessons of human experience. We can see who was right, who was wrong, and who suffered for being either.

The reader will notice that in some instances I have quoted original sources at length. This was done because the truth at times seems unbelievable, and I did not want the reader to have any doubts as to who said, did, or believed what. In instances where I have quoted other historians and biographers, I have done so mainly to verify and substantiate my own narration, so that the reader would understand that, regardless of my own preferences and opinions in this controversy, I have adhered strictly to the facts of history.

If ever a book owed its existence to the interest and help of others, this one is it. The project was begun under a research and writing fellowship from the Institute for Humane Studies at Menlo Park, California. The Institute, founded in 1961, assists scholars who seek to expand our knowledge and understanding of political and economic freedom. I am deeply grateful to George H. Pearson and Kenneth S. Templeton, Jr., of the Institute for their encouragement and support while I grappled with the research problems that changed the character of the original project. I am grateful to William Johnson, director of the Center for Independent Education, for his early reading of the manuscript and helpful suggestions. I wish to thank the able and amiable staff at the Boston Public Library's research facilities, where much of the work was done. Other research facilities and archives used were the Humanities Library at the Massachusetts Institute of Technology; the Widener and Houghton libraries at Harvard University; the Monroe C. Gutman Library at the Harvard Graduate School of Education; the Kress Library of Business and Economics at the Harvard School of Business, whose curator, Kenneth E. Carpenter, was most helpful; the Concord Free Public Library at Concord, Massachusetts; the Bentley College Library; and the New York Public Library. To all of those who facilitated my work in these various institutions I owe a debt of gratitude. My greatest debt, however, is owed to Madeline P. Gilbert, a most sympathetic friend, whose fine editorial sense and insightful assessment of the work in progress was especially valuable to the writer. Without her help and kindness this book could not have been completed.

Boston   —S.L.B.

IS PUBLIC EDUCATION NECESSARY?

1. What is Public Education?

THE MOST COMMONLY held view of public education—the view that persuades many of us to preserve it—is, without doubt, the least accurate, in that it tells us very little about the realities of public education. It is based on a collection of myths which most Americans are quite reluctant to give up. The first myth is that public education is a great democratic institution fundamental to America's prosperity and well-being. The second myth is that public education is necessary as the great equalizer in our society, bringing together children from different ethnic, social, racial, and religious groups and molding them into homogenized "Americans"—which we are all supposed to want to be. Included in that myth is the notion that public education, because of our separation of church and state, is ideologically neutral and preaches no religious doctrine. The third myth is that it provides the best possible education because we are the best possible country spending the most possible money. The fourth myth is that the neighborhood school with its cadre of dedicated teachers and administrators belongs to the community and is answerable to it through an elected school board. The fifth myth is that our

1

society cannot survive without it—that is, public education and all the people who run it.

Why are these myths so hard to discard? Because it requires discarding an even greater myth that props up the whole edifice: that all men are created equal and that government, as the great equalizer, is the most benevolent dispenser of human goodness, generosity, and justice on earth. After all, there are several million benevolent bureaucrats to prove it. But the inequality in human beings is not only the primary fact of the human condition, it is the basic justification for a free society in which human beings in their great diversity can live according to their own values and consciences. The framers of the Declaration of Independence did not mean "created equal" in the egalitarian sense it is used today. Egalitarianism leads to monotonous sameness, in which individuality, free choice, and the expression of individual values are suppressed for a supposed higher value of collective sameness. It is one thing to believe that each unique human being should have the maximum freedom and opportunity to lead his or her life according to that individual's values. But the current trend in public education is to eradicate or deny the existence of differences, particularly sexual, racial, and religious differences, to a point of such confusion that individual identity becomes more and more difficult for youngsters to define, let alone achieve. The only way an individual can achieve a sense of identity today in public education is to rebel against it. And perhaps this is one of the reasons for the steadily increasing destruction of school property by American students.

But identifying the mythology that sustains public education does not necessarily define it. Like any large, complex institution, public education defies simple definition because it is more than one thing. And as such, it must be viewed from a number of perspectives before we can understand what it is and why it creates a myriad of social, intellectual, moral, and financial problems that seem to defy solution.

First, there is its physical existence, which is visible to all of us across the American landscape. The public school, especially the American high school, with its spacious lawns and playing fields, is a quasi-sacred landmark in every American town, as indelibly part of the community government as the town hall, the fire station, the police station, the court house, the public library. But the public school represents something more than merely a government service or the enforcement of law. It represents a body of intellectual, moral, and philosophical values based on the concepts that created it and expressed in the activities that go on within its walls. The youngster who passes through its classrooms emerges indoctrinated in a body of secular values as if he had gone to a sort of governmental parochial school. It may not be a very coherent body of values and it may conflict with the values of his parents or religion; but that very incoherence and conflict, combined with a general philosophical confusion, become the dominant frame of mind of the graduate.

Thus the school building itself seems to have its own spiritual aura, as palpable as that of any church with its peculiarly spiritual architecture. The textbook, with its litany of questions and topics for discussion, takes the place of the prayer book, dispensing moral as well as instructional information. This is particularly true in the social sciences, where a secular humanist view of the world is presented virtually as a revealed religion based on an unquestioned faith in science and materialism. Thus, the rituals of school life replace the rituals of the church to fill the youngster's days with a formalism called "education." No one is sure what it all means, for there is in America as much confusion and vagueness surrounding the word "education" as there is surrounding the word religion.

The physical plant also represents a considerable public

investment and indebtedness. There are about 70,000 elementary schools and 24,000 high schools in America, representing substantial community investments in real property and equipment, all financed by the taxpayer. Maintenance of this property is a perpetual burden on each community, which is periodically reassured by the educators that the burden is well worth bearing.

Taxation for the local school tends to fortify the myth that the community not only controls the school property but also what goes on within its buildings. But the truth is that the neighborhood school is controlled by a national educational and bureaucratic hierarchy completely insulated from local community pressures and answerable only to itself. Curriculum is determined by remote educational commissions in far-off universities, while national school policies are determined by federal judges and the dispensers of federal funds, without which more and more public schools cannot get along. And as the local schools and teacher salaries become more and more dependent on the financial largesse of the Department of Education, they become the instruments of federal policy rather than of the community.

Public education is also an employer in every town and city in the nation. There are over two million teachers and administrators for whom public education is a primary source of livelihood. To them the public school is a place for building careers and professional reputations, with the students merely passing through and the townspeople paying the bills. But the teachers and administrators are on the receiving end of this vast government payroll. For them, public education is an economic lifeline that determines their standard of living and their status in the community.

Public education is therefore money. Apart from national defense, public education now represents the largest single tax-based system of cash flow in the United States. In 1977 about 81 billion dollars flowed through its channels. More than two million educators have developed a vested interest in seeing that the cash not only continues to flow but increases in volume. It is far easier to increase the flow of cash in an established and accepted public channel than to create an entirely new flow of cash, public or private. The statistics for public education bear this out. In 1970 public school enrollment was 45,909,088. In 1977 it had declined to 40,201,000, a loss of some 5,708,088 students. Yet, during that same period, the number of teachers rose from 2,061,115 in 1970 to 2,197,000 in 1977, and total expenditures rose from $44,423,865,000 in 1970 to $81,097,000,000 in 1977. For some reason, five-and-a-half million fewer students required some 135,000 more teachers and 36 more billion dollars.[1]

A cash flow of 81 billion dollars represents considerable economic power for those who can control even a small fraction of it. It is the financial foundation on which the educational "establishment" rests. A vast army of professionals and careerists populate this establishment, from lofty professors of education to lowly first-grade teachers, not to mention the bureaucrats in the state departments of education and the administrators who run the schools. A network of teachers' colleges—like a system of religious seminaries—has been built to train all of those who would become professionals in the educational establishment. In these colleges future teachers and administrators are indoctrinated in the dogma of the public religion. The combination of vast sums of money, sacrosanct institutions of learning, and an army of professionals make up this formidable establishment. Supporting it is an interlocking network of professional organizations and publications, which tend to create an even more closed environment, with its own special language developed for the benefit of those who manage and run the establishment.

The educational establishment's political power is great and grows greater each year. Washington has its well-oiled contingent of educational lobbyists whose only interest is in increasing the volume of cash flow in their direction. The power of the public educator to command so large a slice of the government's revenues is an extraordinary financial success story. However, the fact that Americans are paying an enormous amount of money for an institution that no longer seems to know what it is doing is slowly making its way into the American consciousness.

Public education is also a complex legal structure that not only requires communities to build and operate schools but also places severe limits on the freedom of parents to educate their children according to their own wishes. Every state in the Union, except Mississippi, has a compulsory attendance law, requiring parents to send their children to the government schools or to private schools that meet the requirements set by law. Private schools and home instruction by parents or tutors are permitted provided that certain requirements set by school committees are complied with. In other words, there is no true educational freedom in the United States as there once was. One of the prices we have paid for public education is the loss of educational freedom. The power of the educational establishment depends largely, if not entirely, on the monopoly the law has given it. Obviously, public educators will be the strongest defenders of the legal structure that supports and maintains their monopoly.

Besides being buildings, cash flow, a powerful establishment of professionals, and a legal structure that maintains and regulates it all at taxpayer expense, public education is also a process whereby the American youngster is molded into an American adult. The nature of this process has changed over the years as educational theorists have changed their ideas about education and put them into practice. Today, most of the young adults who emerge from the process read poorly, write miserably, have stunted vocabularies, cannot do arithmetic well, know little geography and less history, and know virtually nothing about the economic system in which they live. At school they fall under strong peer pressure, are introduced to drugs and sexual promiscuity, while their teachers preach the moral relativism of secular humanism as a substitute for the outmoded moral codes of religion. Traditional discipline has been replaced by behavior modification techniques, which include the use of powerful drugs developed by behavioral psychologists. Some students, puzzled by the deeper, spiritual questions of life, which neither the humanists nor behaviorists can address, turn to astrology, black magic, or religious cults for answers. The average graduate, however, tries to make his way into the adult world with a serious deficiency in basic skills and the use of logic. The process, in short, is a stunting of intellectual and spiritual growth. Every September a new generation of American children are fed into this crippling process, and American parents are at a loss to understand why the young adults emerging at the end are the way they are. The school buildings look fine from the outside. But parents are only vaguely aware of what goes on inside.

Last, but hardly least, public education is an instrument of government policy. The public educator, as a government employee, is obliged to implement that policy whatever it may be. At the moment, the integration of the races seems to be the primary goal of the government's social engineers. Through the courts, the social engineers, in concert with various interest groups, have been able to use the government schools as instruments of social change. Costly, wasteful, disruptive forced-busing edicts have been handed down by federal judges, requiring the massive crosstown movement of students who may no longer attend their neighborhood schools because of their skin color. The public schools, in other words, are required to discriminate on the basis of skin color in order to eliminate racial prejudice! All of this is permitted to take place despite the existence of a serious energy shortage, the threat of fuel rationing, and the enormous cost the program imposes on the taxpayer. What educative value this massive forced integration program may have has not been determined and probably never will be. But what has been clearly demonstrated is that the American public educator is quite willing to do whatever the government bids him or her do—today, in favor of racial integration, tomorrow, in favor of something else. This does not bode well for American freedom. But we ought not to be surprised, since totalitarian governments have long considered public education as their most important tool for indoctrinating and controlling the young.

Public educators are not freedom fighters. They are more likely to be the loyal servants of the political master, the willing tools of government dictates. Any teacher who is not will leave public education on his own or will be forced out by his colleagues.

It is obvious that public education is far more than simply a community system of free instruction financed by taxes. It is so much more that we must ask ourselves if this is really what we want, what we bargained for. When all is said and done, we must ask ourselves if public education, as it has become, is really necessary at all. Does it educate? *Can* it educate? Public educators will argue that it all depends on what you mean by education. Since there is no agreement in this country on the meaning of education, the latter becomes impossible under the circumstances. In the days of educational freedom it was possible to deal with education more realistically. The values one expected to gain from education were quite apparent and identifiable. The benefits of acquiring strong academic skills were understood by parents, students, and teachers. This is no longer the case in our socialized system, where the social dominates the academic, where mythology supersedes objective history, and where the mystique of "mind expansion" has replaced the concrete world of skills.

Which brings us to a basic question: Why did Americans give up educational freedom for educational statism so early in their history? The answer is not to be found in the standard histories, because it has always been assumed by educational historians that whatever preceded public education had to be less desirable than, and therefore inferior to, what came after. Otherwise, why would Americans have adopted public education? But the truth is that the system that prevailed prior to the introduction of public education and compulsory attendance was not only quite adequate for the young nation, but served the public need far better than anything we have today.

The reasons why this country adopted universal public education really had very little to do with education. This is what history teaches us, and this is what we must now carefully consider. Public education does not fail in a totalitarian state where its purposes are clearly defined by the rulers. But in a country like our own, the incompatibility of public education with the values of a free society have become more and more apparent each year. This incompatibility has created insoluble, ongoing conflicts within our society. That is why it is necessary to go back to the origins. For if we discover that the seeds of public education's failures are to be found in the errors of its original premises, then we shall know that it was doomed from the start and that the only cure to its many chronic ills may be its total dismantlement.

2. Beginnings

THE MODERN IDEA of popular education—that is, education for everyone—first arose in Europe during the Protestant Reformation when Papal authority was replaced by Biblical authority. Since the Protestant rebellion against Rome had arisen in part as a result of Biblical study and interpretation, it became obvious to Protestant leaders that if the Reform movement were to survive and flourish, widespread Biblical literacy, at all levels of society, would be absolutely necessary. The Bible was to be the moral and spiritual authority in every man's life, and therefore an intimate knowledge of it was imperative if a new Protestant social order were to take root.

In 1524, Martin Luther, in his famous letter to the German princes, urged the establishment of public schools and compulsory attendance by all children. Luther himself had translated the New Testament into German to make its message available to the common people. In persuading the German rulers to apply state power in the establishment of schools, the leader of the Reformation argued that if the state could compel its citizens to serve in the military in time of war, it had a right to compel its people to send their children to school to better arm themselves in man's never-ending struggle against the devil.

The German rulers agreed with Luther and subsequently established state-supported schools in Gotha and Thuringia. In 1528, schools were established in Saxony according to a plan drawn up by Luther himself. The first compulsory attendance system was established in Württemberg in 1559 by the duke of Württemberg. Detailed attendance records were kept, and fines levied on the parents of truants. The Saxon and Württemberg systems became the models for compulsory public schools in most of the Protestant German states and later in Prussia.

The Reform movement was not the only impetus to popular education. The invention of moveable type in Europe around 1450, the expansion of book publishing (twenty complete translations of the Bible alone were printed in Germany between 1466 and 1522), the growth of universities, the expansion of commerce, and the emergence of a middle class in the towns increased the desire and need for literacy throughout society. Indeed, literacy was already so widespread among the middle class in Germany prior to the Reformation that this fact alone made the Reformation possible. For the first time in human history a great reading public judged the validity of revolutionary ideas through a mass medium—the book. It was through the printed book that Luther was able to make precise, uniform and indelible impressions upon the minds of men in Europe.

In 1536, in Geneva, Switzerland, at the urging of the Protestant reformers there, the town's General Assembly created public schools for the same religious reasons they had been established in Germany. Later, under the leadership of John Calvin, the educational system was more fully developed to become a very important part of the new religious order. Calvin, a remarkable Frenchman whose transcendent ability as a theologian was enhanced by a brilliant intellect and superb literary style, clearly recognized the role that education would have to play in securing the gains of the Reformation and aiding its spread.

It was the Academy in Geneva, founded in 1559 by Calvin, that was considered the crown of the Reformer's work. It was second only to his *Institutes of the Christian Religion* as a force in the spread of Calvinism. No school in all of Protestantism ranked higher in public repute for a century after Calvin's death in 1564. It attracted students from all over Europe.

In Geneva, under the famous *Ordonnances* of 1541, in which the church was granted a measure of independence and self-government unknown elsewhere, an entire school system under ecclesiastical control was created. One Calvin biographer wrote:

> Calvin viewed the office of teacher as of divine appointment, having as its highest duty that of educating "the faithful in sound doctrine" from the Old and New Testaments. But he felt no less strongly that before the learner "can profit by such lessons he must first be instructed in the languages and worldly sciences." Calvin therefore sought to develop the Genevan school system under this ecclesiastical conception of the teachership. A "learned and expert man" was to be appointed as head of the school, and teacher-in-chief, with "readers" to give secondary instruction, and "bachelors" to teach the "little children" under his control. The teacher was reckoned in the ministry, put under its disciplinary regulations; and, in Calvin's intention, was to be installed on ministerial approval,—an exercise of ministerial authority which the jealous Little Council modified by the provision that he first be "presented" to the government and examined in the presence of two of its members. In Calvin's judgment, the school was an integral factor in the religious training of the community.[1]

Calvinists elsewhere followed the example set in Geneva. For the sake of maintaining doctrinal purity and survival in politically hostile environments, the school became a vital adjunct to the church. The Puritans who founded the Massachusetts Bay Colony in 1630 brought these ideas with them to the New World. They had left England in order to be free to create in the wilderness as perfect a Calvinist society as they could, as free from interference from king or the hierarchal Anglican church as possible. Their charter permitted them to govern themselves—to elect their own governor and legislators. They organized their town churches in the Congregational form as outlined by Calvin in his *Institutes*. The church, composed of God's elect, was to maintain ecclesiastical independence of the civil authority and exert an exacting but brotherly discipline over its members up to the point of excommunication. The church membership elected its ministers and other officers, and no church dominated any other church.

As for civil government, "Its object," wrote Calvin, "is not merely to enable men to breathe, eat, drink, and be warmed (though it certainly includes all of these, while it enables them to live together); this, I say, is not its only object, but it is, that no idolatry, no blasphemy against the name of God, no calumnies against his truth, nor other offences to religion, break out and be disseminated among the people; that the public quiet be not disturbed, that every man's property be kept secure, that men may carry on innocent commerce with each other, that honesty and modesty be cultivated; in short, that a public form of religion may exist among Christians, and humanity among men." Thus, in the ideal Calvinist society, the civil government served the broader purposes of religion rather than vice versa. Laws and courts were created "to foster and maintain the external worship of God, to defend sound doctrine and the condition of the Church, to adapt our conduct to human society, to form our manners to civil justice, to conciliate us to each other, to cherish common peace and tranquillity."[2]

In Germany, Luther had placed the Reform church under the control of the princes. In Geneva, Calvin insisted that the Church be self-governing but maintain an active partnership with the civil government. All, however, were subservient to God.

As for monarchs, Calvin took great pleasure in cutting them down to size. "Great kings," he wrote, "should not think it a disgrace to them to prostrate themselves suppliantly before Christ, the King of kings; nor ought they to be displeased at being judged by the Church. For seeing they seldom hear anything in their courts but mere flattery, the more necessary is it that the Lord should correct them by the mouths of his priests."[3]

It is for this reason that monarchs in Europe in general distrusted Calvinists. The latter, who considered themselves to be God's elect, found it their duty to resist any king or government that tried to exact an allegiance or loyalty higher than the one they owed to God. Calvin had written, "We are subject to the men who rule over us, but subject only in the Lord. If they command anything against Him let us not pay the least regard to it, nor be moved by all the dignity which they possess as magistrates—a dignity to which no injury is done when it is subordinated to the special and truly supreme power of God."[4]

The Puritans in the Massachusetts Bay Colony, in a position to build a new society from the ground up, endeavored to create a civil government that would indeed serve the higher purposes of religion. To do so, they limited the voting franchise to church members only, thus guaranteeing a civil government maintained in the hands of the elect. The Bible commonwealth was thereby established as a working partnership between church and civil authority, over which God's law reigned supreme.

Not everyone who migrated to Massachusetts agreed with this arrangement. The earliest and most notable dissenter was Roger Williams, a devout Calvinist who believed that the path to heaven was so straight and narrow that no community could possibly be made up entirely of true believers. Therefore, he concluded, the best policy was not to mix church and state. Needless to say, the Massachusetts magistrates disagreed with him. "The prosperity of church and commonwealth," said one of them, "are twisted together. Break one cord, you weaken and break the other also."[5] In 1636 Williams was banished from the colony. He subsequently migrated southward, where he established the colony of Rhode Island based on complete religious tolerance and a clear separation of church and civil government.

In the same year that Williams was banished, barely six years after the first settlement of Boston, the Massachusetts legislature, known as the General Court, began to lay the foundation of another important institution of the Bible commonwealth: its education system. It appropriated 400 pounds toward the establishment of what was to become Harvard College. Considering that there were less than 5,000 persons in the entire colony at the time and that the grant was larger than all of the taxes levied on the colony in a single year, it indicated how essential education was considered in the Bible commonwealth. Calvin had stressed the importance of an intelligent, learned clergy, knowledgeable in Hebrew, Latin, and Greek, familiar with the writings of the Church Fathers, the Scholastic Philosophers, and the Reformers. He had also stressed the secular and economic benefits of education. All of this greatly appealed to the Puritan leaders, among whom were a large number of graduates from Oxford and Cambridge.

In 1638, John Harvard, one of the founders of the college, died, leaving to the new institution the sum of 778 pounds and a library of over three hundred books, a considerable legacy for that period. In appreciation of this, the college was named after him. In 1640 the legislature granted to the college the income from the Charlestown ferry, and in 1642 the Governor, along with the magistrates, teachers, and elders, were empowered to establish statutes and constitutions for the infant institution. In 1650, a charter was granted.

Meanwhile, in 1642, the General Court enacted its first law concerning the education of the colony's children. The text of the law summed up the colonists' concerns:

> Forasmuch as the good education of children is of singular behoof and benefit to any commonwealth; and whereas many parents and masters are too indulgent and negligent of their duty in this kind:
>
> It is therefore ordered by this Court and the authority thereof, That the selectmen of every town, in the several precincts and quarters where they dwell, shall have a vigilant eye over their brethren and neighbors, to see, first, that none of them shall suffer so much barbarism in any of their families, as not to endeavor to teach, by themselves or others, their children and apprentices as much learning as may enable them perfectly to read the English tongue, and knowledge of the capital laws, upon penalty of twenty shillings for each neglect therein; also, that all masters of families do, once a week, at least, catechise their children and servants in the grounds and principles of religion, and if any be unable to do so much, that then, at the least, they procure such children or apprentices to learn some short orthodox catechisms, without book, that they may be able to answer to the questions that shall be propounded to them out of such catechisms by their parents or masters, or any of the selectmen, where they shall call them to a trial of what they have learned in this kind. . . .

The selectmen were expected to exert a quasi-ecclesiastical discipline over their communities in matters of education. This was quite in keeping with Calvin's idea of church discipline. For, while Christian doctrine was the "life of the Church," discipline was the "sinews" whereby the church was held together. "All who either wish that discipline were abolished," wrote Calvin, "or who impede the restoration of it, whether they do this of design or through thoughtlessness, certainly aim at the complete devastation of the Church. For what will be the result if everyone is allowed to do as he pleases? But this must happen if to the preaching of the gospel are not added private admonition, correction, and similar methods of maintaining doctrine and not allowing it to become lethargic. Discipline, therefore, is a kind of curb to restrain and tame those who war against the doctrine of Christ, or it is a kind of stimulus by which the indifferent are aroused."[6]

In addition to the education law, the following School Code was enacted in 1647. It was the first public school law to be passed in the English colonies:

It being one chief project of that old deluder, Satan, to keep man from the knowledge of the Scriptures, as in former times, keeping them in an unknown tongue, so in these latter times, by persuading from the use of tongues, so that at least the true sense and meaning of the original might be clouded and corrupted with false glosses of deceivers; and to the end that learning may not be buried in the grave of our forefathers, in church and commonwealth, the Lord assisting our endeavors;

It is therefore ordered by this Court and authority thereof, That every township within this jurisdiction, after the Lord hath increased them to the number of fifty householders, shall then forthwith appoint one within their town to teach all such children as shall resort to him, to write and read, whose wages shall be paid, either by the parents or masters of such children, or by the inhabitants in general, by way of supply, as the major part of those who order the prudentials of the town shall appoint; provided that those who send their children be not oppressed by paying much more than they can have them taught for in other towns.

And it is further ordered, That where any town shall increase to the number of one hundred families or householders, they shall set up a grammar school, the masters thereof being able to instruct youths so far as they may be fitted for the university, and if any other town neglect the performance hereof above one year, then every such town shall pay five pounds per annum to the next such school, till they shall perform this order.

Thus, the emphasis on education was twofold: to encourage learning in general and religious study in particular. In a community committed to doctrinal purity, compulsory education was as much a religious discipline as it was a means of insuring literacy.

Because its ruling elect insisted on doctrinal purity, Massachusetts, of all the English colonies, became the least tolerant of publicly expressed heretical teachings. As Perry Miller, the historian, aptly describes it: "Those who did not hold with the ideals entertained by the righteous, or who believed God had preached other principles, or who desired that in religious belief, morality, and ecclesiastical preferences all men should be left at liberty to do as they would—such persons had every liberty, as Nathaniel Ward said, to stay away from New England. If they did come, they were expected to keep their opinions to themselves; if they discussed them in public or attempted to act upon them, they were exiled; if they persisted in returning, they were cast out again; if they still came back, as did four Quakers, they were hanged on Boston Common."[7]

Thus, the Massachusetts education laws of 1642, 1647, and 1648, which educational historians cite as the basis of American public education, must be understood in the context of the society that enacted them. They were the ordinances of a religious community upholding the orthodoxy of its doctrines and providing for its future leadership. None of the other English colonies, with the exception of Connecticut which had been settled by Massachusetts Calvinists, enacted such education laws. The other colonies, settled by a variety of religious sects and governed by charters that gave the crown and the Church of England greater power and influence than they had in New England, left education entirely up to the parents, individual religious sects, private teachers and philanthropy.

The Puritan oligarchy governed Massachusetts until their charter was revoked by Charles II in 1684. In 1691 a new charter was procured for the colony, which greatly diminished the power of the Congregationalists. Henceforth, the governor would be appointed by the king and the voting franchise would rest upon property rather than membership in a Congregational church. It spelled the legal end to the Bible commonwealth.

Under the new charter, the General Court tried to reinstate all of the laws in effect before the colony lost its charter. But the king's Privy Council vetoed the action. In 1692, the General Court reenacted the compulsory education law of 1647, but now the measure was resisted and ineffectively obeyed. In 1701, the law was stiffened. But it had no great effect. In 1718, fines on scofflaw towns were raised to new heights. But towns found a variety of loopholes to get around compliance with the law.

In all, the Bible commonwealth lasted no more than sixty years. The growth of the colony, the development of trade, the influx of other religious sects, the increased general prosperity, the emergence of religious liberalism, and the revocation of the original charter greatly weakened the hold of the austere Puritan orthodoxy. New secular interests began to take the place of religion as the main topics of thought and conversation. With the end of religious discipline came a relaxation of compliance with the school laws. This did not mean a loss of interest in education. It meant a shift in emphasis and a change in organization in keeping with the other changes taking place in colonial society. Private academies run by educator proprietors sprang up to teach the more practical commercial subjects. By 1720 Boston had far more private schools than public ones, and by the close of the American Revolution, many towns had no common schools—as the public schools were then called—at all.

Because of the stress Puritan society placed on education, Massachusetts gained a reputation for having the best schools in the English colonies. But the other colonies were not far behind. All of the Protestant sects placed high value on education. Colleges were founded in Virginia (1693), Connecticut (1701), New Jersey (1746 and 1766), New York (1754), Pennsylvania (1755), Rhode Island (1764), and New Hampshire (1770). All were private colleges, and there were usually preparatory academies in the larger towns to supply the students.

Prof. Lawrence Cremin, in his study on colonial education, estimated that, based on the evidence of signatures on deeds, wills, militia rolls, and voting rosters, adult male literacy in the American colonies ran from 70 to 100 per cent. It was this high literacy that, indeed, made the American Revolution possible. Like the Reformation, it was a Revolution among literate men in which the written word was crucial to the spread of revolutionary ideas and projects. Prof. Cremin writes:

> If one considers the 89 men who signed either the Declaration of Independence or the Constitution or both, it is clear that the group is a collective outcome of provincial education in all its richness and diversity. Of the 56 signers of the Declaration, 22 were products of the provincial colleges, 2 had attended the academy conducted by Francis Alison at New London, Pennsylvania, and the others represented every conceivable combination of parental, church, apprenticeship, school, tutorial, and self-education, including some who studied abroad. Of the 33 signers of the Constitution, who had not also signed the Declaration, 14 were products of the provincial colleges, one was a product of the Newark Academy, and the remainder spanned the same wide range of alternatives.[8]

Yet, out of such educational freedom and diversity came enough consensus and agreement to make possible not only the Declaration of Independence, but also the pursuit of a long, difficult war against Great Britain, and the establishment of a national government based on an ingenious Constitution. Anyone who reads the debates and essential documents of that period must conclude that colonial education was of a very high order and that its freedom from government control was conducive to the spirit of independence the colonists had.

The fact is that the men who founded the United States were educated under the freest conditions possible. George Washington was educated by his father and half-brother. Benjamin Franklin was taught to read by his father and attended a private school for writing and arithmetic. Thomas Jefferson studied Latin and Greek under a tutor. Of the 117 men who signed the Declaration of Independence, the Articles of Confederation, and the Constitution, one out of three had had only a few months of formal schooling, and only one in four had gone to college.

It is therefore not surprising that the United States Constitution made no mention of education in its provisions. Its framers left education up to the parents, communities, churches, educator proprietors of schools, and the individual states. There were some statesmen, like Thomas Jefferson and John Adams, who did advocate free, state-supported education on a rather modest scale. But they were clearly in the minority. Thus, at the beginning of the American nation, education, except for some tax-supported common schools in New England, was on a completely laissez-faire basis.

In 1780, Massachusetts drafted a new constitution in which was inserted an article that both confirmed the special legal status of Harvard and emphasized the commonwealth's continued interest in public education. John

Adams framed the article, and its strongest support came from the Harvard-Boston establishment, made up mostly of Harvard graduates, who wanted to maintain the link between government and education. Harvard had been created with the help of a government grant and had been the recipient of many such grants over the years. In addition, members of the government had been on the Harvard Board of Overseers since 1642. The new constitution maintained the continuity of that relationship.

In 1789, Massachusetts entered the Union and enacted the first comprehensive state school law in the new nation. Although many towns in the commonwealth had abandoned the common schools entirely during the Revolutionary War and there were many citizens who would have liked to be relieved of tax-supported education altogether, the legislators decided to reinstate the common school system. No matter how much they might have disagreed on matters of theology, the legislators agreed for the most part on the social value of the common schools, even though the trend toward private education was clearly evident throughout the state. In fact, during the 18th century the towns either openly defied the compulsory school law or were generally indifferent to it. If there were any common schools still in existence in 1789, it was by force of law rather than by popular will.

The new law merely maintained the continuity of the Puritan educational legacy. The law required every town to support an elementary school for six months out of the year. Larger towns were required to maintain at least one school all year round. Grammar schools that prepared students for the Boston Latin school had to be maintained in towns containing two hundred families or more. To justify this additional tax burden on the citizens, the advocates of the law argued that the government schools were needed to inculcate among the young respect and devotion to America's political, moral, and religious institutions.

What it indicated was that the religious discipline that had given rise to the compulsory school law of 1647, over which the elect exerted control, had been replaced by a concept of social discipline exerted by a governing elite. The idea that individual behavior should be restrained or regulated through some instrument in the hands of government had survived the transition from Bible commonwealth to republicanism.

In complying with the new state law, Boston passed its own Education Act of 1789 and thereby laid the foundation for the first system of public schools in any American city. But before the law was passed, there was a heated battle over the issue of control. The conservatives had advocated the same direct control of the schools by the town selectmen and their appointees as had prevailed prior to 1789. But a new, more democratically oriented faction wanted the schools to be controlled by an elected committee with representatives from each ward of the city. Federalists like John Adams, Fisher Ames and Daniel Cony opposed the idea because it negated the very concept of a government school system controlled by a moral elite. Adams was one of those who greatly distrusted democracy and had written that it "never lasts long. It soon wastes, exhausts, and murders itself." While Adams was a theological liberal, he had nevertheless inherited the Calvinist distrust for pure democracy which the Genevan reformer disfavored because of its strong "tendency to sedition." Calvin favored an aristocracy modified by popular government—which is what the American republic resembled most at its start.

The democratic faction won. Its success was mainly due to the efforts of its leader, Samuel Adams, the fiery revolutionary, who, on the matter of public education, differed with his cousin John only on the issue of control. The egalitarians won, and henceforth the school committee would be chosen by popular vote. But if Boston had a public school system, it was hardly a comprehensive one. All primary education was still private, and a child had to be able to read and write to be eligible for the public grammar school at age seven. In addition, the public grammer schools had to compete with a large number of private schools for the school-age population. Also, the crowning glory of the public system was not a school for the poor but the elitist Boston Latin School, which provided, at public expense, the classical preparatory training needed by those intent on pursuing higher studies at Harvard College. Some of its students came from the wealthiest families in Boston. Thus, the purpose of the city school system was not to insure literacy for all or to provide special educational opportunities for the poor. Its purpose was simply to perpetuate a government institution created in earlier times, which could now serve a socially useful purpose in the new political order.

A large body of influential people stood to benefit from the continuation of the common school system. These included educators, textbook writers, publishers and suppliers, all of whom had a vested interest in this tax-supported cash-flow system. In fact, the authors of the Boston Educational Reorganization Act of 1789 took whatever prudent measures they could to enlarge the public school's constituency. The new system was to be coeducational, and henceforth Boston Latin teachers were forbidden to offer private tutoring to students preparing to enter the Latin School from private schools. Students from private schools were now permitted to attend the public grammar school while also attending the Latin School. These measures increased public school expenditures.

Elsewhere in New England, Connecticut and New Hampshire adopted state education laws similar to those in Massachusetts. They too voted to maintain the old Calvinist institutions for new social purposes. Rhode Island, however, abstained. Since the common schools were viewed there as a religious institution controlled by the church that had created them, they had no place in a society which maintained a strict separation of church and state. "To compel a citizen to support a school would have been to violate the right of conscience," commented the *North American Review* in 1848. "To compel him to educate his children would have been an invasion of his rights as a free-born Rhode Islander, which would not be endured."[9] In 1800, however, an attempt was made to establish public schools in Rhode Island, but the law was repealed in 1803.

In Virginia, in 1779, Thomas Jefferson submitted a bill to the legislature that would have established a compulsory statewide public school system. It was, however, an idea that Virginians were not quite ready for. They set aside the bill until 1796 when they passed it in a noncompulsory and therefore ineffective form. Without compulsion, public education could not come into being. Citizens simply refused to tax themselves for public schools when the private sector seemed to be satisfying the need quite well.

Although one of the arguments in favor of public schools was that it provided equal education for the poor, it could be counter-argued that it was possible to provide education for the poor through other means. Pennsylvania, for example, passed a law providing tuition grants to poor children so that they could attend private schools. Other states made similar provisions.

While the new national government left educational matters entirely up to the states, its land grant policies did encourage the establishment of schools. In 1785 and 1787, the Continental Congress, in order to raise revenue to pay its heavy Revolutionary War debts, passed two Land Ordinances whereby it sold millions of acres of public lands in six-mile-square areas called "Congressional townships." Each township was divided into thirty-six equal parcels of one-mile square for sale to the public. The Ordinance prohibited the sale of section #16 in each township, and reserved that section "for the maintenance of public schools, within the said township." Income from the use of that land could be applied to a general school fund. While the purpose of the land grants was to provide incentives to those who wished to establish communities in sparsely settled areas, the net effect was to encourage state governments to become involved in subsidizing education.

In New York State, in 1795, the legislature created a large school fund based on income from the land grants. Towns and cities were encouraged to take advantage of the fund and establish schools. Many towns did indeed establish common schools, but these were only partially financed by the state fund. The counties were required to raise matching funds, and tuition was also paid by parents. While there was no law compelling towns to establish common schools, the existence of the fund did much to encourage their development. Since most of the inhabitants of Upper New York State were migrants from New England, the common school was a familiar idea to them. That, plus the state subsidy, made it easy to accept the idea of government involvement in education.

3. The Emergence of a Liberal Elite

APART FROM NEW ENGLAND, where tax-supported schools existed under state law, the United States, from 1789 to 1835, had a completely laissez-faire system of education. Although the idea of the town-supported common school had spread westward with the migration of New Englanders and was encouraged by the federal land grants, there were no compulsory attendance laws anywhere. Parents educated their children as they wished: at home with tutors, at private academies, or church schools. This did not mean that poor children were neglected. Some states paid the tuition of poor children, enabling them to attend the private school of their choice. Virtually every large city in the country had its "free-school" societies that built and operated schools for the poor and were supported by the community's leading benefactors and philanthropists. Such schools were considered extremely worthwhile causes for philanthropy. Often these schools also received small grants from local governments in recognition of their public service. Thus, there was no need for any child to go without an education. The rate of literacy in the United States then was probably higher than it is today.

27

Nor were these free schools inferior to the private schools. The McKim School in Baltimore, for example, founded in 1817 on a bequest of John McKim, was designed as a replica of the temple of Theseus at Athens and is today regarded as one of Baltimore's architectural treasures. In Philadelphia, an entire system of charity schools was created around the William Penn Charter School, founded by Quakers in 1701. Its support came from rents, gifts, legacies and fees, but instruction for the poor was always free.

Even in New England, the spirit of educational freedom had begun to erode support for the public schools. Despite the new school laws of 1789 which reaffirmed the concept of public schools, many towns were abandoning the tax-supported common school for the private academy. Free-market forces were slowly shifting public favor from the poorly managed public school to the more efficiently managed private school. Only in Boston did the public schools receive unflagging public support despite the competition from private academies, mainly because of a special situation in that city: the growth of the Unitarian movement which strongly favored public education.

It is ironic that Unitarianism, the heresy that Calvin considered to be the most dangerous, should have arisen in the heart of the Puritan commonwealth. But it was clearly a reaction against the Calvinist world view, with its pessimistic evaluation of human nature; its awesome, omnipotent God, more to be feared than loved; its doctrine of salvation limited to the elect.

Actually, Unitarianism first arose in Europe at about the same time that Calvin was formulating his own view of Christianity. It arose as a rebellion against the orthodox doctrine of the Trinity, and it specifically denied the divinity of Christ. The most noted promoter of this idea was Michel Servetus (1511-1553), a Spanish physician, whose treatise, *De Trinitatis Erroribus*, was published in 1531, five years before the first edition of Calvin's *Institutes* was published. In the ensuing years a considerable antagonism developed between Calvin and Servetus which was climaxed by the latter's arrest in Geneva in 1553. Servetus was tried for heresy, found guilty and burned at the stake.

Servetus's heresy was considered particularly subversive by Catholics as well as Calvinists and other Protestants because it undermined the entire foundation of Christianity which is based on the divinity of Christ. The Old Testament teaches that God revealed himself to Abraham and made a covenant with him and his descendants. The New Testament teaches that Christ, God's son, was sent by God to permit the rest of fallen mankind to enjoy a similar covenant. Christ, as mediator between man and God, provided the means whereby those enlightened by the Holy Spirit could become one with God and thereby achieve everlasting life. It was through Christ that the God of Abraham had made himself accessible to the elect in the whole of humanity. Thus, the Trinity—Father, Son, and Holy Spirit—was the essential cornerstone of Christianity. To deny it was to make the entire process of salvation through grace theologically unworkable. Unitarianism required nothing less than a new concept of God, if not the creation of a new god.

All of this was quite well understood by the New England Calvinists, who watched Unitarianism grow within their midst with no small alarm. Unitarianism had come to England, mainly through the teachings of Socinus, in the middle 1600s. It crossed the Atlantic and gained a foothold at Harvard College where the first "liberal" president was elected in 1707. That election was the beginning of a century-long struggle between orthodox Calvinists and religious liberals for control of Harvard. The "Great Awakening" religious revival led by Jonathan Edwards in 1735 was in part a strong popular reaction against the liberal tendencies of the clerical elite. In 1785, under the ministry of Harvard-educated Unitarian James Freeman, the congregation of King's Chapel in Boston purged their Anglican liturgy of all references to the Trinity, thus establishing the first Unitarian church in America. Twenty years later the Unitarians finally took full control of Harvard.

The takeover of Harvard in 1805 by the Unitarians is probably the most important intellectual event in American history—at least from the standpoint of education. The circumstances that signaled the takeover were the election of liberal theologian Henry Ware as Hollis Professor of Divinity and the subsequent retreat of the Calvinists to a new seminary of their own in Andover. From then on Harvard became the Unitarian Vatican, so to speak, dispensing a religious and secular liberalism that was to have profound and enduring effects on the evolution of American cultural, moral, and social values. It was, in effect, the beginning of the long journey to the secular humanist world view that now dominates American culture.

It is improbable that we shall find a more crucial turning point in American intellectual history, and it is not without significance that it involved such basic issues as the nature of man, the nature of God, and the nature of evil. While the controversy over the Hollis professorship had been a long time in the making, the election of Ware was the opening salvo of a long, bitter, protracted struggle between Unitarians and Calvinists for control of the cultural and religious institutions of New England and for the minds and hearts of its people. It made Harvard not only the seat of liberalism but also, by necessity, the seat of anti-Calvinism. There was no such thing as neutral ground, or academic impartiality, in this religious struggle, and therefore Harvard's strong anti-Calvinist bias became part of the world view it imparted to its students.

The primary Calvinist doctrine the Unitarians rebelled against was that concerning man's nature. Calvin argued that it was Adam's innate depravity that caused him to fall from grace in the Garden of Eden. "Let Adam excuse himself as he may," wrote Calvin, "saying that he was deceived by the enticements of the wife God gave him; within himself will be found the fatal poison of infidelity, within himself the worst counsellor of all which is ambition, within himself the diabolical torch of pride."[1]

It was Adam's disobedience to God's commandment that was the cause of man's suffering and mortality, the cause of his damnation. In practical terms, it meant that since man was by his very nature corrupt, only obedience to God's law could save him from the miserable consequences of his own unbridled depravity.

The Unitarians who took over Harvard in 1805 were all brought up in a Puritan society of high moral standards. They were the beneficiaries of the industry and productivity of their ancestors who lived within the framework of Calvinist order. Within that framework, few men were permitted the opportunity to express their potential corruption to the full. People seemed by nature to be decent, cooperative, responsible, and benevolent. Children, especially, appeared angelic and pure of heart. It hardly seemed that man was the depraved, corrupt, fallen creature depicted by Calvin, Augustine, and other theologians. On the contrary, it seemed that man was innately good, rational, benevolent, and cooperative. It was civilization that caused corruption, said Rousseau. Yes, man did have his faults, but he was eminently perfectible. All he really needed to be saved from his negative impulses was the right education. To the Unitarians, therefore, education became the road to salvation.

It is easy to find the sources of Unitarian optimism. The American people, strongly Christian in moral beliefs, had waged a successful war of independence and had created the best of all possible governments in the best of all possible worlds. Science was achieving breakthroughs in human knowledge, and mankind was on the threshold of the industrial era. People were freeing themselves from political tyranny. They were now ready, for the sake of intellectual and moral freedom, to free themselves from what they believed to be theological tyranny. There were no limits to the good that man could achieve with the guidance of education.

There was, of course, the nagging problem of evil. What caused it? How could it be eliminated? William Ellery Channing (1790-1842), who was graduated from Harvard College in 1798 and became the leader of the Unitarian movement, touched on the problem in a letter written in 1799 to William Shaw, a former classmate. In his biography of Channing, Arthur Brown describes the contents of that letter:

> Avarice was the chief obstacle to human progress, [Channing] declared. The only way to eliminate it was to establish a community of property. Convinced that virtue and benevolence were natural to man, he blamed selfishness and greed upon the false ideas of superiority of the body over the mind and the separation of individual interest from that of the community as a whole. Men must be educated to understand that the powers and dignity of their minds were unlimited. To this end he sketched, in his letters to Shaw and Arthur Walter, another Harvard classmate, a scheme for a fraternal organization that would have as its goal the foundation of human happiness.[2]

Although Channing was later to modify his communist ideas concerning property, he typified the liberal New Englander's approach to the problem of evil. Evil was created by the way society was organized, not by anything innately evil in men. Change society and evil could be eliminated.

Channing and his classmates, who were to become leaders of the Unitarian elite, had become religious liberals while at Harvard. Arthur Brown writes:

At Harvard, Channing . . . discovered the Edinburgh Enlightenment. Through Professor David Tappan and Harvard in general, he discovered Francis Hutcheson and his theory of benevolence and then the other Scottish liberals. While reading Hutcheson's *Inquiry* one day in his favorite retreat, he came upon the doctrine of an innate moral sense and the theory of disinterested benevolence. . . . From this time on, he remained convinced that altruism rather than self-love provided the only suitable motive for human beings living in a world of order and beauty.[3]

Harvard, indeed, became the fountainhead of a new cultural, social, and moral elite centered around Unitarianism. By 1805, that elite was strong enough to put its ideas in motion and exert its influences more broadly. Unitarian leaders had coalesced around the Boston Anthology Society, a highly influential literary club that published the *Monthly Anthology and Boston Review*. The members met in private homes to discuss literature, politics, education, theology, and other topics of the day. Its members included William Emerson (Harvard 1789), minister at the First Unitarian Church and father of Ralph Waldo; Joseph Buckminster (Harvard 1800), minister at the fashionable Brattle Street Church; William Shaw (Harvard 1798), secretary to President John Adams and founder of the Boston Athenaeum in 1807; Joseph Tuckerman (Harvard 1798), who became Channing's minister-at-large to the poor; William Tudor (Harvard 1798), future editor of the influential *North American Review;* George Ticknor (Dartmouth 1807), who became the epitome of the Boston Brahmin, a Harvard professor, and the arbiter of taste and social mores; Samuel Thacher (Harvard 1804), acting headmaster at Boston Latin School, later librarian at Harvard and then a Unitarian minister; John T. Kirkland (Harvard 1789), a Unitarian minister who became both president of the Anthology Society and of Harvard in 1810; Andrews Norton

(Harvard 1804), who, as professor of divinity at Harvard, became known as the Unitarian Pope; Alexander Everett (Harvard 1806), older brother of Edward Everett and assistant to Ambassador John Quincy Adams when the latter was sent to Russia by President Madison; James Savage (Harvard 1803), the workhorse of the group who founded the Provident Institution for Savings in 1816 and became a member of the state Senate in 1826. Tuckerman, Tudor, and Shaw had all been classmates of Channing's at Harvard.

Channing's influence on his friends was quite profound. During his two-year postgraduate stint as tutor to the children of John Randolph in Virginia in 1798-99, Channing immersed himself in the authors of the Enlightenment, reading Hume, Wollstonecraft, Godwin, Rousseau and Voltaire. During it all he corresponded profusely with his friends. Channing's biographer, Jack Mendelsohn, writes of that period:

> When [Channing] drove off the deep end for a communistic scheme of society, as he did during his second year in Richmond, he was experiencing only what many young idealists of his time felt. He dreamed for a time of rejecting private property forever and signing on as spiritual mentor to a utopian-minded group of Scottish immigrants. . . .
>
> He implored his friends Shaw and Walter to join him in a lifelong crusade to "beat down with the irresistible engines of truth those strong ramparts consolidated by time, within which avarice, ignorance, and selfishness have entrenched themselves. We will plant the standards of virtue and science on the ruins, and lay the foundation of a fair fabric of human happiness to endure as long as time."[4]

In 1807, William Shaw founded the Boston Athenaeum as a direct offshoot of the Anthology Society. The Athenaeum was to become the elite's new gathering place, the richest private library in America. It was to become the temple of the new trinity: Harvard, Unitarianism, and money. According to Ronald Story in the *American Scholar Quarterly* of May 1975:

> Of the 26 original organizers, incorporators and trustees [of the Athenaeum], two-thirds left estates of $25,000 or more, which placed them in roughly the top 2.1 per cent of the population; almost 40 per cent left $100,000 or more, thus ranking in the top 0.3 per cent. . . . Of the officers and trustees elected by the proprietors from 1816 to 1830, almost 90 per cent left estates of $100,000 or more, ranking in the top 0.6 per cent of the population; two-thirds left $200,000 or more, placing them in the top 0.2 per cent; five were millionaires.

Among the first trustees was Samuel Eliot, a wealthy merchant, whose family was destined to play prominent roles in the future of Harvard, Unitarianism, and public education. Eliot, a benefactor of Harvard, founded in 1814 the Eliot Professorship of Greek, giving Harvard $20,000 for the purpose. Kirkland was by then president of Harvard. Russel Nye, in his biography of Brahmin historian George Bancroft, describes how that money was used to forge the German connection that was to have a profound influence on American educators in later years:

> [George] Ticknor's and [Edward] Everett's enthusiastic interest in Germany infected Kirkland, and in 1814 when Samuel Eliot of Boston endowed a professorship of Greek literature with $20,000, the progressive-minded president recognized the opportunity. The position was offered to Everett, with the suggestion that he study abroad at full salary to fit himself for the chair. Everett sailed for Germany in 1815, to return two years later trained in the best traditions of European scholarship. Ticknor went with him; later Joseph Green Cogswell; and still later George Bancroft followed them. Everett became the greatest classical scholar in America, Ticknor the father of modern language study in America, Cogswell the first great American librarian, and Bancroft the first great American historian.[5]

The four Unitarians all shared the belief that virtue, if not salvation itself, was more attainable through learning and culture than through religion. David B. Tyack, in his biography of George Ticknor, writes:

> As academic missionaries, Ticknor, Everett, Bancroft and Cogswell all returned to Harvard hoping they could show Americans the meaning of scholarship and culture. . . . They were convinced that "mere power, unaccompanied by intellectual refinement, never failed of being a scourge, whether possessed by a despot or a republic. . . ." Significantly, Everett called the library, not the chapel, "the life and soul of any university."[6]

In Boston, the Unitarians provided the public schools with unflagging support. To emphasize their commitment to public education, leading Unitarians such as Channing, Kirkland, Tudor, and James Freeman served on the school committee.

Meanwhile, things were happening in Europe that would greatly influence the course of action Unitarians would take regarding public education. With the emergence of nationalism on the continent during the Napoleonic era, the idea of a national system of education became a widely accepted tenet of statist policy. The state was now viewed as the guardian of national character and culture. In 1806, Holland became the first country to create a national system of popular education regulated by the state. By 1811, Holland had 4,451 public primary schools. The Prussians followed suit in 1819, adopting a centralized state system which was to become the very model the Unitarians and their allies would later apply to America. Describing the Prussian system, Hugh Pollard, in *Pioneers of Popular Education*, writes:

> One is amazed on studying the 1819 Code today to discover the extraordinary powers which the state assumed to coerce

unwilling and negligent parents to have their children educated. . . . Every year a census of all children of school age was made. Baptismal registers and the records of the civil authorities were laid open for inspection and the police were asked to give every assistance. . . . When this information had been obtained, it was used not merely to coerce unwilling parents to send their offspring to school, but also to ensure that the children arrived at school punctually. Thus, the state increased its power over the very lives of the people.[7]

It would take some years before Americans would be ready to accept such state control over their lives. Meanwhile, in Scotland, other experiments in education were taking place that would have a more immediate impact on the Boston Unitarians than those taking place on the continent. An Englishman by the name of Robert Owen, who would some day become known as the father of modern socialism, had gained widespread fame by establishing a model community for his workers and a special school for their children at his spinning mills at New Lanark, Scotland. Owen, born near Wales in 1771, was a self-made social reformer of little formal education who became an atheist at the age of ten and worked out in his own mind a creed concerning the nature of man and the causes of his misery, which he preached tirelessly from about 1813 to the day of his death in 1858.

Some called him a man of one idea, but it was an idea that had wide ramifications and appealed to many idealists and closet atheists because of its utter simplicity. His idea was this: that man was not responsible for his own character, that it was given to him by the society he lived in. This simple idea led to two other ideas Owen was to preach: that capitalism and religion created a competitive, irrational environment that made men evil, and that a totally new form of education was needed to create cooperative, rational men, free of superstition, who would forever be wise, good, and happy. Owen explained the evolution of his thinking in his autobiography:

It was with the greatest reluctance, and after long contests in my mind, that I was compelled to abandon my first and deep rooted impressions in favour of Christianity,—but being obliged to give up my faith in this sect, I was at the same time compelled to reject all others, for I had discovered that all had been based on the same absurd imagination, "that each one formed his own qualities,—determined his own thoughts, will, and action,—and was responsible for them to God and to his fellowmen." My own reflections compelled me to come to very different conclusions. My reason taught me that I could not have made one of my own qualities,—that they were forced upon me by Nature;—that my language, religion, and habits, were forced upon me by Society;—that Nature gave the qualities, and Society directed them. Thus was I forced, through seeing the error of their foundation, to abandon all belief in every religion which had been taught to man. But my religious feelings were immediately replaced by the spirit of universal charity,—not for a sect or a party, or for a country or a colour,—but for the human race, and with a real and ardent desire to do them good.[8]

In 1800, Owen, then only 29, assumed full management of New Lanark Mills which he and several partners had purchased. The mills had been located at the Falls of the Clyde to take advantage of a natural source of power. Because of the remoteness of the area, a village had been built around the mills and its houses rented at low rates to the workers who were recruited in distant towns. When Owen took over management of the mills, he found conditions deplorable. "The people had been collected hastily from any place from whence they could be induced to come, and the great majority of them were idle, intemperate, dishonest, devoid of truth, and pretenders of religion, which they supposed would cover and excuse all their short-comings and immoral proceedings."[9]

Owen found the situation at New Lanark ideal for the implementation of his educational ideas. He was ready, he stated modestly, "to commence the most important experiment for the happiness of the human race that had yet been instituted at any time in any part of the world. This was, to ascertain whether the character of man could be better formed, and society better constructed and governed, by falsehood, fraud, force, and fear, keeping him in ignorance and slavery to superstition,—or by truth, charity, and love, based on an accurate knowledge of human nature, and by forming all the institutions of society in accordance with that knowledge. It was to ascertain, in fact, whether replacing evil conditions by good, man might not be relieved from evil, and transformed into an intelligent, rational, and good being;—whether the misery in which man had been and was surrounded, from his birth to his death, could be changed into a life of goodness and happiness, by surrounding him through life with good and superior conditions only."[10]

After eight years of "training the people, improving the village and machinery, and in laying the foundation for future progress," the community began to take shape. The workers were better off, more sober, and more productive. Eight years of Owen's paternal care and attention had produced noteworthy results. But there was a limit to what could be done with adults whose characters were already formed. One had to start with the youngsters. "Children are," wrote Owen, "without exception, passive and wonderfully contrived compounds; which, by an accurate previous and subsequent attention, founded on a correct knowledge of the subject, may be formed collectively to have any human character. And although these compounds, like all other works of nature, possess endless varieties, yet they partake of that plastic quality, which, by perseverence under judicious management, may be ultimately moulded into the very image of rational wishes and desires."

And so Owen decided to create a school for the workers' children, which was to be called the Institution for the Formation of Character. He had no faith in the ability of the poor to raise their own children correctly, for, after all, the poor were the chief victims of the environment and therefore totally corrupted by it.

The Institution for the Formation of Character was opened on January 1, 1816, and its curriculum bore a striking resemblance to what John Dewey and other progressive educators would be doing eighty years later. The school was divided into three divisions: the first for children from one to three years of age; the second for children three to six; and the third for youngsters from six to ten. It was not easy to find teachers for the new school, but Owen did find a few and he described how he wanted them to conduct themselves:

> [T]hey were on no account ever to beat any one of the children, or to threaten them in any manner in word or action, or to use abusive terms; but were always to speak to them with a pleasant countenance, and in a kind manner and tone of voice. That they should tell the infants and children that they must on all occasions do all they could to make their playfellows happy,—and that the older ones, from four to six years of age, should take especial care of the younger ones, and should assist to teach them to make each other happy. . . .
>
> The children were not to be annoyed with books; but were to be taught the uses and nature or qualities of the common things around them, by familiar conversation when the children's curiosity was excited so as to induce them to ask questions respecting them.[11]

At two years of age the children were taught to dance, at four to sing, and also instructed in military exercises. Owen wrote: "Dancing, music, and the military discipline, will always be prominent surroundings in a rational system for forming characters. They give health, unaffected grace to

the body, teach obedience and order in the most impercep-
tible and pleasant manner, and create peace and happiness
to the mind, preparing it in the best manner to make
progress in all mental acquisitions.''

For Owen the experiment at New Lanark was to be a
model for the whole world to copy. Thousands of visitors
came to see this new educational marvel. Owen was particularly anxious to influence the rulers of Europe who
could easily implement his ideas on a national scale. Prior
to the creation of the school, he had written about the need
for a national system of education to be used to mold
character. These ideas were published in 1813 in a work
entitled *A New View of Society or Essays on the Formation
of the Human Character* which Owen distributed widely
among the influential people of society. He even took credit
for having inspired the Prussians to create their new national system of education in 1819, for he had written in
1813:

> It follows that every state, to be well governed, ought to
> direct its chief attention to the formation of character, and that
> the best governed state will be that which shall possess the best
> national system of education.
>
> Under the guidance of minds competent to its direction, a
> national system of training and education may be formed, to
> become the most safe, easy, effectual, and economical instru-
> ment of government that can be devised. And it may be made to
> possess a power equal to the accomplishment of the most grand
> and beneficial purposes.[12]

Concerning his influence on the Prussians, Owen wrote in
his autobiography how in 1816 the Prussian ambassador had
conveyed a copy of his essays to the King of Prussia, ''who
so much approved of them as to write an autograph letter to
me, expressing his high approbation of my sentiments on
national education and on government, and stating that he
had in consequence given instruction to his minister of

interior, to adopt my views on national education to the extent that the political condition and locality of Prussia would permit. And the next year (1817) this measure was commenced, and it has been carried out to the present time."[13]

Owen's ideas had reached the Boston Unitarians soon after their publication in 1813. "At this period," Owen wrote, "John Quincy Adams was the American minister of our government, and when I was introduced to him, a short time before he left this country, he asked me for a sufficient number of copies of my Essays, which were now become very popular, for the governor of each state in the union, and he would undertake that they should be faithfully delivered, and with his recommendation."[14] There were other channels through which European ideas on education reached Boston, primarily through Edward Everett and George Ticknor, who had been sent by President Kirkland of Harvard to the University of Göttingen.

The Unitarians were very selective in what they drew from Owen. They rejected his socialistic ideas but they liked what he had done to improve the conditions of the poor and they were greatly persuaded by the idea that a child could be molded into a rational, virtuous human being by education. Since the Unitarians believed in the innate goodness of man and his perfectibility, the experiment at New Lanark was of great interest to them. The idea of a national system of education was not new to the Unitarians, since both Jefferson and Adams had put forth the notion, but they easily realized that America was not yet ready for such a system. Yet, one had to make a start.

And so, in May 1817, a small group of Bostonians petitioned the town meeting to extend public education to the primary level. At that time children were taught to read and write at home or at a private dame's school. A child could not enter the public school at age seven unless he or she could already read and write. To find out if indeed there was a need for public primary schools, the Boston School Committee appointed a subcommittee, chaired by the distinguished architect Charles Bulfinch, to conduct a survey, the first such survey ever to be conducted in America.

The survey, which was made public in November 1817, revealed that Boston, with a population of about 40,000, supported eight public schools, including the Latin School, an African School for Negro children, and a school in the Almshouse for the children of paupers. Total enrollment of the eight schools was 2,365 pupils. This was approximately 33 per cent of the school-age population. The report also revealed that there were scattered throughout the city 154 private schools for both boys and girls with a total enrollment of 3,767. There were eight "charity free schools" with an enrollment of 365 pupils. All told, over 4,000 students between the ages of four and fourteen attended private schools of one sort or another, at a total cost to their parents of almost $50,000. The survey reported that there were 283 children aged seven and under who attended no schools. Thus, an astonishing 96 percent of the town's children were attending school, and the 4 percent who did not, had charity schools to attend if their parents wanted them to. Thus, there was no justification at all for the creation of a system of public primary schools, and Bulfinch reported as much to the School Committee, which accepted the subcommittee's recommendation.

But the Bulfinch report was not to be the last word. Behind the scenes the Unitarians were marshalling their forces to wage a campaign for public primary schools as part of this general campaign to alleviate the conditions of the poor. The campaign, promoted by meetings and newspaper appeals, reached its emotional peak in the early months of 1818. Finally, on May 25, 1818, a new petition on primary schools, authored by James Savage and Elisha Ticknor, was presented to the town meeting. James Savage, the activist Unitarian, had founded the Provident Institution for Savings in 1816 with the help of fellow Unitarians to encourage savings among the poor. Elisha Ticknor, a former master of the Boston public schools, was the father of George Ticknor who was then studying at Göttingen with Edward Everett. The petition was signed by almost two hundred leading citizens, including William E. Channing and other members of the Harvard-Boston Athenaeum elite.

The Town Meeting referred the petition to a committee composed of nine men, eight of whom had signed the petition. The result was not unexpected. The committee urged the formation of primary schools as "highly expedient and necessary." However, the majority of the Selectmen and School Committee still adhered to the recommendations of the Bulfinch report. With 96 per cent of the town's children attending school, they could not justify the expense of creating an entire system of public primary schools. In addition, Bulfinch had raised important moral issues. He claimed that public primary schools were unnecessary because most parents who sent their children to private tuition schools did not look upon the expense as a burden: they paid the cost willingly out of love and a sense of duty. This in turn made them better parents. They were more likely to devote their attention to the business of education "where a small weekly stipend is paid by them for this object, than where the whole expense is defrayed by the public treasury." Bulfinch further implied that moral degeneration would result if public taxes usurped the province of private responsibilities. Family solidarity might break down if government assumed the cost of what rightfully belonged to the private sphere. "It ought never to be forgotten," he argued, "that the office of instruction belongs to parents, and that to the schoolmaster is delegated a portion only of the parental character and rights."[15]

But these arguments fell on deaf ears, for Robert Owen had preached that the children had to be separated from their parents as early as possible so that their characters could be molded by their educators. Thus, child-parent alienation was a deliberate part of the Owen program, and apparently the Unitarians went along with it but under altered circumstances. Boston was not New Lanark. Nor did the Unitarians advertise the source of their ideas. In August 1817, Owen had made what he considered to be the most important speech of his life, in which he denounced all religion as the cause of human misery. His name, thereafter, became anathema to believers, and any educational program that could be linked to him would immediately be suspect.

Besides, most of Owen's ideas were "in the air." Pestalozzi in Switzerland had experimented with ways to elevate the poor through education. Lancaster, to whom Owen had lent support, had worked out a scheme for educating the poor multitudes at minimal expense through the use of a monitorial program. Rousseau's *Emile* described natural, informal education that was to provide the pathway to the progressive school. Also, the very institution of the public school was part of the New England heritage. Thus, it was not difficult to overcome Bulfinch's arguments by a fervent appeal to sentiment and moral duty. The promoters of the public primary schools focused their attention on the several hundred poor and delinquent children who were not in school. What are these children doing, they asked. Who has charge of them? Where do they live? Why are they not in school? They warned that unless these children were rescued from neglect, they would surely become the criminals of tomorrow, and their cost to society would be far greater than the cost of public primary schools.

What is curious about this campaign is that the promoters never suggested that perhaps the city might subsidize the tuition of children whose parents could not afford to send them to the dames' schools, thereby saving the taxpayers the cost of an entire public primary system. What they insisted on was an expansion of the public system to include the primary grades, and they would not settle for anything less. Their persistence paid off. On June 11, 1818, the Town Meeting accepted the recommendations of Savage and Ticknor and ordered the school committee to organize a Primary School Board to implement the new system of public primary schools. James Savage was chosen as secretary of the new Primary School Board and Ticknor a member. It was a great victory for the Unitarians.

The Calvinists, of course, did not oppose public education. They supported it as it then existed, but they were wary of its potential misuse as Unitarians took control of the religious, educational, and cultural institutions of Boston. The moral purpose of the public school, they believed, was to provide literacy to the child so that he could uphold his religion. It was not to mold the character of an innocent plastic glob into the perfect adult. As far as the Calvinists were concerned, the child was already a vessel of depravity. The purpose of teaching God's law was to provide the child with the necessary restraints that would protect him from his own inner evil. Thus, the Calvinists advocated Christian moral education for both public and private schools. This sentiment was well expressed by one noted Calvinist minister of the time, Dr. Heman Humphrey, in an address he gave in 1823:

> What would a finely cultivated mind, united to the best physical constitution be, without moral principle? What but mere brute force, impelled by the combined and terrible energies of a perverted understanding and a depraved heart? How much worse than physical imbecility is strength employed in doing evil? How much more to be dreaded than the most profound ignorance, is a high state of mental cultivation, when once men have broken away from the control of conscience and the Bible.
>
> Without fear of God nothing can be secure for one moment. Without the control of moral and religious principle, education

is a drawn and polished sword, in the hands of a gigantic maniac. In his madness he may fall upon it, or bathe it in the blood of the innocent. Great and highly cultivated talents, allied to skepticism, or infidelity, are the right arm that "scatters firebrands arrows and death." After all the dreams of human perfectibility, and all the hosannas which have been profanely lavished upon reason, philosophy and literature, who, but for the guardianship of religion, could protect his beloved daughters, or be safe in his own house for one night? What would civil government be in the profound sleep of conscience, and in the absence of right moral habits and feelings—what, but an iron despotism on the one hand, or intoxicated anarchy on the other?[16]

4. Toward the Conquest of Evil

THE YEAR 1819 was an important one for both public education and the Unitarians. In Prussia, the new national system of education had been organized by the Prussian state. In the United States, Boston was the first city to have a complete public school system, from the primary to the secondary level. It was also the year when both Edward Everett and George Ticknor returned to Boston from their European studies and travels. On their return, both men immediately assumed their posts at Harvard: Everett as Eliot Professor of Greek and Ticknor as Abiel Smith Professor of the French and Spanish Languages and Literatures and Professor of Belles Lettres.

But the most important event for the Unitarians in 1819 was William E. Channing's sermon at the ordination of Jared Sparks in Baltimore. It had all started in 1816 when a group of prominent Baltimore citizens had appealed to the Boston liberals to help them establish a Unitarian church in strong orthodox territory. James Freeman (Harvard 1777), the Unitarian patriarch of King's Chapel, answered the call and preached in Baltimore. By February 1817, the Baltimore group felt strong enough to found a church, and they built an impressive new structure to house the congregation. For minister, they chose Jared Sparks (Harvard 1815), one of Channing's protégés and a future president of Harvard. Sparks's ordination was planned for May 5, 1819, and the Unitarians decided to take full advantage of the occasion to make their views widely known. Channing's biographer, Mendelsohn, describes how the event was organized:

> A considerable amount of stage-managing, under Sparks's personal direction, went into the planning of the ordination. By mutual consent among Boston's leading liberal clergy, the time had come for their cause to make a national impact. Baltimore, a vital outpost far removed from Boston, was just the place to bring it off. No less than seven of the most potent Unitarian spokesmen in New England were lined up by Sparks to participate in the Baltimore event. Channing was appointed to make the hard-hitting, comprehensive statement of the Unitarian position. The legion of brethren backing him would make certain that his remarks received the widest possible public notice.[1]

Channing's Baltimore sermon would go down in history as the true parting of the ways between the Congregationalist-Trinitarian-Puritan-Orthodox Calvinists and the liberal-Harvard-Brahmin Unitarians. To the Calvinists, Unitarianism was the "halfway house" to atheism. For the Unitarians, the Baltimore event was a declaration of spiritual independence, a cutting of the moorings to the religion of their Puritan forebears and the beginning of a long voyage on the unchartered seas of religious imagination and moral relativism.

Channing's sermon addressed itself to three key issues: the concept of the Trinity, which he said was "an enormous tax on human credulity"; the differing views between Calvinists and liberals on the nature of God, and the nature of piety or "Christian virtue." On the nature of God, Channing said:

> We believe in the moral perfection of God. . . . It is not because he is our Creator merely, but because he created us for good and holy purposes; it is not because his will is irresistible, but because his will is the perfection of virtue, that we pay him allegiance. We cannot bow before a being, however, great and powerful, who governs tyrannically. We respect nothing but excellence, whether on earth or in heaven. We venerate, not the loftiness of God's throne, but the equity and goodness in which it is established. . . .
>
> To give our views of God in one word, we believe in his Parental character. . . . We look upon this world as a place of education, in which he is training men by prosperity and adversity, by aids and obstructions, by conflicts of reason and passion, by motives to duty and temptations to sin, by a various discipline suited to free and moral beings, for union with himself, and for a sublime and ever-growing virtue in heaven.
>
> Now we object to the systems of religion which prevail among us, that they are adverse, in a greater or less degree, to these purifying, comforting, and honorable views of God that they take from us our father in heaven, and substitute for him a being, whom we cannot love if we would, and whom we ought not to love if we could.[2]

Unlike Calvin, who was satisfied to know and accept God as He was revealed in the Bible, Channing and the Unitarians made their worship of God conditional on His being what they wanted Him to be. "We cannot bow before a being, however great and powerful, who governs tyrannically," as Channing put it. It was a subtle shift from the objective to the subjective, a warning that if God was not what they thought He ought to be, they'd create a god who was. When *man* creates God, he reverses the divine process and ends up worshipping himself.

It was easy enough to pick apart Calvin's system. How could you reconcile man's innate depravity with God's omnipotence? Did God deliberately create a being predestined to damnation? Edward A. Dowey, Jr., writes of Calvin:

> He developed each doctrine as he found it to its logical end, no matter how violently the conclusion might be controverted by some other theme similarly developed. In this pursuit Calvin was one of the most relentless of theologians and was sometimes called upon to borrow words from Augustine or Bernard to express his own wonderment before these antinomies of his thought that were to him none other than the mysteries of God's will.[3]

Calvin had no sympathy with those intellectuals who could not accept the unanswerable mysteries of the Bible. He wrote:

> . . . what wonder if the immense and incomprehensible majesty of God exceed the limits of our intellect? . . . those who seek to know more than God has revealed are crazy. Therefore let us be pleased with instructed ignorance rather than with the intemperate and inquisitive intoxication of wanting to know more than God allows. . . .
>
> Far be it from any of the faithful to be ashamed of ignorance of what the Lord withdraws into the glory of His inaccessible light. . . . For the Lord is my witness, and my conscience attests it, that I daily so meditate on these mysteries of His judgments that curiosity to know anything more does not attract me; no sinister suspicion concerning His justice steals away my confidence; no desire to complain entices me . . . if the ears of any so itch that they will have none of the mysteries of God hidden and closed to them, it would be a mad master who would attempt to satisfy such people.[4]

Compared to Calvin, Channing was a theological lightweight, and had Calvin lived in Boston in 1819 he would have used against Channing the same relentless logic he had used during his lifetime in arguing with others who had objected to these very same Bible-based doctrines. The Unitarians objected to the doctrine of election simply because it did not guarantee everyone salvation. According to Calvin, doing good on earth was no guarantee of a reserved place in heaven:

The offer of salvation is made equally to all, but salvation itself is for those who are elect.[5]

God, by His eternal goodwill, which has no cause outside itself, destined those whom He pleased to salvation, rejecting the rest; those whom he dignified by gratuitous adoption He illumined by His Spirit, so that they receive the life offered in Christ, while others voluntarily disbelieve, so that they remain in darkness destitute of the light of faith.[6]

Faith therefore from beginning to end is the gift of God; and that this gift is given to some and not to others, no one can at all doubt . . . and why God delivers one man and not another are matters constituting His inscrutable judgments and His univestigable ways.[7]

Salvation of the faithful depends upon the eternal election of God, and that for this no cause can be given except His gratuitous good pleasure.
God did not choose us because we believed, but in order that we might believe, lest we should seem first to have chosen Him. Paul emphasizes that our beginning to be holy is the fruit and effect of election. Hence, they act most preposterously who place election after faith.[8]

The Unitarians, of course, found the Calvinist idea of election unacceptable. In its place they adopted a doctrine of Christian virtue. If indeed man had been created for "good and holy purposes," as Channing argued, what other purpose could it be for than doing good through social altruism? Since the Unitarians rejected salvation through election, over which they had no control, to salvation by works, over which they had control, they embraced altruism as the sure road to heaven, an altruism exercised through social and political activism.

In 1820, the Unitarians won another important victory. The Unitarian-dominated Massachusetts Supreme Court ruled that "where a majority of the members of a Congregational Church separate from a majority of the Parish, the members who remain, though a minority, constitute the Church in such Parish, and retain the rights and property belonging thereto." This ruling became known as the Dedham decision. Jack Mendelsohn writes:

> Everywhere the orthodox screamed foul, as well they might. Isaac Parker, the judge who wrote the decision, was a staunch Unitarian. It was clear to church conservatives that they were about to be "plundered," in community after community, of properties they considered to be rightly theirs. As the tide ran, there was no choice for convinced evangelicals, in the steadily mounting number of towns where liberal parish majorities were insisting upon liberal ministers, but to withdraw to form their own theologically pure churches. A careful, though probably incomplete, report prepared in 1836 by a committee of the Massachusetts General Association lists eighty-one "exiled churches," which by withdrawing from their parishes surrendered parish and church funds valued at some $366,000 and meeting-houses valued at $243,000.[9]

While the Unitarians, without doubt, acquired all of this Calvinist property in the interest of true religion, one must admire their ability to increase their material base without having to go out into the wilderness. They had a decided affinity toward material power. The Unitarian elite was particularly successful in creating a very powerful economic network through marriage. For example, in 1815, Channing married his first cousin, Ruth Gibbs, daughter of one of New England's richest merchants. In 1821 both Andrews Norton and George Ticknor married daughters of Harvard benefactor Samuel Eliot. Edward Everett and Charles Frances Adams, son of John Quincy Adams, married daughters of Peter Chardon Brooks, one of Boston's earliest millionaires. Thus was created an interlocking directorate of wealthy families linking Harvard, the Unitarian Church, the Boston Athenaeum, and some of New England's largest economic enterprises. This combination created a group philosophy of political and economic conservatism, moral relativism, altruistic piety, and intellectual elitism.

As a religion, Unitarianism was particularly suited to this highly cultivated, worldly, self-righteous, morally smug elite. Calvinism was a religion for both rich and poor, kings and commoners, the intelligent and the ignorant. After all, social status did not determine election. Unitarianism, on the other hand, was strictly for the well-to-do, because only they could afford it. What could you do for the poor if you yourself were the poorest? What could you do for Harvard if you had never gone beyond grade-school? But the rich Unitarian could be "saved" or get to heaven—if he believed in such a place—by becoming a benefactor of Harvard, or helping the poor, usually by getting the taxpayer to bear the ultimate burden. Channing urged the rich to "regard property as a trust for the good of those who are in want." Unless they turned their attention to the less fortunate, the elite would become corrupted by power and money. "Let there be no literary *class*," Channing preached, "no *class* of the rich. The learned, when forming a distinct class become jealous, exacting, domineering, and seek to maintain their sway, even at the expense of truth. Scholars already begin to find the benefit of quitting their pedantic cells and mingling with general society; but still they associate too much with the rich and refined,—still they seek honor and power. Their high office, of being lights to society, is overlooked. How the rich injure themselves by a clannish spirit, corrupting one another by rivalries in show and expense!"

Since the only way the Unitarians could practice their

religion was by doing something for the poor and the underprivileged, they organized groups through which their efforts could be carried out. One such group was the Wednesday Evening Association, whose purposes were to extend the knowledge and practical influence of "true religion," to promote plans for the reform and improvement of society, and "to produce a unity of purpose and effort among Unitarian Christians." Channing, since his days in Virginia, had given much thought to some sort of fraternal organization that would have as its goal the foundation of human happiness. The Unitarian movement now provided the means to create such concerted, organized effort. In 1822 Channing and his wife went to Europe which they toured for over a year. Appalled by the poverty he found in the great cities, Channing began to think of some practical plan to reform society. His biographer writes:

> So Channing began to mobilize and organize on paper precisely what the pressure points of enlightened social policy should be: education that opens the "faculties and affections" of every person whatever his rank or condition; economic arrangements that put human improvement first, property and profits second; an end to the "ruinous" notion that respectability and high social status are identical; replacement of civil society's abounding "restraints" with a new, great aim of "development"; reentry into society's mainstream of the poor; recognition that government, with its array of institutions, laws, and resources exists primarily to promote respect and progress for *all* of its citizens, but especially, because of their degraded condition, for "the poor, weak, helpless, suffering."
>
> To flesh out his Elysian prospectus, Channing called for an intellectual elite—"a body of enlightened, studious men," who do not form a "party" or faction, but "consider their light as a good given to be diffused, and as a means to maintain an improving intercourse among all orders."[10]

The idea of an intellectual elite formulating and promoting social policy appealed to the Unitarians because it gave their lives a higher purpose. The Calvinists had predestination, God's purpose, to provide a sense of destiny and meaning to their lives. Channing tried to evoke a similar sense of mission based on being superior or "enlightened" and therefore fit to lead others. Their "light" was "a good given to be diffused." Given by whom? Had the "light" in a liberal professor's head been put there by God?

Meanwhile the Boston Unitarians increased their efforts to help the poor. In 1821 Unitarian mayor Josiah Quincy (Harvard 1790), who was to become president of his alma mater in 1829, issued a report on pauperism and outlined steps to be taken to deal with it. James Savage proposed a new public workhouse for the indigent. The following year a House of Industry for the poor was opened.

The year 1821 also saw the establishment of the first American public high school in Boston—English High School. It was created to complement the elitist Boston Latin School and provide the same kind of practical education the private academies offered. Its first principal was George B. Emerson (Harvard 1817). As of 1820, only about 22 percent of Boston's school-age population was enrolled in the public schools. Outside of Boston, the private academy movement was spreading rapidly, and the state legislature was under pressure to modify the laws requiring towns to maintain public grammar schools. While the Harvard-Boston elite did not like the trend, they lacked sufficient statewide political power to stop it.

Meanwhile, in other states, particularly New York where large numbers of New Englanders had settled, common schools were being established. The availability of funds through the land grant program made the creation of these schools possible. They were not elaborate schools, and their cost to the taxpayer was nominal since low tuition fees were also contributed by parents. In New York State support of the common schools by a State School Fund distributed among school districts began in 1795, to which was also added funds locally collected by majority vote. No town was compelled to establish a common school, but the State School Fund was a strong inducement to establish one. By 1798 there were 1,352 voluntarily established common schools in New York State instructing 59,660 pupils. In 1823 there were 7,382 school districts, instructing 400,534 pupils. The *Third Annual Report of the Superintendent of Common Schools in the State of New York* boasted that, in 1823, "182,802 dollars, 25 cents, of public monies (being the whole amount drawn last year from the treasury, raised by tax and received from the *local school fund,*) were expended for the support of common schools during that year, and it is estimated that, in addition to this amount, more than 850,000 dollars from the private funds of individuals were appropriated, in like manner, during the same period, (exclusive of public and private appropriations and benefactions for the support of colleges and academies,) making a grand total of more than *a million of dollars.*"[11] Thus, it was clear that despite the prevalence of the common-school idea, these "public" schools were supported by many more private dollars than public ones. The distance between subsidized common schools locally controlled by those who voluntarily established them and a national compulsory system of education run by a hierarchal elite as practiced in Prussia was considerable. It would take at least thirty years to bridge the gap, and the Harvard-Unitarian elite would be the principal builders of that bridge.

Was the American system inadequate because it was not a centrally controlled national system? Not according to Charles J. Ingersoll, a noted lecturer of the time. He told an audience of the American Philosophical Society in Philadelphia in 1823:

Not one of the eleven new states has been admitted into the Union without provision in its constitution for schools, academies, colleges, and universities. In most of the original states large sums in money are appropriated to education, and they claim a share in the great landed investments, which are mortgaged to it in the new states. Reckoning all those contributions federal and local, it may be asserted, that nearly as much as the whole national expenditure of the United States is set apart by laws to enlighten the people. The public patronage of learning in this country, adverting to what the value of these donations will be before the close of the present century, equals at least the ostentatious bounties conferred on it in Europe. In one state alone, with but 275,000 inhabitants, more than forty thousand pupils are instructed at the public schools. I believe we may compute the number of such pupils throughout the United States at more than half a million. In the city of Philadelphia, without counting the private or the charity schools, there are about five thousand pupils in the Commonwealth's seminaries, taught reading, writing, and arithmetic, at an expense to the public of little more than three dollars a year each one. Nearly the whole minor population of the United States are receiving school education.[12]

Clearly, by 1823, the American people had about as much public education as they needed. In Massachusetts they had had too much, and the trend outside of Boston was away from the public school on the secondary level to the private academy. However, the Harvard-Unitarian elite, moved by their exalted vision of human perfectibility, had only begun to do their work. Flushed with their success in establishing public primary schools in Boston and encouraged by the national reception given Channing's sermon in Baltimore, the Unitarians optimistically proceeded to weave their network of intellectual, economic and political power. Samuel Eliot Morison, in his history of Harvard, describes the Unitarian mood at the time:

The eighteen-twenties were the palmy days of Unitarianism, when Thomas Jefferson predicted that it would sweep the

South, and when young Harvard missionaries of liberal Christianity preached in Southern legislative halls. Unitarianism seemed so simple and logical that its swift progress and early triumph were confidently anticipated. Faith in the divinity of human nature seemed the destined religion for a democracy, closely allied to confidence in the power of education to develop the reason, conscience, and character of man. But, alas for them, the Unitarians overlooked the emotional and aesthetic side of human nature; nor were the theological dogmas of the Protestant churches so obliging as to crumble at the touch of reason, like the wonderful one-hoss shay. The fundamentalist tide that had ebbed Southward flowed back; the transcendentalists floated off, and the Roman tide rolled in; but not before Harvard had become a fortress of the liberal outlook and faith. In that sense, but in no other, Unitarianism sealed Harvard with its spirit. We can never measure the relief, the stimulus, the exhuberant joy, felt in the last century by thousands of young men who, after a stern upbringing in expectation of a hard struggle to escape eternal damnation, entered a college where hot-gospelling was poor form, hell was not mentioned, and venerable preachers treated the students, not as limbs of Satan, but as younger brothers of their Lord and Saviour.[13]

And yet, in 1823, these "younger brothers of their Lord and Saviour" gave President Kirkland his most difficult year. Morison writes: "The class of 1823 was uncommonly rowdy. A class history kept by a member chronicles class meetings and forbidden dinners, battles in commons, bonfires and explosions in the Yard, cannon-balls dropped from upper windows, choruses of 'scraping' that drowned tutors' voices in classroom and chapel and plots that resulted in drenching their persons with buckets of ink-and-water. . . . The Faculty, determined to rule, expelled forty-three students out of a class of seventy."

The perfect man had yet to be created, but the Unitarians would not get a chance to create him if the people of Massachusetts kept whittling away at public education. It is interesting that the only thing the Unitarians liked about the Calvinist commonwealth was its education laws, which compelled communities to establish public schools. Time and again, in their drive to revive and expand public education, the Unitarians would piously quote these laws and bemoan their erosion and disuse. In an article in the *North American Review* of October 1824, the writer reviewed the history of that erosion, starting with the school laws of 1647 and their weakening in 1693 under the new royal charter. Reviewing the post-Revolutionary period, he wrote:

> A still greater falling off followed the settlement of the constitution of 1780, though that constitution solemnly recognised the duty of cherishing the grammar schools, for by the act of 1789, towns of fifty families are required to support a reading and writing school only six months in the year instead of twelve as before, and towns of two hundred families are required to have a grammar school, instead of towns of one hundred as before. And finally, by the act of February 18, 1824, any town may refuse to have a grammar school, whose inhabitants fall short of five thousand; or, in other words, no town in Massachusetts, except five or six, is now required to furnish the higher branches of a common education to all its children.
>
> We confess that we regard this course of legislation on the subject of free schools with much regret. The laws have been continually diminishing their requisitions, until, at last, these requisitions are altogether nominal; until in fact they are made where they are not wanted, and omitted where they are.

The article was a review of a new book by James G. Carter entitled *Letters to the Hon. William Prescott, LL.D., on the Free Schools of New England, with Remarks upon the Principles of Instruction.* Carter, 29, had been graduated from Harvard in 1820 and had started his own school in Lancaster, Massachusetts, his home town. The school specialized in handling students suspended from Harvard, "correcting the errors and supplying the deficiencies in the education, both moral and intellectual, of this class of pupils.''

Carter began his post-graduate career as an activist for public education with a series of letters which he wrote to the Boston newspapers and which were published in book form in 1824. The article in the *North American Review* was a review of that book. The letters, the book, and the very favorable review suggest that Carter received special encouragement from those who promoted him. The *North American Review* was the nation's most prestigious literary journal—a cross between the *Atlantic Monthly* and *Foreign Affairs*—specializing in worldly tastes and impeccable scholarship. It was very selective in what it gave its attention to. The periodical had been founded in 1815 as a successor to the *Monthly Anthology and Boston Review* by W. E. Channing's brother, Edward Tyrell Channing and Richard Henry Dana, Josiah Quincy, William Tudor, and President Kirkland of Harvard. E. T. Channing became Boylston Professor of Rhetoric and Oratory at Harvard in 1819; Josiah Quincy succeeded Kirkland as president of Harvard in 1829. Tudor became the *Review*'s first editor, and Edward Everett became editor in 1820.

At the time Carter's book was reviewed, Jared Sparks was editor. Sparks had left his Baltimore ministry in 1823, returned to Boston and bought a controlling interest in the *Review*, of which he became editor. The *North American Review*, reflecting the tastes and interests of the Harvard-Unitarian elite, exerted a strong influence on New England intellectuals. It became the main channel through which German ideas filtered into the intellectual community. Bancroft, Cogswell, Ticknor, and Everett, all of whom wrote for the Review, were quite at home with German literature and scholarship. They all admired the Prussian system of education. In fact, in 1823, on their return from Germany, Bancroft and Cogswell actually founded a private school based on the German *gymnasium*. The Round Hill School, as it was called, was located in Northhampton, Massachusetts, and became somewhat of a model school. But it was destined to fail, as American youth would not adapt itself to the German methods. The school closed its doors in 1834.

Carter's book of 1824 is of value today because it gives an excellent account of the trend away from public education in areas where the Unitarian influence was weakest. It also reveals where the resistance to public education was coming from. Carter wrote:

> The middling and poorer classes find their equivalent, in having their families educated at a small expense to themselves. For these classes of society to refuse ample provisions for public instruction, is virtually to refuse to have their children educated at other's expense. Yet it is here, oftener than any where, we find a backwardness and indifference upon the subject. . . . In the appropriations for schools in the towns, that class of inhabitants, who are to be the greatest gainers at the least expense, are often most reluctant at the expenditure. . . . Notwithstanding the burden of the schools comes principally upon the rich, they are the strongest advocate for their support.[14]

In other words, the poor and the middle class were mainly responsible for the trend away from the public schools, while the rich were their strongest supporters. The private academies were particularly suited to the needs of the middle class. Carter wrote:

> These schools, or academies, as they are more frequently called, have been generally founded by individuals, and afterwards made corporations with grants of land or money from the State authorities. They have now become very numerous throughout New England. In Massachusetts, they are found in every county, and oftentimes within ten or fifteen miles of each

other. They have generally been made a class above the *grammar schools*. Here, young men are prepared for teachers in the primary schools,—for mercantile life,—or for the University. This class of schools is not entirely free. The instructor is supported in part by the proceeds of funds, which have arisen from private or public munificence; and in part, by a tax on each scholar. For the rich and those in easy circumstances, these schools answer the same, and probably a better purpose, than the grammar schools, contemplated by the late law; but they are out of the reach of the poor.[15]

That last point was to become a favorite argument against the private academy: that it deprived the poor of equal educational opportunity. It never occurred to the "friends of education" to advocate state scholarships or tuition grants for poor youths so that they could attend the private academy in their town. Instead, they promoted the idea of free public schools for *all*—including all of those who could afford private schooling. The reason for this is obvious. Only in free public schools could the characters and minds of all be manipulated by the controlling few. The end result was to be a social utopia that would bring unparalleled happiness to the human race. Carter evoked that utopian vision in the final paragraph of his book, which is worth reading in its entirety because of how well it reveals the all-encompassing nature of that vision:

The subject of education has never excited so deep and lively an interest, in every part of our country, as at present. If this interest can be directed by the wisdom and experience of the more enlightened, it can not fail of a great and happy effect. The *importance* of the subject has long since been felt; the time has come when attention should be turned to the *nature* of it. We may then hope for those improvements of which the subject is susceptible; and those splendid results in the state of society, which the more ardent and philanthropic anticipate. . . . But when the influence of education is more duly estimated, and when the cultivation of the head and heart shall be united, and form one distinct and dignified profession, drawing to its practice the greatest and best of men; we may then hope a proper direction will be given to the opening minds and expanding hearts of the young; and that all the deep and permanent prepossessions of childhood and youth, will be upon the side of truth and virtue. Science, philosophy, and religion will then be blended with their very natures, to grow with their growth, and strengthen with their strength. The whole earth will then constitute but one beautiful temple, in which may dwell in peace all mankind; and their lives form but one consistent and perpetual worship.

It was a vision of heaven on earth, attainable through universal public education "directed by the wisdom and experience of the more enlightened," at the taxpayer's full expense.

In 1826 Carter published a second book entitled *Essays upon Popular Education containing a particular Examination of the Schools of Massachusetts, and an Outline of an Institution for the Education of Teachers.* In this book Carter complained at length about the private tuition academies and the negative effects they were having on the free public schools in the towns outside Boston. He was particularly critical of the legislature's neglect of the public schools which had received "almost no legislative attention, protection, or bounty, for nearly forty years." He had only one good thing to say about the academies, that they were producing competent young instructors for the free schools. Otherwise their influence was "pernicious." Carter wrote:

But the academies have had another influence upon the public town schools, which has much impaired their usefulness, and, if not soon checked, it will ultimately destroy them. This influence, operating for a series of years, had led already to the abandonment of a part of the free school system, and to a depreciation in the character and prospects of the remaining part. And it is working, not slowly, the destruction of the vital principle of the institution, more valuable to us than any other, for the preservation of enlightened freedom.

Carter could not deny that parents were creating private schools because they were dissatisfied with the public ones. He also realized that public opinion favored the coexistence of both private and public schools. But he argued that coexistence in the long run would undo public education entirely. He described how that would happen if the trend were not reversed:

Take any ten contiguous towns in the interior of this commonwealth, and suppose an academy to be placed in the center of them. . . . In each of these ten towns, select the six individuals, who have families to educate, who set the highest value on early education, and who are able to defray the expenses of the best which can be had, either in a private school among themselves, or at the academy, which, by the supposition, is in their neighborhood. Now of what immediate consequences can it be to the six families of each town, or to the sixty families of the ten towns, whether there be such a thing as a free school in the commonwealth or not! . . .

As soon as difficulties and disagreements, in regard to the free schools, arise, as they necessarily must, upon various topics; such as, the amount of money to be raised, the distribution of it among the several districts, the manner of appropriation, whether it be to the ''summer schools'' or to the ''winter schools,'' to pay an instructor from this family or from that family, of higher qualifications or of lower qualifications, of this or that political or religious creed, or a thousand other questions which are constantly occurring; if any of our six families happen to be dissatisfied or disgusted with any course which may be adopted, they will, immediately, abandon the free schools, and provide for the education of their children in their own way. They may organize a private school, for their own convenience, upon such principles as they most approve. Or, they may send their scholars, at an expense trifling to them, to the academy in their neighborhood. . . .

But the evils of this course, and of the general policy of the state government, which has led to it, are very serious ones. When the six individuals of any country town, who are, by the supposition, first in point of wealth and interest in the subject, and who will generally be also first in point of intelligence and influence in town affairs, withdraw their children from the common schools; there are, at the same time, withdrawn a portion of intelligence from their direction, and heartfelt interest for their support. This intelligence is needed, to manage the delicate and important concerns of the schools.[16]

Wherever academies were established, asserted Carter, the common school declined because the most intelligent people in town were no longer interested in it. But there was a solution to the problem, wrote Carter: "Abolish the academy and leave these six families of each town to the free schools alone, and you would find all their powers assiduously employed to put them in the best condition possible. Or rather put the free schools in a state to afford as good instruction as the academies now do, and you would supercede, in a great degree, the necessity of them."

The free market in education was clearly phasing out the public schools because the latter were not supplying the services that more and more parents wanted. The private schools were more efficiently organized, provided better instruction, pupil supervision, and social atmosphere. They were less crowded and offered a more practical curriculum. How could the common schools compete with them? Only by improving their quality. And how was this to be done? By training teachers in the science of instruction. And who would train the teachers? The State.

Carter was one of the first Americans to publicly advocate the establishment of state-owned teachers' colleges for the training of public school teachers. If the ultimate purpose of a public school system was to fulfill the social vision of an enlightened elite, then it would be necessary to train a cadre of teachers to carry out the policies of that elite. Teacher training implied uniformity of curriculum. This had been demonstrated in Prussia, where teachers' institutes were an integral part of the national system of education. Carter wrote:

> An institution for the education of teachers . . . would form a part, and a very important part, of the free-school system. It would be, moreover, precisely that portion of the system which should be under the direction of the State, whether the others are or not. Because we should thus secure at once, a uniform, intelligent, and independent tribunal for decisions on the qualifications of teachers. Because we should then relieve the clergy of an invidious task, and insure to the public competent teachers, if such could be found or prepared. An institution for this purpose would become, by its influence on society, and particularly on the young, an engine to sway the public sentiment, the public morals, and the public religion, more powerful than any other in the possession of government. It should, therefore, be responsible immediately to them. And they should carefully overlook it, and prevent its being perverted to other purposes, directly or indirectly, than those for which it is designed. It should be emphatically the State's institution. And its results would soon make it the State's favorite and pride, among other literary and scientific institutions.[17]

Thus, as early as 1825, educational statism, modelled on the Prussian design, was already a well-developed idea in the heads of the Harvard-Unitarian elite. George Ticknor, the epitome of the "enlightened," took time out from a bitter academic controversy at Harvard to review Carter's book in the January 1827 issue of the *North American Review*.[18] Since Americans were enjoying the fullest measure of freedom any people in history had ever enjoyed and were in no mood for a national system of education controlled by the state, in turn controlled by a self-anointed elite, the subject had to be handled delicately. Ticknor wrote:

> We have read these Essays with more than a feeling of interest and pleasure. . . . They are judicious and able, full of sound and liberal views, and important suggestions.
>
> . . . We cannot let this number of our Journal go forth, without yielding the full measure of all the encouragement, which it is in our power to give, to the plan that Mr. Carter has laid before us. We say the plan, for it is the projected Institution for the Instruction of Teachers . . . that we shall principally direct our observations. . . .
>
> In the first place, better schools are wanted. We mean, that the Free Schools, or what are usually called, the Common, and in the country, District Schools, need to be made better, and more efficient organs of instruction and influence.[19]

Ticknor then went on to complain about the state of instruction in the common schools. "They learn nothing, or, what amounts very much to the same thing, nothing that they care to know," he asserted. How this Harvard Brahmin knew what was being learned in the common schools, which he probably never visited, is not explained. But he did admit that learning to read wasn't the problem. "They learn to read. Very well. . . . and it is our boast, that of the whole mass of our population, it is rare to find an individual, who has not made this acquisition." Literacy was not the problem. The problem was how this reading skill was later applied in school work. According to Ticknor, most common schools were doing a poor job in this department. But there were a few exceptions. Some of the common schools were quite good. And what was the "secret of their superiority?" Ticknor asked. Superior teachers, of course. And that was why the free schools had to have their own teacher training institutes. Ticknor explained:

The graduates from our colleges, almost without exception, are employed in private schools; and it is a sufficient evidence, we may remark in passing, of the low estimation into which the systems of free instruction have fallen, that all, or almost all, who are able to afford it, send their children to these (private) schools. . . .

. . . [S]omething should be done to raise the character of our common schools. An institution for the education of teachers, to be employed in these schools, would be emphatically the people's institution. Such a seminary would be most consonant with the genius of our political condition.

Shall we build school houses, and purchase books, and collect large sums of money, and stop here, and leave undone the very thing that is to give efficiency to all the rest?[20]

It is ironic that when there were no teachers' colleges in existence even the worst common schools could teach children to read "very well" and illiteracy was a rarity. Today, with more teachers' colleges and stricter certification requirements than Ticknor or Carter could have ever dreamed of, functional illiteracy among students is greater than ever. Ticknor closed his article with the usual exalted vision:

From the spirit of this age, and the advantages of this country combined, we are looking for better results than have yet appeared. Mr. Owen will not accomplish them for us, nor will any enthusiast, however much more generous and philanthropic, or less vain and shortsighted. . . . [T]he grand lever, which is to raise up the mighty mass of this community is *education*. . . . The *schools* hold, in embryo, the future communities of this land. The *schools* are the pillars of the republic. To these, let the strong arm of government be stretched out. Over these, let the wisdom of our legislatures watch.[21]

Thus, the call for the "strong arm of government" to take control of education came directly from the Harvard-

Unitarian elite. When Ticknor spoke of "education" as the "grand lever" with which to raise up the masses, or of "schools" as the "pillars of the republic," he was engaging in a form of semantic sleight of hand which would become standard practice among the promoters of public education: that of associating "education" with "public education" and "schools" with "public schools," as if private schools were neither schools nor providers of education. It was a form of intellectual dishonesty that confused the public and lent credence to the idea that anyone who opposed public education was not only opposed to schools in general but to the improvement of the republic as well. This was easy for men like Ticknor and Carter to do, for they knew exactly what they wanted, the grand design being quite clear in their minds.

Ticknor's reference to Owen was quite appropriate, for Owen had come to the United States in 1825 to set up his experimental communist colony at New Harmony, Indiana. While Ticknor was certainly no Owenite, he found it useful to use Owen as an example of the dreamer whose plans, however laudable, were nowhere as practical as those of the Unitarian elite. Owen really believed in utopia, and he had come to America to demonstrate that utopia was just around the corner and that education was the primary means of getting there. Thus, both Owen and the Unitarians shared a similar exalted vision of education leading to a perfect society, which gave them much in common. How this common view was translated into activism toward a common goal will be seen in the chapters that follow.

5. The Road to Utopia

IT IS SOMEWHAT ironic that the first experiment in modern secular communism should have taken place here in the United States when this country was barely fifty years old and Karl Marx was a seven-year-old boy in Germany. It is also ironic that modern secular communism should have been founded by an Anglo-Saxon rather than a Russian or a Chinese. Yet these are the facts of history. We tend to associate communism with those unfortunate nations who now live under it, forgetting that the original source of modern communist ideology is Anglo-Saxon. Today, New Harmony, Indiana, is little more than a quaint tourist attraction on the banks of the Wabash. But who in 1825 could have known that it was the beginning of the long road to the Gulag Archipelago?

Robert Owen had decided to establish his communist colony in America because only in America could such a radical, anti-religious social experiment be tried. In addition, he was convinced that Americans would voluntarily adopt his system once they saw how marvelously it worked. After all, who in his right mind would reject heaven on earth once it had been proven that such an earthly paradise was possible?

And so, in 1825, Robert Owen set out to bring communism to America. He had bought a village named Harmonie, founded in 1813 by a primitive German sect of Christians known as the Rappites, who believed in communal property, celibacy, and complete obedience and submission to their pastoral leader, George Rapp. The Rappites had achieved great economic success, but they wanted to move elsewhere. They sold the houses and two thirds of the acreage to Owen for $150,000. Thus, with a ready-made village, which was renamed New Harmony, and 20,000 acres of rich alluvial land on the banks of the Wabash, Owen now had the opportunity to put his social ideas into practice and prove that they could work on a scale large enough to impress everyone. He was encouraged by the economic success of the Rappites, and was certain that under a system of voluntary, secular communism his success would be even greater. Utopia was, indeed, just around the corner.

The key dogma in Robert Owen's system was the notion that man's character had been deformed by religious brainwashing and that only "rational" education could correct it. The term "brainwashing" was not used in those days, but the idea was the same. Owen's cure for all of society's ills was the reformation of mankind through a new kind of secular, scientifically oriented education, the methodology for which he had developed at New Lanark. Thus, in founding New Harmony, education was to be of prime importance in creating social utopia. To that end, Owen assembled a distinguished group of scientists and educators who were ready and willing to put his ideas to the test.

The central figure in this group was wealthy amateur geologist William Maclure, a 62-year-old retired businessman who had been one of the founders of the Academy of Natural Sciences of Philadelphia in 1812 and was also president of the American Geological Society. Maclure had visited New Lanark in 1824, become a convert to Owenism, and decided to join Owen in the New Harmony experiment. Maclure recruited three other distinguished natural scientists and an educator to go with him: Charles LeSueur, a French geologist whom Maclure had brought to the United States and made curator of the Academy of Natural Sciences; Thomas Say, an entomologist and professor of natural history at the University of Pennsylvania; Gerard Troost, a minerologist and chemist who was also the first president of the Academy of Natural Sciences and professor at the Philadelphia College of Pharmacy; and Francis Joseph Neef, a disciple of Pestalozzi, whom Maclure had recruited in 1805 during a visit to Switzerland and brought to the United States to head up the first Pestalozzian school in this country. Along with his scientific colleagues, Maclure brought with him to New Harmony his extensive library, his museum of minerology, and much valuable scientific equipment.

That education would be at the heart of the communist experiment was made clear in the first issue of the *New Harmony Gazette,* which appeared on October 1, 1825. The "Prospectus" stated:

> In our Gazette we purpose developing more fully the principles of the Social System; that the world, with ourselves, may, by contrast, be convinced—that INDIVIDUALITY DETRACTS LARGELY FROM THE SUM OF HUMAN HAPPINESS.
>
> It is intended to point out what we believe to be the most *rational,* therefore the *best* mode of educating human beings from infancy to manhood: knowing, that any character, from the best to the worst, from the most ignorant to the most enlightened, may be given to any individual, community, or to the world at large, by different modes of education.

In 1825, the words "socialist" and "socialism" had not yet been coined. The words "social system" stood for socialism. Robert Owen himself explained what he meant by "social system" in his address to the New Harmony colonists on April 27, 1825, which the first issue of the *New Harmony Gazette* published in full. The address presented a very clear, detailed picture of how the father of British socialism viewed the world. Its premises are still operative today in communist countries and among Western socialists. It is therefore worth quoting at length:

> I am come to this country, to introduce an entire new state of society; to change it from the ignorant, selfish system, to an enlightened, social system, which shall gradually unite all interests into one, and remove all cause for contest between individuals.
>
> The individual system has heretofore universally prevailed, and while it continues, the great mass of mankind must remain, as they comparatively are at present, ignorant, poor, oppressed, and, consequently, vicious, and miserable; and though it should last for numberless ages, virtue and happiness cannot be attained, nor can man, strictly speaking, become a rational being.
>
> Until the individual system shall be entirely abandoned, it will be useless to expect any substantial, permanent improvement in the condition of the human race; for this system ever has been, and must ever remain, directly opposed to universal charity, benevolence and kindness; and until the means were discovered, and can be brought into practice, by which universal charity, benevolence and kindness, can be made to pervade the heart and mind of every human being, a state of society in which "peace on earth and good will to man" shall exist, must remain unknown and unenjoyed by mankind.
>
> These invaluable blessings can be obtained only under a social system; a system derived from an accurate knowledge of human nature, and of the circumstances by which it is, or may be, governed.
>
> This knowledge has been, until now, hidden from man; he therefore knew not how to put the social system into practice; for without this knowledge, the social system is utterly impracticable. . . .

The knowledge of our nature, and of the circumstances, which govern the character and conduct of man, are to be acquired only by attending to the facts which exist around us, and to the past history of the human species.

These facts and this history demonstrate, that all men are formed by a creative power, and by the circumstances which are permitted to surround them from birth; and that no man has ever had any will, or power, or control, in creating himself, nor in forming the circumstances which exist around him at birth, in his childhood, in youth, or in manhood. He is a being, then, whose general nature, whose individual, or personal nature, and whose artificial acquirements, or character, have been formed for him. He cannot, therefore, become a proper subject for praise or blame, nor for artificial reward or punishment, or artificial accountability; but he becomes a being capable of being formed into the extremes of good or bad, and to experience the extremes of happiness or misery, by, and through the circumstances which shall exist around him at birth, in childhood, in youth, and in manhood; he cannot, therefore, become a rational object for anger or displeasure of any kind; but in whatever deplorable circumstances he may be found, and whatever may be the character which nature and these circumstances may have formed for him, he is a being who justly claims our compassion, care, attention and kindness, in proportion to the extent of the evil and misery which he has been made to experience; and to this rule there can be no exception.

These fundamental principles being understood, and the real nature of man being thus laid open to us, the proceedings requisite to produce good instead of evil, and happiness instead of misery, become obvious and easy of practice.

I have bought this property, and have now come here to introduce this practice, and to render it familiar to all the inhabitants of this country.

But to change from the individual to the social system; from single families with separate interests, to communities of many families with one interest, cannot be accomplished at once; the change would be too great for the present habits of society; nor can it be effected in practice, except by those who have been long acquainted with each other, and whose habits, condition and sentiments, are similar; it becomes necessary, therefore, that some intermediate measures should be adopted, to enable all parties, with the least inconvenience, to change their individual, selfish habits, and to acquire the superior habits requisite to a social state; to proceed, if I may so express myself, to a halfway house on this new journey from poverty to wealth; from ignorance to intelligence; from anxiety to satisfaction of mind; from distrust of all, to confidence in every one; from bad habits and erroneous ideas, to good habits and a correct mode of thinking in all things; . . .

On May 1, 1825, the Constitution of the Preliminary Society of New Harmony was adopted by the inhabitants, and the experiment got underway. Owen then returned to England to attend to affairs there. During the spring of 1825, the New Harmony experiment was a subject of general discussion all over the country. The colony became the gathering place of so-called "enlightened and progressive" people from all over the United States and northern Europe. The large majority were freethinkers attracted by Robert Owen's antireligious views. New Harmony was called "the focus of enlightened atheism." This fact accounted, in no small degree, for the exodus of scientific men to the colony at a time when there was thought to be an irreconcilable disagreement between science and religion.

In November of 1825, Robert Owen returned to the United States, this time accompanied by his sons Robert Dale and William. They remained in New York for several weeks where they were joined by the Maclure party of scientists and educators. They all made their way to Pittsburgh where they purchased a keel boat to take them down the Ohio River to New Harmony. The "Boatload of Knowledge," as it was dubbed, arrived at New Harmony on January 18, 1826.

Owen was so pleased by the progress made during the preliminary stage that he decided to institute full communism—"a community of common property"—at New

Harmony as soon as possible. By February 5, 1826, a Constitution had been drawn up and accepted by the inhabitants. But failure came faster than Owen's optimism would have indicated. In his autobiography, Robert Dale Owen describes what happened.

[A] little more than a year after the Community experiment commenced, came official acknowledgment of its failure. The editorial [in the New Harmony Gazette] containing it, though without signature, was written by my brother William and myself, as editors, on our own responsibility; but it was submitted by us, for revision as to the facts, to my father. We said: "Our opinion is that Robert Owen ascribed too little influence to the early anti-social circumstances that had surrounded many of the quickly collected inhabitants of New Harmony before their arrival there; and too much to those circumstances which his experience might enable them to create around themselves in future . . . We are too inexperienced to hazard a judgment on the prudence and management of those who directed its execution; and the only opinion we can express with confidence is of the perseverence with which Robert Owen pursued it at great pecuniary loss to himself. One form of government was first adopted, and when that appeared unsuitable another was tried; until it appeared that the members were too various in their feelings and too dissimilar in their habits to govern themselves harmoniously as one community. . . . New Harmony, therefore, is not now a community."[1]

The great lesson learned by Owen and his followers was that education had to *precede* the creation of a communist society, for people educated under the old system were too selfish, too uncooperative, too incorrigible. Owen explained as much to the inhabitants of New Harmony in an address delivered on April 13, 1828. He said:

I tried here a new course for which I was induced to hope that fifty years of political liberty had prepared the American population: that is, to govern themselves advantageously. I supplied land, houses, and the use of much capital; and I tried, each in their own way, all the different parties who collected here; but experience proved that the attempt was premature to unite a number of strangers not previously educated for the purpose, who should carry on extensive operations for their common interest and live together as a common family. I afterwards tried, before my last departure hence, what could be done by those who associated through their own choice and in small numbers; to these I gave leases of large tracts of good land for ten thousand years upon a nominal rent and for moral conditions only; and these I did expect would have made a progress during my absence; but now, upon my return, I find that the habits of the individual system were so powerful that these leases have been, with a few exceptions, applied for individual purposes and individual gain; and in consequence they must return again into my hands.

This last experience has made it evident that *families* trained in the individual system, founded as it is upon superstition, have not acquired those moral qualities of forbearance and charity for each other which are necessary to promote full confidence and harmony among all the members, and without which communities cannot exist. Communities, to prosper permanently, must consist of persons devoid of prejudice and possessed of moral feelings in unison with the laws of human nature.

All systems of religion train men to be prejudiced, to be without charity and to be opposed to each other. With these qualities they never can unite as brethren of one family having one interest and sincere kind feelings for each other.

But is the population of the world to be left in this miserable and hopeless state? If all we desire cannot be effected for this generation, so as to produce honesty, industry, intelligence, independence and happiness, by reason of the habits and feelings that have arisen out of their superstitious training; ought we to abandon them and their offspring to their errors and miseries? Ought we not rather redouble our exertions to stop the evil from proceeding any farther and never be weary to well doing? If we cannot do all now, let us do what is practicable; and make as great an advance towards the right road as we can make with the means we possess.[2]

Thus, the failure of the New Harmony experiment neither discouraged Owen nor put an end to his influence. On the contrary, it marked the beginning of a whole new phase of Owenite activism. From then on the Owenites would promote national public education as the preliminary step to socialism. Adults educated under the old system were simply incapable of creating and sustaining a communist society. Only a new generation, rationally educated, could bring socialism to pass. For Owen it meant that it would take years before the new social order would come voluntarily into being. But communists in the future would not have Owen's patience. Once they took power, they would exterminate the incorrigibles by the millions. Owen never believed that violence or force would be necessary to bring about the new social order. He was convinced that once people were exposed to his ideas, they would recognize their superiority and accept them. The Marxists who were to succeed Owen were to differ with him radically on the matter of means. The Owenite socialists would work to bring about socialism democratically through political activism and education. The Marxists would preach the violent overthrow of the existing system and the extermination of the opposition. But in 1828 Robert Owen would have been the last to believe that his "benevolent" ideas could possibly lead to such barbarism. But John Calvin would not have been surprised. He would have noted that man was innately corrupt and that once man had renounced God's law, his unrestrained nature would lead to unbelievable excesses of evil. What prevented Owen from going the way of the Marxists was his vestigial belief in a supreme power and a messianic vision of his own purpose. It was enough of a difference to distinguish him from the pure atheists and nihilists who would become the socialist revolutionaries of the future.

But to the Owenites in 1828 it was clear that national public education was the essential first step on the road to socialism and that this would require a sustained effort of propaganda and political activism over a long period of time. About a thousand people had taken part in the New Harmony experiment. Through lectures, writings, discussions, and the experience of communal living, the participants came away from New Harmony not disillusioned by socialism, but convinced like Owen that socialism would work among people given a new character through rational education. Some returned to their homes fired up and anxious to press for educational reform in their own communities.

One such group became active in Philadelphia. In the summer of 1827 a group of journeymen carpenters in Philadelphia went on strike for a ten-hour day. As a result of the strike there came into existence late in 1827 the Mechanics' Union of Trade Associations, the first city central union in the United States, if not in the world. We know from its official organ, the *Mechanics' Free Press*, that Harmonites were involved in this incipient labor movement which was to become politically oriented and make the cause of public education the center of its program. The organization of labor to fight the exploitation of the employer had become part of Owen's activist program. John Commons, in his *History of American Industrial Society*, writes:

> Some six or eight months after its organization, indeed, the Mechanics' Union decided that it was necessary for the working men to go into politics to obtain their rights, and a little later took the initial steps toward the organization of a Working Men's Party. It appears to have attempted, however, to maintain its own separate existence as a trades' union at the same time that it fostered the political movement. On October 4, 1828, the *Mechanics' Free Press* announced a meeting of the Mechanics' Union of Trade Association to consider "business of the greatest importance." Gradually, however, it lost vitality, and it probably existed for little more than a year. . . .
> In 1829 public education took its place distinctly and

definitely at the head of the list of measures urged by the Working Men's Party.[3]

The two people most responsible for making the Working Men's Party a vehicle for promoting the idea of a national education system were Owen's son, Robert Dale Owen, and Frances Wright, one of the earliest of the radical women reformers. Owen had met her at New Harmony in the summer of 1826 after her own experimental colony for the emancipation and rehabilitation of slaves had failed at Nashoba, Tennessee. In his autobiography, *Threading My Way*, published in 1874, Robert Dale Owen recounted how he, then 25, became involved with Frances Wright, who was ten years his senior:

> Frances Wright was a cultivated Englishwoman of good family, who, though left an orphan at an early age, had received a careful and finished education, was thoroughly versed in the literature of the day, well informed on all general subjects, and spoke French and Italian fluently. She had travelled and resided for years in Europe, was an intimate friend of General Lafayette, had made the acquaintance of many leading reformers. . . . Refined in her manner and language, she was radical alike in politics, morals, and religion.
>
> She had a strong, logical mind, a courageous independence of thought, and a zealous wish to benefit her fellow-creatures; but the mind had not been submitted to early discipline, the courage was not tempered with prudence, the philanthropy had little common-sense to give it practical form and efficiency. . . . A redeeming point was, that to carry out her convictions she was ready to make great sacrifices, personal and pecuniary . . .
>
> Miss Wright's vigorous character, rare cultivation, and hopeful enthusiasm gradually gave her great influence over me; and I recollect her telling me, one day when I expressed in the New Harmony Gazette, with more than usual fearlessness, some radical opinions which she shared, that I was one of the few persons she had ever met, with whom she felt that, in her

reformatory efforts, she could act in unison. Thus we became intimate friends, and in the sequel co-editors.

After the failure of New Harmony, Robert Dale Owen, Frances Wright, and a fellow Harmonite named Robert L. Jennings set up shop in New York City to publish *The Free Enquirer* as a continuation of the defunct *New Harmony Gazette*. The publication appeared under its new name on October 29, 1828, and in the issues that followed there was to be frequent editorial cooperation with the *Mechanics' Free Press*, its sister publication in Philadelphia. Both newspapers were mouthpieces for the Owenite movement, vigorously socialist, anti-religious, and strongly in favor of a national education system. They became the major intellectual force behind the Working Men's Party, developing the party's program with its main emphasis on public education.

Orestes A. Brownson, who joined the Owenites at about that time, described why the party was formed in his autobiography, *The Convert:*

The purpose in the formation of this party was to get control of the political power of the state, so as to be able to use it for establishing our system of schools. We hoped, by linking our cause with the ultra-democratic sentiment of the country, which had had, from the time of Jefferson and Tom Paine, something of an anti-Christian character, by professing ourselves the bold and uncompromising champions of equality, by expressing a great love for the people, and a deep sympathy with the laborer, whom we represented as defrauded and oppressed by his employer, by denouncing all proprietors as aristocrats, and by keeping the more unpopular features of our plan as far in the background as possible, to enlist the majority of the American people under the banner of the Working-Men's Party; nothing doubting that, if we could once raise the party to power, we could use it to secure the adoption of our educational system.[4]

The Owenite plan for "a national republican education for all the children of the land" was outlined by Frances Wright in a series of lectures she gave in many cities. Out of the lectures came the formation by Owen and Wright in September 1829 of the Association for the Protection of Industry and for the Promotion of Popular Instruction. In a lecture given in Buffalo on November 19, 1829, addressed to "the intelligent among the working classes," Wright made it clear that the state was to play the major role in the reformation of human character. "National, rational" education, she said, was to be "free for all at the expense of all; conducted under the guardianship of the state, at the expense of the state, and for the honor, the happiness, the virtue, the salvation of the state." She urged the audience to:

> Fix your eyes upon the great object—the salvation and regeneration of human kind, by means of the rational education and protection of youth. . . .
>
> Bind all your efforts to the one great measure of a uniform plan of education for all the children and youth of your several states; and let that plan be in perfect unison with the nature of man, the nature of things, and with the declaration of your country—all men are free and equal.[5]

Although both Owenites and Unitarians agreed that the government should take full control of education, the Owenite plan was far more radical in total concept than anything the Unitarians advocated. The Owenites wanted children to be separated from their parents as early as possible—age two was suggested—and placed in district boarding schools away from the influences of the prevailing system. Each school would house a different age group and be furnished with "instructors in every branch of knowledge, intellectual and operative, with all the apparata, land, and conveniences necessary for the best development of all knowledge." What about problem youngsters? "Those entering with bad habits," Frances Wright told her audiences, "would be kept apart from the others until corrected. How rapidly reform may be effected on the plastic disposition of childhood, had been proved in your houses of refuge, more especially when such establishments have been under liberal superintendance, as was formerly the case in New York. Under their orthodox directors, those asylums of youth have been converted into jails." What about parental rights? Parents, she said, "could visit the children at suitable hours, but, in no case, interfere with or interrupt the rules of the institution."

The Owenite vision of equality was summed up by Wright in these descriptive words:

> In these nurseries of a free nation, no inequality must be allowed to enter. Fed at a common board, clothed in a common garb, uniting neatness with simplicity and convenience; raised in the exercise of common duties, in the acquirement of the same knowledge and practice of the same industry, varied only according to individual taste and capabilities; in the exercise of the same virtues, the enjoyment of the same pleasures; in the study of the same nature; in pursuit of the same object—their own and each other's happiness—say! would not such a race, when arrived at manhood and womanhood, work out the reform of society—perfect the free institutions of America?[6]

Already, in 1829, it was possible to see in the Owenite vision, the drab, monotonous, communist states of the future, in which children would be considered malleable globs of plastic to be shaped by the state, which was to become the supreme and omnipotent power in every child's life. The materialism of Wright and Owen reduced man to mere chemicals devoid of any spiritual substance. There was at least something exalting in the Unitarian view of perfectible man running the world in a kind of partnership with God who would help man achieve utopia. But in the

Owen-Wright concept of pure egalitarian materialism, there was a depressing lack of anything spiritual. It is not without irony that Robert Owen and Robert Dale Owen both turned to spiritualism in their later years, unable to deny the spiritual spark within them that leads human beings to a belief in a higher being. By itself, it might lead to a sort of generalized deism or pantheism or some other religious expression. In the case of Robert Owen, however, it led to something far more eccentric: a belief that he was some sort of Christ. In 1857 he wrote in his autobiography:

> Unknowing in what form or manner the Intelligence and Power exists, which creates, un-creates, and recreates all forms eternally throughout the universe—an Intelligence and Power far beyond the faculties of humanity hitherto to comprehend—yet am I compelled to believe that this Intelligence directs all things within the universe to produce the best possible ultimate results that the eternal elements of the universe will admit. And this supreme Creating Mind, Intelligence, Energy, or call it what you will, has to me, in a wondrous manner, directed all my measures, without a particle of merit being in any way due to me, so as to enable me to sustain this long contest, not only without physical or mental injury, but, as far as I can judge from my knowledge of human nature under its present most unfavourable conditions and surroundings, with a greater degree of continually sustained happiness than has fallen to the lot of any I have known.[7]

Apparently, without Calvin's help, Owen had arrived at his own views of predestination, election, and an all-powerful but inscrutable God. But Owen lacked the most important ingredient in the Calvinist character as it relates to God: total humility; for he refused to believe that he was anything less than a messiah himself. If God had a son, it was Robert Owen, not Jesus Christ, for Owen, not Christ, had discovered the "true religion," and Owen, not Christ, was the messiah to bring it to mankind. Owen wrote:

Now this true religion of love and charity, evident in voice, manner, and act, daily to all of human-kind, and in showing mercy to all sentient life, will create an entirely *new system* in forming the character of the human race, in constructing society through all its ramifications, and in governing all human affairs. This great change, as it will be given to the world through me as the human agent, would be, according to past unfortunate custom, called the "Owenian" system of society. Now "Owenism" has no more meaning than any of the names of authority through past ages, and which have created such deadly feud, hatred, and sufferings between different divisions of the human race; and in future every means should be adopted to prevent this most lamentable practice through the future history of man upon the earth.[8]

Owen needn't have worried that his name would be used to designate the new religion or become the object of veneration. Other socialists would modify and take credit for his doctrines and throw out the religious junk before anyone could get a chance to worship Owen as the new savior of mankind.

Meanwhile, back in 1829, Robert Dale Owen and Frances Wright were busily trying to convince Americans to accept the "true religion," but under the name of popular education, which was the first step to be taken toward a socialist society.

The Working Men's Party was to spearhead the way. In Philadelphia, the Working Men's Party appointed a city and county committee in September 1829 to look into the matter of public instruction and come up with recommendations. The committee completed its report in February 1830, and it is obvious from its contents that Owen and Wright helped write it. The report attacked the present state of education—both private and public—in Pennsylvania as inadequate and recommended establishing a public system much like the one Wright had outlined in her lectures.

At that time, Pennsylvania had a completely laissez-faire

system of education. Although the land ordinances had divided areas of the state into "school districts," only a small number of such districts provided free public instruction. A state law, however, provided tuition grants for poor children so that no one in the state need be deprived of an education because of poverty. But the report of the Working Men's Party criticized the law as being "incomplete and frequently inoperative." It also criticized the whole idea of private education:

> The elementary schools throughout the state are irresponsible institutions, established by individuals, from mere motives of private speculation or gain, who are sometimes destitute of character, and frequently, of the requisite attainments and abilities. From the circumstance of the schools being the absolute property of individuals, no supervision or effectual control can be exercised over them: hence, ignorance, inattention, and even immorality, prevail to a lamentable extent among their teachers.[9]

It was to be expected that the private school would be attacked as intrinsically immoral because its owners made a profit. But the strongest objection to private education was in the fact that it could not be controlled or supervised by the state.

The report also criticized the public system for providing no care or instruction for children under five. It recommended the creation of "infant schools" which would "prevent much of that vicious depravity of character which penal codes and punishments are intended to counteract." It also suggested that the public schools not only teach "words and cyphers" but extend its influence "to the production of a just disposition, virtuous habits, and a rational self-governing character."

Accompanying the report was a proposed bill for establishing common schools throughout the state and the equivalent of trade schools in each county. The trade school was to be modeled, in part, after the experimental school at Hofwyl, Switzerland, founded in 1809 by Emanuel von Fellenberg, in which manual labor, for the first time, was combined with literature and science to form a unique curriculum. All four of Robert Owen's sons had attended Hofwyl, which suggests that Robert Dale Owen was probably the chief author of the Working Men's Party report, for the latter described the Swiss school in some detail.

The senior Robert Owen had visited Hofwyl in 1817 and converted Fellenberg to his way of thinking. In his autobiography, Owen wrote: "I agreed to send my sons and place them under M. de Fellenberg's especial care and direction. I have ever remembered this visit with unmixed pleasure, from the gratification I experienced in the friendly, frank, confidential communication of mind to mind on all subjects, enhanced by the mutual confidence each had in the other."

The Hofwyl establishment consisted of a primary school, a college for young aristocrats, an industrial school for orphaned or destitute boys, and workshops for agricultural implements. Robert Dale Owen and his brother William were enrolled in the college, and two younger brothers, David and Richard, were enrolled several years later. Explaining Fellenberg's philosophy, Robert Dale Owen later wrote in his autobiography:

> The one great idea of his life appears to have been, not to fuse, in the crucible of equality, what are called the upper and the lower classes, but to seize the extremes of society, and carefully to educate them both: the one to be intelligent, cultivated workers; the other to be wise and considerate legislators, enlightened and philanthropic leaders of civilization. I believe he imagined that there would be rich and poor to the end of the world; and he restricted his endeavors to making the rich friends of the poor, and the poor worthy of such friendship. To carry out this last he considered agriculture, when intelligently followed as a calling, to be an essential aid.

On his estate of Hofwyl, purchased in 1809, he commenced first a workshop for improved farm implements: ten years later an industrial school. . . . I think M. de Fellenberg considered this industrial experiment of more importance, as a reformatory agency, then our college.[10]

Fellenberg's industrial school was in fact the first real reform school. The whole idea behind it was that human character could be reformed through a combination of work and education. It was an idea that appealed greatly to the Unitarians, who were seeking evidence that education was indeed the means of human salvation. Thus, both the Unitarians and the Owenites found much to admire in Hofwyl.

However, the people of Pennsylvania were hardly convinced that the educational reforms outlined in the Working Men's Party report were necessary or even desirable. Throughout the summer of 1830, the Philadelphia *National Gazette* published a series of editorials critical of the report and expressing what could be considered today rather libertarian social views. On July 12, 1830, it wrote:

It is an old and sound remark, that government cannot provide for the necessities of the People; that it is they who maintain the government, and not the latter the People. Education may be among their necessities; but it is one of that description which the state or national councils cannot supply, except partially and in a limited degree. They may endow public schools for the indigent, and colleges for the most comprehensive and costly scheme of instruction. To create or sustain seminaries for the tuition of all classes—to digest and regulate systems; to adjust and manage details, to render a multitude of schools effective, this is beyond their province and power. Education in general must be the work of the intelligence, need, and enterprise of individuals and associations. At present, in nearly all the most populous parts of the United States, it is attainable for nearly all the inhabitants; it is comparatively cheap, and if not the best possible, it is susceptible of improvement and likely to be advanced. Its progress and wider diffusion will depend, not upon government, but on the public spirit, information, liberality and training of the citizens themselves, who may appreciate duly the value of the object as a national good, and as a personal benefit for their children. Some of the writers about universal instruction and discipline, seem to forget the constitution of modern society, and disclaim as if our communities could receive institutions or habits like those of Sparta.[11]

The editorial of July 16, 1830 was particularly interesting. Pennsylvania had not started out as a Puritan colony with laws compelling communities to support schools. It could therefore look at the New England common schools with much less reverence than James Carter, George Ticknor, and the other Unitarian promoters of public education. To the Pennsylvanians, the general decline of the New England common school system was a strong argument against public education, not an argument for extending it. The editorialist quoted the Hartford *Courant* of July 13, 1830, which painted quite a dismal picture of the common schools in Connecticut:

"The prevailing mode of managing our common schools renders them comparatively useless. Exclusive reliance is placed upon the avails of the fund, and in a great majority of instances, no addition is made to the amount obtained from this source, by tax or otherwise, and consequently adequate means are not provided for employing competent instructors, and introducing the improvements which have been suggested by modern investigations. In most cases, the public provision which has been made for schools, instead of operating as an encouragement to liberality and effort for their improvement, is regarded as a sufficient excuse for doing nothing. Accordingly the public money is used while it lasts, and when this is exhausted the school is discontinued. A cheap instructor is employed for a few months, and the remainder of the year the school-house is closed."

This is but a faint illustration of what would happen if the new project of Universal Education, by means of the Government, was at all practicable and should be attempted. The higher colleges, military and naval schools, and schools for the indigent, may be endowed by government and administered by persons of its choice; but education generally, to be effective, must be left to the enterprise and competition of individuals, to the sagacity and liberality of parents, and to the efforts of enlightened associations. In this country, nothing could prevent it from becoming a political job, if a government concern.[12]

The editorial of August 19, 1830, argued convincingly against the forced redistribution of wealth called for by the advocates of universal public education who wanted direct taxation to pay for it all. The newspaper criticized the idea as being a form of "Agrarianism," a property redistribution scheme thought up by Thomas Skidmore, one of the New York radicals in the Working Men's Party. Oddly enough, Robert Dale Owen was strongly opposed to Agrarianism on the ground that it was "devoid of common sense." The New Harmony failure had convinced Owen that education had to precede any sort of property redistribution, for only men educated in advance to be socialists could make socialism work. Therefore, the aim of the Working Men's Party was equal education for all. The *National Gazette* was quite critical of this educational egalitarianism. It wrote:

We have no confidence in any compulsory equalizations; it has been well observed that they pull down what is above, but never much raise what is below, and often "depress high and low together beneath the level of what was originally the lowest." By no possibility could a perfect equality be procured. A scheme of universal equal education, attempted in reality, would be an unexampled bed of Procrustes, for the understandings of our youth, and in fact, could not be used with any degree of equality of profit, unless the dispositions and circumstances of parents and children were nearly the same; to accomplish which phenomenon, in a nation of many millions, engaged in a great variety of pursuits, would be beyond human power.[13]

One of the strongest arguments used by the proponents of public education was that the poor would benefit greatly from such a system. But were the poor taking advantage of the facilities that already existed? The *National Gazette* editorialist commented on that problem on August 23, 1830:

We do know that it has been found extremely difficult to induce the poorer classes of Philadelphia to avail themselves, for their children, of our Common Schools; and that they neglect the benefit in a degree which would be deemed almost incredible. It is not that they are averse to the charity education, as such; they prefer, or are obliged, to use their offspring at home, or consign them to manufactories.

In New York, the same reluctance or refusal is experienced. There is room in the schools there, for thousands more of pupils than are given. The real state of the case may be known by reference to the New York official reports. Good private teachers abound in Philadelphia, if they could obtain scholars. We are acquainted with men of excellent capacity, who have failed wholly or partially, in the attempt to form establishments, though asking for their instruction, a price within the means of the great majority of our citizens. The due encouragement of private enterprise would answer every salutary purpose.[14]

The picture thus drawn of American education in 1830 was one of great freedom and opportunity for anyone willing to take advantage of what was available. That the poor found more value in earning money than sitting in classrooms should come as no surprise. It is also true today, and accounts for the huge dropout problem that plagues modern public education.

All of the arguments against public or government education were of no avail to the Owenites or the Unitarians.

The socialists were out to do away with the individual, competitive system of which private education was a part, and the Unitarians, driven by the need to prove that man was not the hopeless, fallen creature portrayed by Calvin, saw public education as the instrument of human salvation. Neither group would be denied its opportunity to prove the rightness of its cause.

6. The Socialist Purpose in Public Education

THE WORKING MEN'S Party, during its short existence from 1827 to 1831, was little more than a front for Owenite ideas and political activism. Owen and Wright had come to New York in 1829 because it provided them with the best possible platform from which to wage their campaign for universal public education. *The Free Enquirer,* owned and edited by Owen and Wright from 1829 to 1832, provides us with a detailed weekly chronicle of their activities and thoughts during those years. It was the mouthpiece of the socialist movement, advocating the communal way of life, the redistribution of wealth, women's liberation, atheism or at best a sort of pantheism, and above all, a national public education system. It attracted a great deal of attention and a great deal of opposition. The working men were not at all attracted by such radicalism, and when it became known who were the true minds behind the party, it disintegrated.

The fact is that intellectuals, educators, and clergymen were far more inclined to be drawn to Owen and Wright than were the working men. Among clergymen drawn to Owenism were Abner Kneeland (1774-1844) and Orestes A.

Brownson (1803-1876). Kneeland, a Universalist minister from New England, became intimate with Owen and Wright in New York, contributed frequently to *The Free Enquirer*, then moved to Boston where he became the leader of a group known as the First Society of Free Enquirers, and in 1831 began publishing his own weekly, the *Boston Investigator*. In 1835 he was tried and convicted of blasphemy, whereupon a group of noted Unitarians, including William E. Channing, Theodore Parker, and Ralph Waldo Emerson, protested in his behalf. Kneeland, however, served sixty days in jail, after which he migrated to Iowa to start a communal settlement which never materialized.

Brownson, also a Universalist clergyman, became a corresponding editor of *The Free Enquirer* in 1829 and was active in the Working Men's Party as a covert organizer. In 1832, he became a Unitarian minister in the Boston area, where there was an active branch of the Working Men's Party, indicating that one could be both a Unitarian and an Owenite without any conflict. Brownson was also drawn to the Transcendentalists who were later to found the celebrated Brook Farm communal experiment. Brownson published the *Boston Quarterly Review* and knew Channing, Emerson, Thoreau, Bancroft, George Ripley and a host of other Unitarian intellectuals. After twelve years as a Unitarian, he renounced his religious liberalism and converted to Catholicism. In his autobiography he revealed that the Owenites went underground in 1829 and organized their activities nationwide in the form of a secret society in order to attain their goal of universal public education. Brownson wrote:

> The great object was to get rid of Christianity, and to convert our churches into halls of science. The plan was not to make open attacks on religion, although we might belabor the clergy and bring them into contempt where we could; but to establish a system of state,—we said *national*—schools, from which all religion was to be excluded, in which nothing was to be taught

but such knowledge as is verifiable by the senses, and to which all parents were to be compelled by law to send their children. . . . The first thing to be done was to get this system of schools established. For this purpose, a secret society was formed, and the whole country was to be organized somewhat on the plan of the carbonari of Italy, or as were the revolutionists throughout Europe by Bazard preparatory to the revolutions of 1820 and 1830. This organization was commenced in 1829, in the city of New York, and to my own knowledge was effected throughout a considerable part of New York State. How far it was extended in other states, or whether it is still kept up I know not, for I abandoned it in the latter part of the year 1830, and have since had no confidential relations with any engaged in it; but this much I can say, the plan has been successfully pursued, the views we put forth have gained great popularity, and the whole action of the country on the subject has taken the direction we sought to give it. I have observed too that many who were associated with us and relied upon to carry out the plan, have taken the lead in what has been done on the subject. . . . It would be worth inquiring, if there were any means of ascertaining how large a share of this secret infidel society, with its members all through the country unsuspected by the public, and unknown to each other, yet all known to a central committee, and moved by it, have had in giving the extraordinary impulse to godless education which all must have remarked since 1830, an impulse which seems too strong for any human power now to resist.[1]

We can assume that Robert Dale Owen and Frances Wright were members of the central committee guiding this secret society. Was William Maclure also a member? Brownson had observed that "many who were associated with us and relied upon to carry out the plan, have taken the lead in what has been done on the subject."

Among educators who were drawn into the Owenite movement was Henry Darwin Rogers, a 20-year-old natural scientist teaching at the Maryland Institute, who had been converted to Owenism in 1828 after attending a lecture series given by Frances Wright in Baltimore. Rogers was one of four closely knit brothers who were to distinguish themselves as educators and scientists in the years to come. The most important of the four, William Barton Rogers, would one day found the Massachusetts Institute of Technology. In 1828, Henry Rogers wrote his brother William, describing his meeting with Miss Wright:

> The populace of Baltimore throughout all last week have been wonderstruck by the matchless eloquence of a most daring reformer. Miss Frances Wright, a coadjutor of Owen the Harmonist, and joint conductor with him of the "Harmony Gazette," an infidel in all religion and an avowed opponent of existing institutions, has, in association with a gentleman of the name Jennings, been preaching a crusade throughout the chief of the Atlantic cities. A prodigy in learning, in intellect and in courage, she awes into deference the most refractory bigots. . . .
>
> . . . That you may know more accurately her views, I should inform you of the purport and topics of her lectures. Her first was on free inquiry, tending to lull the prejudices of those who recoil at the discussion of subjects at all implicating religion. The two subsequent ones regarded knowledge, its importance, its true nature, and its source primarily in the senses: this had a powerful bearing on the substantiality of religious belief. The fourth lecture was devoted to a disproof of the justice of any science of theology, and contained some highly philosophical discussion on the distinction between belief and knowledge. In the last she treated of morals. The whole might be regarded as a happy extension and application of the sound philosophy of Brown to the existing condition of human institutions; but there were throughout such clearness and reach of thought, sublimity of diction, and often such powerful philippics against the clergy, that every mind seemed spell-bound throughout the term of her lectures.[2]

Henry Rogers joined the movement and became one of the inner circle. In 1832, he wrote a series of articles on education which were published in *The Free Enquirer*. The first article, published on April 28, 1832, re-echoed Robert Owen's conviction that education would have to precede social reform. Rogers wrote:

> The true struggle for human liberty is in the field of education. . . . The tide of political improvement in a nation, may be arrested and turned back for a day by the barriers thrown against it by the hand of tyranny, the conflict of a heroic people for their dearest rights and liberties may for a reason end in their ruin and defeat, but let them only once free education from its abuses, (and this they are never too powerless to do,) and their final emancipation from inequality and servitude is certain. . . . If the extension of education in an equal share to all, be a necessary preliminary in securing equality in political and social rights, quite as necessary to that preliminary itself, must I regard many previous reforms in the style and manner of conducting instruction. . . .
>
> There are many abuses in government, in law, in social institutions generally, and to overthrow these, many hard conflicts must be fought, but at the foundation of them all, lies a previous reform in education. It is on that ground then, that the champions of improvement in the present day should take their most decided stand; and surely the advocates of man can find no fitter field on which to contest his glorious cause. Let but a sound plan for instruction overtake the place of that which now prevails, and though every other plan now on foot for the benefit of society should fail of success, it would not lessen for one moment my present confidence in the speedy melioration of the race.

Rogers was convinced that the struggle to reform education would be a long one, but that it was the surest road to socialist success. In short, there was "no fitter field" on which the "advocates of man" could do battle. With the demise of the Working Men's Party in 1831, the Owenites had indeed shifted their activities and resources into education. For Rogers, the most important task now was to reform "the style and manner of conducting instruction," for it would be useless to create universal public education without devising in great detail a new plan of instruction or curriculum to go with it. In all, Rogers wrote eight essays, the last of which appeared on June 30, 1832. The essays outlined a program of progressive education a good seventy years before John Dewey "originated" it all. As in the progressive education of the future, Rogers advocated a stronger emphasis on the natural sciences and a lesser emphasis on language studies.

In several of the essays, Rogers outlined in considerable detail a plan for a new educational institution to be devoted to scientific and technical instruction, based on observation of the material world, devoid of any moral values or inferences. He believed that such an education would lead to the adoption of a scientific, rational approach to the world, free of religious superstition and dogma. Out of these ideas, he and his brother William later developed a plan for a polytechnical institute which would in 1861 be established as the Massachusetts Institute of Technology, with William Barton Rogers its first president. It is not without significance that America's leading scientific university should have been founded by a socialist working in concert with Harvard Unitarians determined to remake the character of man. In 1849, William Barton Rogers married the daughter of James Savage, one of the leading Unitarian activists in the cause of public education.

In May 1832, Henry Rogers sailed for Europe with Robert Owen and Robert Dale Owen. Rogers stayed in London with the Owens through the winter, studying geology with some of the most eminent scientists of the day. From London, Rogers wrote a letter to *The Free Enquirer*, dated July 13, 1832, which was published on September 8, 1832. In the letter Rogers reiterated his conviction that education had to precede any radical reform of society. He wrote:

Benevolent spirits in different regions of the world have of late been active in devising new systems of legislation and new forms of society for the purpose of better meeting the social necessities of man. I revere the noble goodness of their intentions. I partly anticipate beneficial consequences to their labors, but their efforts radically to cure the evils of society by legislative invention, I look upon as visionary. Robert Owen, the St. Simonians in France, and the Agrarians in America, all overlook, it seems to me, the previous necessity of cultivating in man a new character, before great definite change in social arrangements can prevail—of qualifying men for a new state before forcing them into it.

The lesson of New Harmony had been learned so well that Rogers probably thought he could teach Robert Owen something. But Robert Dale Owen had said the same thing many times before many audiences: that no permanent change in the organization of society could come about without *first* changing the character of man. *The Free Enquirer* of July 28, 1832 published one of Robert Dale Owen's more fiery speeches on national education, in which the lesson of New Harmony was implicit in every line. He said:

Suppose the ill-gotten treasure of the speculator, and the well earned savings of the fortunate and industrious, alike thrown into common stock, and equal partition made to each adult throughout the republic. Suppose that to-night each purse was equally filled, and each citizen an equal landed proprietor. How long, think you, would the artificial equality last? A year? a month? a single week? . . . In a word, in destroying the inequality of the moment, ye would leave all the thousand causes that at first produced, still reproduce it. . . .

No! Ye must have some better substitute for religion than moral preaching or agrarian laws. Ye must touch the root of the evil. . . .

Ye must take human mind—not the adult mind of this degenerate age, that has learnt all the tricks of dishonesty, and stooped to all the caprices of folly, that is warped by prejudice and blotted by vice—but the pure, unstained, unwritten mind of infancy. And there ye must engrave those characters of rational wisdom and republican virtue. . . .

Less than this is but to trifle with reform. Less than this is but to play the old game of inequality and ignorance over again. Less than this cannot rescue the national character or cure the national disease. If this country is to be redeemed, National Education, extended through all her states, must be her redeemer.

Owen realized that one of the greatest obstacles to his father's utopian plan was the general Calvinist belief in the innate depravity of human nature. It was this belief that compelled the founding fathers to devise a form of government of checks and balances to limit the power of politicians and to make political tyranny as difficult as possible to succeed. The confidence the founding fathers had in human nature was clearly demonstrated by the legal bulwark they built to constrain it. The Calvinist distrust of human nature was the cornerstone of the American system. But Owen tried to convince his Working Men's Party audiences otherwise. He said in the August 4, 1832 *Free Enquirer:*

Priests may traduce our nature by preaching of innate depravity; and moral teachers deny the existence of virtues which they are too blind to discriminate and too ignorant to call forth,—there *is* in the human mind a deep spring of lovely feeling and generous sentiment. . . .

Do ye ask me wherein I put my trust, if religious responsibilities are annihilated? In human goodness. Do ye enquire what I propose as a substitute for religion? Cultivation of the noble faculties of the human mind. Will ye tell me that I lean on a broken reed, and propose an inefficient substitute?—that fear is stronger than love, and religious enthusiasm more powerful and endearing than human integrity? Will ye tell me that the heart of the smiling infant is irredeemably corrupt, and that all its artless thoughts are only evil continually? Alas for the degrading slander that has stolen from man his self-respect! Alas for the priestly humility that bids us cry out weekly that we are miserable sinners, until, by dint of repetition, we begin, in very truth, to merit the name! . . .

Let us train children to integrity, and we shall have honest men and women;—to temperance, and temperance will cover the land;—to equality, and we shall see a republic. Let us give children facts for spiritualities, good habits for long sermons, the truths of science for the mysteries of creeds, kindness for fear, and liberality for sectarianism. I said liberality for sectarianism, and I would not be misunderstood. I do not mean irreligion when I say liberality. I would as little prejudice a child against any religion as in its favor; I would not speak to it on the subject. It should learn first what it could see and understand: its judgment should be carefully matured, and its reasoning powers sedulously cultivated. And if at riper age, when it opened its eyes on the creeds that now distract the world, it found one among the number that bore the impress of reason and truth, it is not I who would complain of conversion.

This was a perfect description of what was meant by a liberal, secular education. It was to be scientific and impartial, devoid of any religious content. Thus, public education, which had been instituted in the Puritan colony as a means of guaranteeing the survival of pure religion, would now be used to destroy it. And in time, secular American education would become largely socialist and atheist in content and values. Owen continued:

Let us, then take the infant mind; let us seclude it from the temptations that corrupt its tender virtue—from the tyranny that blunts its sensibilities; from the ignorance that confounds its nascent conceptions; from the mysteries that becloud its expanding reason; let us take the infant mind, and train it from youth to manhood in seclusion from the corruption of a vicious age, to reason and virtue, and then we shall have an intelligent and happy world.

Who doubts the omnipotence of National Education? Let

him read of Sparta, and learn how her infant citizens were trained to belie almost every weakness of their nature. Let us learn of Lycurgus—of him who moulded a nation's character to his will,—let us learn of him the secret of government. Let us, like him, "resolve the whole business of legislation into the bringing up of youth," ere we presumptuously assert, that human nature is, and always will be, deceitful above all things and desperately wicked.

Of course, Robert Dale Owen did not live to witness the incredible excesses of evil in the twentieth century: the killing of millions in Russia by Lenin and Stalin, the rise of Hitler and the extermination of the Jews, the enslavement of Eastern Europe, the rise of Mao Tse Tung and the murder of millions in China, the bloody reign of Pol Pot and the mass murders in Cambodia, and all the other atrocities and acts of barbarism perpetrated by National Socialists and communists in the name of human progress. No one could have predicted what "trust" in human nature would produce.

In any case, the Owenites had decided that national education must precede everything else in their program, and that political and academic activism in its behalf, overt and covert, must become socialism's first priority. This was spelled out at a public meeting of the Association for the Protection of Industry and for the Promotion of Popular Education reported in *The Free Enquirer* of November 7, 1829. Among the resolutions unanimously adopted at that meeting were the following:

Resolved, the opinion of this meeting, that any peaceful and effectual measures which shall tend permanently to equalize the possession of landed property and of all other property, will prove eminently useful to society.

Resolved, that, hitherto, in this republic, professing the principles of equality, there has been in practice, a most unequal division of wealth, power, and privileges.

Resolved, that the most grievous species of inequality is that produced by unequal education: and that a National System of Education and Guardianship which shall furnish to all the children of the land equal food, clothing and instruction, at the public expense, is the only effectual remedy for this and for almost every other species of injustice.

Resolved, that we will support as candidates for members of Assembly or of the Senate those men, *and those men only*, whom we believe to be favorable to a National System of Education.

Resolved, that if any candidate, elected to any office whatever should, in word or deed, *seek to oppose the passing of a law for the promotion of National Education, as in a former resolution defined, we will* FOR EVER AFTER, (or until unequivocal evidence be afforded us, of a conscientious change of opinion in that candidate) *withhold our votes from him*, be his class, talents, profession and political creed what they may.

It was perhaps this single-minded, unbending stand on public education which gave the Owenite effort "an impulse," as Brownson later wrote, "which seems too strong for any human power now to resist." The same issue of *The Free Enquirer* that published the above resolutions also published a statement by Robert Dale Owen entitled "My Creed." Was this the oath that members of the secret society were required to take? It read:

I believe in a National System of Equal, Republican, Protective, Practical Education, the sole regenerator of a profligate age, and the only redeemer of our suffering country from the equal curses of chilling poverty and corrupting riches, of gnawing want and destroying debauchery, of blind ignorance and of unprincipled intrigue.

By this, my creed, I will live. By my consistency, or inconsistency with this, my professed belief, I claim to be judged. By it I will stand or fall.

Robert Dale Owen was to remain true to his creed. As a member of the Indiana state legislature from 1836 to 1838 he was instrumental in getting the state to allocate half its surplus funds from the federal government for public education. Then as a Congressman (1843–47) he introduced a bill in 1845 for the establishment of the Smithsonian Institution for the dissemination of scientific knowledge. In 1850, at the Indiana constitutional convention he was instrumental in getting the state to adopt a full state-supported educational system. In many respects he had the same single-minded determination to further the cause of socialism as his father had. While in England in 1832, Owen worked with his father for six months as co-editor of *The Crisis*. In a letter to *The Free Enquirer* (September 22, 1832) dated London, July 18, 1832, Robert Dale Owen drew this fascinating picture of his father:

> My father (if a son's opinion may be received in evidence) is a most extraordinary man. Now, at the age of *sixty-one* . . . he is, more active, far more zealous, a hundred times more sanguine, than I, thirty years his junior, ever was or ever shall be. . . . From seven in the morning until ten at night, he thinks of nothing, speaks of nothing, acts for nothing, save only and alone the furtherance of his system of reform. . . . Nothing interests him but that one engrossing theme; nothing seems to him of value, but with direct reference thereto; no one useful, but as he promotes it; no one intelligent but as he understands it. . .
>
> But that I have seen it, I should not believe it possible for a human being to be devoted so exclusively, so absorbingly, to one great idea; . . . I have seen nothing, even in religious enthusiasm, to match this unchanging confidence, this unvarying self-devotion. Did three or four individuals, of enlightened views and sound practical knowledge, possess the same, it seems to me they might, with ease, revolutionize the civilized world.

Such was the nature of the man determined to establish national education systems in both England and the United

States for the purpose of reforming the human character so that it could live happily ever after in cooperative paradise. The socialist plan for public education was conceived even before the word socialism was invented. We can assume that socialists flocked into education where they were expected to do their major work. How many socialists became educators? We have no sure way of knowing. How many educators became socialists? We know of Henry Rogers and his brother William, and there were obviously many more who attained high positions in the educational world and promoted fellow socialists into key positions. But since so much of this was done covertly, we may never know the full extent of the socialist influence in the American public school movement.

Meanwhile, in England, Robert Owen, convinced by the New Harmony experience that the world would have to pass through a transition stage before it could be ready for socialism, continued to refine his educational concepts. In 1836 he published *The Book of The New Moral World Containing The Rational System of Society, Found on Demonstrable Facts, Developing The Constitution and Laws of Human Nature and Society*. In it, Owen spelled out the world-wide messianic scope of his plan, which would include every human being and strongly influence the future curriculum of public education. He wrote:

[This book] unfolds the fundamental principles of a New Moral World, and it thus lays a new foundation on which to reconstruct society and re-create the character of the human race. It opens to the family of man, without a single exception, the means of endless progressive improvement, physical, intellectual, and moral, and of happiness, without the possibility of retrogression or of assignable limit.

Society has emanated from fundamental errors of the imagination, and all the institutions and social arrangements of man over the world have been based on these errors. Society is, therefore, through all its ramifications, artificial and corrupt, and, in consequence, ignorance, falsehood and grave folly alone, govern all the affairs of mankind.

The religious, moral, political and commercial arrangements of society, throughout the world, have been based, from the commencement of history, upon an error respecting the nature of man; an error so grievous in its consequences, that it has deranged all the proceedings of society, made man irrational in his thoughts, feelings and actions, and consequently, more inconsistent, and perhaps more miserable, then any other animal. . . .

A superior state of human society, therefore, can be formed, only, upon a knowledge that man is not the former of his own nature; that it is organized in a manner unknown to him, and without his consent; and that, when it is comparatively ill-formed in any particular instance, the individual is an object of compassion, calling for our kindest exertions to remedy the evil, and never once for blame or punishment. . . .

It is thus, by the quality and quantity of external circumstances, properly applied for the purpose, that the character of every human being, after he comes into existence, may be principally formed, whatever may be his organization, short of organic disease, to become at maturity very inferior or very superior. It is thus, that future generations may be placed and trained, from their birth, upon principles as certain and permanent in their nature as those of the fixed sciences, to become, without exception, beings of an order altogether different from past generations of men, and greatly superior to them physically, intellectually and morally. . . .

The proper business of man, hereafter, will therefore be to make himself thoroughly acquainted with "the science of the influence of circumstances over human nature"; and by a knowledge of this science he will hold the destinies of future ages, as to their inferiority or superiority, their misery or happiness, under his control. . . .

The easiest mode of training men to be intelligent, superior in their habits, manner and conduct, and to enjoy progressive happiness from birth to death, is to adopt decisive measures to prevent the formation of vicious or inferior habits in a single individual. And when all the laws of human nature, the conditions requisite for happiness, and the science of society, or the social state of man, shall be fully understood, it will be discovered to be for the interest of every one, that not a single individual shall be neglected in the formation of his habits from infancy to maturity, and that it will be much more easy to form arrangements to make *all* really superior, than to train a *few* to be what are now ignorantly considered superior, while the many around them are neglected and allowed to grow up inferior. . . .

This power in the adult, to create so large a portion of the character of his offspring, will enable one generation to see and enjoy the great improvements secured to the coming generation. It will enable those, now living, to adopt a decisive system of progressive and unlimited advance towards human physical, intellectual, and moral perfection. . . .

When the moral science of man, and the science of society, or social science, shall be generally known, the means will become obvious by which the adult part of society will be enabled to teach the young truth only; that is, to make all the impressions which produce convictions on the mind to be in accordance with facts.[3]

Several things come out very clearly from this particular work of Owen's: first, that the radical reformation of human character was at the heart of Owen's socialist program, and that education would be the specific instrument whereby this reformation would be realized, which explains why socialists have so heavily infiltrated the teaching profession; second, that the program was inherently totalitarian in nature in that it included *all* human beings of *all* nations and races and provided no place whatever for any variant or deviant character to exist or for parental preference to be respected; third, that the "science of the influence of circumstances over human nature" would be known as "social science," and that only by the application of "social science" could the entire Owen program be carried out. In fact, the application of "social science" to education would mean that the Owen program was in the process of being carried out.

This is all quite interesting, since progressive educators have given the impression to the lay public that the idea of "social science" was conceived sometime in the nineteen thirties by the followers of John Dewey at Columbia Teachers College. Owen originated the concept one hundred years earlier, before the American or British public educational systems were even in existence. Thus we can easily understand why public education has had, from the outset, such a strong prosocialist bias and why young adults emerging from the public schools are so poorly equipped to defend capitalism and individual freedom.

In the 1830's, however, once the full scope of Owen's program was understood by the public, opposition to it was very strong. It was one thing to create a voluntary communist community for a few true believers, as did the Rappites. It was quite another to preach, believe in, and work for the communization of the entire human race. Owen's program for *everyone*, promoted with his peculiar brand of infallibility and megalomania, repelled most people but attracted enough of a following among people like Maclure, Kneeland, and Henry Rogers to make its influence felt in society. It would take Karl Marx, however, to transform voluntary Owenism into a serious revolutionary threat to Western civilization.

Meanwhile, in December 1832, H. D. Robinson, the new editor of *The Free Enquirer*, complained about the dwindling support the publication was getting. "Christian newspapers," he wrote, "are numerous and well supported, Christian prayer meetings, Christian Sunday Schools, Christian public and private academies and universities, and various other mighty engines of Christian influence, are all planted like the artillery of Heaven against the ramparts of reason and truth." By 1833 such liberal publications as the *Boston Investigator,* the *New York Daily Sentinel,* and the *Delaware Free Press* had folded.

In August of 1832, Robert Dale Owen decided that he had done his work as an editor of *The Free Enquirer* and was ready to move on to other things. He wrote to his readers:

> It is, perhaps, almost as essential to public usefulness, as to private peace of mind, that one should be secure in a pecuniary independence, however small; and this is especially necessary in the case of a heretic. The portion of property which I own in Indiana is sufficient (with my habits) to secure me an independence, while I attend to it myself; insufficient, if I neglect it. Its value depends, in a great measure, on the prosperity or non-prosperity of the town and surrounding lands, (of which it forms a small part.) It is my intention, therefore, to unite my efforts to those of my brother William, already there, so as to secure, if possible, to New Harmony, all the advantages essential to the well-being of a western settlement.
>
> . . . We refrain, at the present, from anticipating, as once we might, the immediate introduction of any radical change in the whole structure of society. . . . I wish I could still believe this change to be close at hand. It is so grateful an idea to anticipate a state of society whence private bargaining and selfish calculations should all be excluded, and where the sordid venalities of commerce should never fall in, to make Cains of us all. Yet, if we cannot at once eradicate the evil, we can mitigate it.

Owen had simply come to the realization that the road to socialism would be a long one. The American people were not about to give up their political liberties, their religions, their property, their children to state guardians for a promised communist utopia. By 1833, the period of highly vocal, radical, anti-religious activism which had begun with the creation of New Harmony was over. The reformers would now toil more quietly but no less diligently on the long educational road to socialism.

7. The Educators Organize

AT ABOUT THE time that the socialists decided to make public education the primary instrument of their efforts to reform the character of man preliminary to their radical reform of society, American educators began to organize into substantial pressure groups in favor of public education. The man most responsible for this development was Josiah Holbrook, founder of the American Lyceum movement. A plan for the Lyceum organization, originally conceived as a "society for mutual instruction," was first made public by Holbrook in a letter to the Editor in the October 1826 issue of the *American Journal of Education*. Holbrook wrote:

Sir, I take the liberty to submit for your consideration, a few articles as regulations for associations for mutual instruction in the sciences, and in useful knowledge generally. You will see they are upon a broad basis; and the reason is that men of views enlightened enough upon education to see its defects and wants, and spirit enough to act, are scattered more or less through the country; and all that is necessary for action, is some definite plan of operation by which their efforts can be united and brought to bear upon one point.

111

Holbrook then went on to describe the various functions the Society for Mutual Education would perform in the field of education, stressing the need to spread scientific knowledge. In that first letter he already envisaged the organization becoming national in scope, with town societies sending delegates to a county board; with county boards sending delegates to a state board. Holbrook wrote:

> Each board of delegates shall appoint a representative, to meet representatives from other boards who shall be styled the Board of Mutual Education for a given State; and it might be advantageous to have also a General Board embracing the United States.
> It shall be the duty of the General or State Boards to meet annually to appoint a president and other officers, to devise and recommend such a system of Education as they shall think most eligible, also to recommend such books as they shall think best fitted to answer the purposes for which they are designed, and to adopt and recommend such measures, generally, as are most likely to secure to the rising generation the best intellectual, moral, and physical education, and to diffuse the greatest quantity of useful information among the various classes of the community.

The plan, in embryo, was an attempt to organize and centralize educational policy in a country of complete educational freedom. To say the least, it was an extremely ambitious plan for anyone to dream up in a country as large and diverse as the United States. One begins to wonder if perhaps Holbrook's plan, particularly in the way it was developed, was not dreamed up by the Owenites. There are circumstances in Holbrook's biography which strongly suggest that he and the Owenites were working in concert toward the same end. In the previous chapter we suggested that some educators became Owenites and some Owenites became educators. It is difficult to say which was the case with Holbrook.

But one thing we do know is that soon after the failure at New Harmony, the Owenites organized themselves in secret cells throughout the country in order to achieve covertly what they could not achieve overtly. Of this secret society Orestes Brownson wrote in his autobiography:

> The members of this secret society were to avail themselves of all the means in their power, each in his own locality, to form public opinion in favor of education by the state at the public expense, and to get such men elected to the legislatures as would be likely to favor our purposes. How far the secret organization extended, I do not know; but I do know that a considerable portion of the State of New York was organized, for I was myself one of the agents organizing it.[1]

We also know that it was under William Maclure's patronage that a "Society for Mutual Instruction" was organized,[2] undoubtedly the same society proposed by Holbrook in his letter to the *American Journal of Education*. Was Josiah Holbrook a member of this secret Owenite organization? Was he a member of its central committee? His known biographical data suggest that he very well may have been.

Josiah Holbrook was born in Derby, Connecticut, in 1788. He was educated at the local district school, entered Yale in 1806, and was graduated in 1810. In 1813 he married. His wife died in 1819 leaving him two sons, and at about the same time his parents died, leaving him their farm. In 1819 he organized an industrial school on his farm, modeled after the institution at Hofwyl, founded by Fellenberg in 1809, the same school attended by Robert Dale Owen and his brothers and well known to Maclure. Prior to founding the school, Holbrook rode regularly to New Haven to attend the lectures of Prof. Benjamin Silliman at Yale, to increase his knowledge of chemistry, minerology and geology. Silliman was the foremost teacher of the natural sciences in the United States, and he was known to all the prominent natural scientists of the day, including William Maclure.

Regarding Maclure, Silliman wrote in his memoirs: "He [Maclure] came to New Haven in the autumn of 1808, and I passed several days with him exploring our geology. He had come from Maine, and had become acquainted with Prof. Parker Cleaveland, whom he greatly admired." Thus began a professional relationship between Silliman and Maclure that was to last more than twenty years. In 1818, Silliman founded the *American Journal of Science and Arts,* the first American scientific journal. An article by Maclure on geology appeared in the first volume. On September 6, 1819, the American Geological Society was organized at Yale. William Maclure was elected president, and the vice presidents included Professors Silliman and Cleaveland, and Col. George Gibbs, brother-in-law of William Ellery Channing. The world of science was very small in those days, and everyone knew everyone else.

It is not stretching the imagination too much to assume that, somewhere along the line, anyone as interested in geology as Holbrook, who knew Silliman quite well, would have eventually met William Maclure, president of the American Geological Society. Anyone who read Silliman's *Journal of Science* would have easily been able to follow the activities of Maclure, which were duly recorded in its pages. Maclure was also president of the Academy of Natural Sciences of Philadelphia, and its work would have been of great interest to Holbrook. Maclure was also interested in all of the educational experiments of the time. In 1805, he had visited Pestalozzi's school in Switzerland, and was so impressed that he brought two of Pestalozzi's associates, Joseph Neef and William Phiquepal (the future husband of Fanny Wright), to the United States in order to set up the first Pestalozzian school in this country. In 1819, Maclure attempted to establish an agricultural school in Spain modeled on Hofwyl, but the project had to be abandoned for political reasons. Thus, Maclure and Holbrook had much in common in the fields of education and geology. In 1824, at about the time that Maclure visited New Lanark and decided to become partners with Robert Owen in his New Harmony experiment, Holbrook established an Agricultural Seminary on his farm. Then, in the fall of 1825, he closed it.

The year 1825 was an important one for the Owenites. Robert Owen came to the United States early in the year and addressed large audiences in the House of Representatives in Washington on February 25 and March 7. American newspapers were full of news about Owen and New Harmony. The June 1825 issue of the *American Journal of Science* carried a letter from Maclure about Owen's experiment, and on October 1, 1825, the *New Harmony Gazette* began publication. Where was Holbrook between the fall of 1825 and the fall of 1826, that is, between the closing of his school and the launching of the Lyceum movement? We know that Robert Owen, Robert Dale Owen, and Maclure's party of natural scientists and educators gathered in New York in the fall of 1825 to prepare for their journey to New Harmony. The Owens had arrived from England on November 7 and for several weeks stayed at the Howard House on Broadway, receiving visitors and preparing for the journey to New Harmony. Robert Dale Owen narrates in his autobiography:

> In the course of two or three weeks several pleasant and intelligent people had joined us, bound for New Harmony; among them Thomas Say, one of the founders of the Academy of Natural Sciences in Philadelphia, who six years before had accompanied Major Long on his expedition to the Rocky Mountains as its naturalist; Charles LeSueur, a French naturalist and designer, who had explored, with Peron, the coasts of Australia; Gerard Troost, a native of Holland and a distinguished chemist and geologist, who was afterwards professor of chemistry in the Nashville University; also several

cultivated ladies, including Miss Sistare (afterwards the wife of Thomas Say) and two of her sisters. Whether William Maclure, president of the Philadelphia Academy of Sciences, and one of the most munificent patrons of that institution, accompanied us, or came on a few weeks later, I am not quite certain. He afterwards purchased from my father several thousand acres of the Harmony estate.[3]

Owen's vagueness about the whereabouts of Maclure during that time matches the vagueness about Holbrook's whereabouts during that same time after the closing of his school. Henry Barnard tells us in a biographic sketch of Holbrook written after the latter's death: "The precise train of thought and of circumstances which led Mr. Holbrook to transfer his efforts from the farm and school at Derby to the wider field of popular scientific lecturing we have no data for tracing."

What we do know is that Owen's party reached Pittsburgh in early December and purchased a keel-boat to take them down the Ohio River to New Harmony. There were from thirty to forty people aboard that famous "boat-load of knowledge," which finally reached New Harmony in the middle of January 1826. Was Holbrook among them? If he was, he might have traveled under an assumed name, for Yale was then a citadel of religious conservatism compared to Harvard, and his association with the atheists and communists at New Harmony would have damaged his future usefulness in the field of education.

By 1826 the full implications of Owen's communist and anti-religious teachings had become well understood by the American public, and to many the experiment at New Harmony was considered not only radical, but clearly the work of the devil. It reached the point where, after an article by William Maclure on "Mr. Owen's Establishment in Indiana," published in the October 1826 *Journal of Science,* nothing further by Maclure about New Harmony appeared thereafter in its pages. In addition, the *American Journal of Education,* which had published a short notice about New Harmony in January 1826, an extract from a letter in June 1826, and a small notice in March 1827, never mentioned Owen, or New Harmony, or Maclure again. Yet, from 1825 to 1832, the Owenites were active and vociferous in their work for public education, and Maclure's school at New Harmony with its distinguished staff was certainly an experiment worthy of attention.

But the simple truth is that any connection with Owen or Maclure was the kiss of death for any organization or movement. This fact was the second lesson the Owenites learned. The first lesson they had learned at New Harmony was that rational education had to precede the institution of socialism. The second was that no movement openly carrying the Owen label could succeed in religious America. Yet, the socialists had decided that public education was to be their first order of business, and it is obvious that the Owenites realized that their operatives would have to work covertly without arousing suspicion to themselves.

A few weeks after Holbrook's plan was first published in October 1826, he lectured at Millbury, Massachusetts, after which he persuaded thirty or forty of his audience to organize themselves into a "society for mutual improvement," which was then designated as Millbury Lyceum No. 1, Branch of the American Lyceum. The formation of the Lyceum at Millbury was closely followed by that of several others in nearby towns, and these were soon combined, as outlined in his plan, into the Worcester County Lyceum. This much accomplished, Holbrook then moved to Boston, which was to be his center of operations for the next few years.

Thus, by 1826, before the word socialism was even coined, the promotion of public education was, to the Owenites, synonymous with the promotion of socialism. The instrument of secular, scientific public education had to be created in order to divest the new generation of the religious myths and superstitions that stood in the way of their becoming rational human beings. The public schools would teach scientific facts only, and that would be enough to create a new race of rational men. Geology, in particular, was a subject that interested the Owenites, for if it could be shown beyond a shadow of a doubt that the earth was older than the Bible said it was, this would prove once and for all that the Bible was myth and not to be believed as infallible authority. This was one line of geological research and investigation that Maclure encouraged, creating a rift between those natural scientists who believed in God and those who didn't. Curiously enough, the U. S. Geological Survey was headquartered at New Harmony until 1856 when it was moved to the Smithsonian Institution in Washington. While Holbrook did not publicly express an opinion in the Biblical argument, he made the study of geology one of the central interests of the Lyceum. Thus, as early as 1826, the socialists were not only working to create the instrument of public education, but also had a clear idea of what its curriculum should be.

The year 1826 also saw the creation of the *American Journal of Education,* the first national journal in the country devoted exclusively to the subject of education. The editor's prospectus in the first issue left no doubt that the Journal would become a mouthpiece for the cause of public education. Its editor, William Russell, was a Scotsman who had come to Boston in the 1820's and, as a teacher of elocution, had quickly become part of the Channing circle. The prospectus in the January 1826 issue read in part:

> The conductors of the Journal will make it their constant endeavor to aid in diffusing *enlarged and liberal views of education.* Nothing, it seems to us, has had more influence in retarding the progress of improvement in the science of instruction, than narrow and partial views of what education should be expected to produce.

Russell then wrote:

There is a deep and strong tide of opinion already undermining all that is useless and cumbrous in instruction. The current of improvement is already flowing; and all that any individual can claim, is the merit of assisting in giving it the most advantageous direction. Our office is not to rouse a dormant attention. Already there is everywhere a stirring of the public mind, and a fervency of public effort, which make it too late for any candidate to hope for the honor of being ranked as a reformer. All that can now be reasonably expected, is the satisfaction of contributing a proportion of service to so good a cause.

In one of the back pages of the first issue there appeared this little notice about New Harmony:

Mr. Owen, whose plans for the melioration of society, have of late excited considerable interest in this country, has instituted, at his settlement of New-Harmony, (Indiana), a school similar to that which attracted so much attention at his establishment in New-Lanark (Scotland). An account of this school will be given in an early number of our work.

That account was never forthcoming. The June 1826 issue published a short extract from a letter from New Harmony, which told very little, and in the March 1827 issue another extract from a letter was published. Among other things, the letter said: "The schools here are independent of all Mr. Owen's religious, political or moral opinions—as much so as those in Boston."

After that, the *Journal of Education* was conspicuously silent on Owen, Maclure, the school at New Harmony, the lectures of Frances Wright and Robert Dale Owen, the program of the Working Men's Party, or anything else connected with the radicals in New Harmony and New York.

What did the *Journal of Education* write about? In that

first year, eight of the issues carried major articles on the Infant Schools, which had become very popular in England and were about to be launched in America. And three issues published large extracts from James G. Carter's books on public education. The lead article in the first issue was an "Account of the System of Infant Schools." The opening paragraphs left no doubt that the interest in the infant mind was more social than educational:

> The cultivation of the infant mind is, of all the departments of education, that in which improvement can be introduced with most ease, and with the greatest certainty of immediate and extensive effect. Here, there are none of those obstacles to be encountered, which the prejudices of ages have successively fastened on institutions devoted to the higher departments of science and literature. Neglect, rather than perverted effort, is to be blamed for the slowness of the progress which has hitherto been made.

In none of the articles was Robert Owen ever to be given credit as the originator of the infant school idea with his school for the formation of character at New Lanark. Owen had particularly focused on the two- to six-year-old group as the crucial period for molding character. William Sargant, in a biography, quotes Owen on this subject:

> Give me a colony of infants; I will suppress all erroneous reasoning and all false conclusions; nothing shall be believed but what is thoroughly understood; I will then so educate my children that they shall grow up to despise those things which now they most value, and unite in a community of interest which will end in universal brotherly love and unity.[4]

But in 1830, after infant schools had been established in many American cities, Robert Dale Owen would write in *The Free Enquirer* (January 30, 1830):

I object to Infant Schools, *as now conducted,* because they are under the control of the clergy, who enlist the sympathies and superstitions of amiable young women to aid them in obtruding on the unsuspecting and immature mind of infancy creeds and doctrines which I believe mischievous at any age, but more peculiarly unsuited to one who is but just opening his senses to perceive the material world around him. . . .

My own father, Robert Owen, was the first individual who imagined and established an infant school. . . . The clergy quickly saw the facilities such a plan afforded, and turned it with zeal and success to their own purposes. Thus that which was designed, by its founder, as a means of storing the young mind with facts, of directing the nascent curiosity upon useful objects, of forming the embryo habits to order and industry, and moulding the docile disposition to kindness and benevolence, has become a tool in the hands of the Christian party in politics, to aid them in their unhallowed designs.

By 1833, however, it was acknowledged that the Infant Schools, great as an idea, were a failure in practice. It was found that children, separated from their mothers at that early age for so many hours, became over-excited and were too difficult to manage.

The *Journal of Education* also became the official organ of Holbrook's Lyceum movement. It was natural for Holbrook to have made Boston his center of operations, for among the Harvard-Boston Unitarians he found the strongest support for his movement and the cause of public education. It took five years, from the creation of the Millbury Lyceum in the fall of 1826 to the first meeting of the National Lyceum in New York in May 1831, for Holbrook to realize his plan for a national organization to centralize and control educational policy. In those five years there were more teacher conventions, more meetings of educators, more educational organizations created than in the previous fifty years of American history. It was a stunning achievement of organization by the indefatigable

Holbrook. By 1833, American educators had been organized into a solid phalanx ready to exert the strongest pressures on town governments and state legislatures in behalf of public education.

What was even more of an accomplishment was the fact that Holbrook had succeeded in enlisting not only the Unitarians and covert socialists to support him but also religious conservatives and many owners of private schools. There was no opposition as such to the Lyceum movement among educators. It promised to improve public support for common schools, improve the lot of teachers, expand the need for more and newer textbooks and teaching equipment. This particularly pleased the textbook writers and publishers, all of whom gave wholehearted support to the Lyceum, because they could see the economic benefits of a centralized policy, particularly if they took part in making that policy.

How was Holbrook able to organize American educators so quickly and so successfully? The first three years were the hardest. But his clear vision of what it was he was aiming for—centralized control—gave his efforts concentrated momentum. In the August 1828 *Journal of Education* he spelled out some of the practical steps to be taken in the direction of centralized control:

> Among the enlightened minds, there is I believe, but one opinion respecting the importance or necessity of a Board of Education. It is quite evident, that no measures of a uniform, general, or efficient character can be taken, until the views and efforts of individuals are concentrated and combined.
>
> Though it cannot be made a question whether it is, or is not desirable and necessary for a society or Board to be organized for the general purpose of diffusing knowledge, and particularly for introducing a uniform and improving system of Popular Education, the manner of organizing and conducting its operations, is a question worthy of mature deliberation. . . . To do this, it will probably be necessary to have such a society so

organized, that it will be supplied with regular channels of communication with every section, and every department of the community, both for diffusing and receiving information.

To infuse life and vigour into every part, and all the extremities of the body on which it is designed to operate, it ought to be connected, both by a vein and an artery with every town and every village of the county for which it is intended.

To establish this connexion, . . . I beg leave to propose through the Journal, that the towns and villages in New England, should have established in each, upon some uniform plan, a society for mutual improvement and the improvement of schools, or for the general purpose of advancing the interests of popular and *practical* education. To have each society supplied with books, particularly a juvenile library, apparatus for familiar and practical illustrations in the sciences, and a collection of specimens in geology and minerology, and such other articles as they shall think fitted to advance their own interests or those of the public. . . . To have all the societies in a county united by a Board of Delegates, which shall be a Board of Education for the county, and auxiliary to a general one for the state. The general Board to consist of delegates or representatives sent from the several county Boards. . . .

If the Legislature of each of the New England states should authorize such a board to act in behalf of schools and of popular education generally, it would not be difficult to establish some connexion or communication by annual meetings of representatives or otherwise, between all the state Boards, and by that means give uniformity, symmetry, energy and effect, to a system of operations, designed to qualify the rising generation to be useful to themselves and the world, to obey and resemble their Creator, and to advance in knowledge and goodness.

The plan thus envisaged a centralized, uniform system of public education, with a revision in the curriculum to stress the sciences and practical instruction. It was, for all practical purposes, the Owen-Maclure program adapted to the realities of the United States at that time. Meanwhile, to encourage the study of the natural sciences and provide himself with an income, Holbrook went into the business of manufacturing all sorts of apparatus for popular instruction in mathematics, physics (then called Natural Philosophy), chemistry, astronomy, and geology.

During 1828 Holbrook's plan received wide and favorable publicity in the New England press. Here's a sample from the *American Traveller,* quoted in the September 1828 *Journal of Education:*

> The fifty or sixty branches of the American Lyceum already established, contemplate a National Institution for the diffusion of knowledge, and the introduction of a uniform and improved system of popular education. It is hoped that, early in the autumn season, every town and village in New England at least, will take its objects into consideration, in regard, both to the instruction it promises to those who associate, and the general diffusion of useful and *practical* knowledge through the community.

William Maclure was in New England during the fall of 1828 to attend a meeting at Yale of the American Geological Society, of which he was still president. Prof. Silliman described the occasion in his memoirs:

> At the meeting of the Geological Society, November 17, 1828, Mr. Maclure appeared decidedly marked by age and infirmity. . . . His friend, Dr. Thomas Cooper, was with him, and these two celebrated men did me the honor to attend one of my lectures in the chemical course, and to call at my house. The principal topic was the moral relations of science and the expositions it gives of the mind and thoughts of the Creator, as they are recorded in his works. . . . Dr. Cooper was well known as a sturdy sceptic in religion, and Mr. Maclure's plans for education did not include the Bible.[5]

Did Holbrook attend the meeting of the Geological Society? Did he meet with Maclure during the latter's stay in

New England? For the moment, we do not know. What we do know is that Maclure, for reasons of health, had spent the winter of 1827-28 in Mexico, and that after his visit to the northeast he returned to Mexico where he became active in promoting his educational ideas. By coincidence, we find that in May 1832 the American Lyceum's second annual meeting in New York was attended by several distinguished Mexicans. Were they friends of Maclure's or his emissaries? This, too, we do not know. Did Holbrook take the opportunity to see Robert Dale Owen while in New York? Such a meeting was certainly possible, for Owen and Henry Rogers did not sail for Europe until two weeks later.

In the spring of 1829, Boston formed its Lyceum under the name of the Boston Society for the Diffusion of Useful Knowledge. Its statement of purpose was signed by William E. Channing and twenty-nine other members of the Boston elite. But Channing's name alone was enough to give it the Harvard-Unitarian seal of approval. The first article in the Society's constitution stated its purpose quite succinctly: "Its object shall be to promote and direct popular education by lectures and other means."

In February 1830, delegates from fourteen county Lyceums met in Boston to form a Massachusetts State Lyceum. Then, in March, Holbrook called a meeting at which a central state committee was chosen, among whose members were Alexander Everett and Horace Mann. Holbrook had also called a teachers' convention in conjunction with the Lyceum meeting. Nearly three hundred teachers and other friends of popular education converged on Boston. At that convention a vote was passed "recommending that a general association of persons, engaged and interested in the business of instruction, be formed." The result was the American Institute of Instruction, the first academic organization of its kind in America. Most of its educator members had written textbooks, and the Institute was to become a platform for academic self-promotion before audiences of teachers long before there was any such thing as a teachers' college. The American Institute of Instruction was also the first organized manifestation of a national academic establishment, and of course it was dominated by the Harvard-Unitarian proponents of public education.

It should be noted, of course, that the academic establishment of the time was indeed minute compared to what it is today. The December 1834 issue of the *American Journal of Education* listed 66 American undergraduate colleges, counting a total of 5,702 students and 547 instructors. Yale had the largest enrollment with 376 students and 26 instructors, while Harvard had 217 students and 30 instructors. But Harvard had the bigger library with 40,000 volumes, while Yale had only 8,500. The worldly tastes of the Harvard liberals no doubt accounted for the disproportionately huge library, the largest in the United States. But despite the literary elitism of Harvard, the rest of the country was just as literate. An item in the *Journal of Education* of January 1828 gave this accounting of American literacy:

> Our population is 12,000,000, for the education of which, we have 50 colleges, besides several times the number of well endowed and flourishing academies leaving primary schools out of the account. For meeting the intellectual wants of this 12,000,000, we have about 600 newspapers and periodical journals. There is no country, (it is often said), where the means of intelligence are so generally enjoyed by all ranks and where knowledge is so generally diffused among the lower orders of the community, as in our own. The population of those portions of Poland which have successively fallen under the dominion of Russia, is about 20,000,000. To meet the wants of which there are but 15 newspapers, eight of which are printed in Warsaw. But with us a newspaper is the daily fare of almost every meal in almost every family.

It was in this context of high national literacy that the Lyceum was achieving its success by appealing to the American thirst for more knowledge and self-improvement. The already educated are logically the biggest market for books and *more* education. Thus, the appeal of the Lyceum to educators was quite strong. In an article on the progress of the Lyceum in the June 1830 *Journal of Education,* which had added *"and Monthly Lyceum"* to its masthead, we learn that:

> More has been done in the last six months to extend the Lyceum system, than in the three years succeeding the attempt to introduce it. . . . The system is already introduced to some extent into every State of the Union, and in many instances, districts and counties have been so organized as to carry the advantages into every family.
>
> By associations of teachers as departments of Lyceums, many towns seem to have changed their character, and in them there is now no complaint of apathy in parents, or indifference in teachers and scholars. . . .
>
> County associations, or conventions of teachers, have been productive of much good, and promise to do more for schools than any measure ever adopted. They are generally held in connexion with Lyceums; and the members, after explaining their mutual views and practice, return to their schools, better qualified for their dignified and responsible profession.

Meanwhile, the centralization of educational policy and control of the teaching profession were the underlying goals of the Lyceum. This was made quite clear by an article on the American Lyceum in the June 1831 issue of the *American Annals of Education:*

> Although the Lyceum, in all its departments, is a *voluntary* association, or an advisory body, and resorts to no law, nor to any other power but *evidence,* and the power of *motives;*—yet

by enlightening and elevating *public sentiment*, before which legislatures, kings, and despots must bow, it may exert *power*, and the only power worthy to be exerted or acknowledged by intellectual and moral beings.

There is every reason to believe that, at the next meeting of the society, every State in the Union will be represented, and a mass of facts collected, which they can apply to the future operations and success of the cause of education throughout the country. The expectation that such a representation will be made, and such facts collected, is founded on the urgent calls made by the friends of education in every part of the country for *co-operation*, and the great and manifest facilities the society will afford for concentrating and combining efforts, and for extending a uniform system of measures into all departments of popular education. . . .

On the qualifications of teachers, seminaries for that purpose were recommended; and as a preparatory step to these institutions, the weekly meetings of teachers in towns, and the semi-annual conventions of teachers in counties, under the direction and aid of town and county Lyceums, were thought to be highly important.

The advantage of these teachers' meetings, both in towns and counties, is, that they can go into operation *immediately*, so that even the summer schools, already commenced, can receive the benefit of them;—that they can act in behalf of *all* the teachers in the country, and can *continue* their operations and their benefits to every teacher during the whole of his engagement, whether it be for three months or thirty years.

It was obvious why the teachers were the central target of Lyceum activities. If public education was to become the primary instrument for the reformation of mankind into rational, co-operative human beings, then the teachers would have the responsibility of conducting that education and would have to be trained themselves to carry it out according to the overall plan.

After forming a state Lyceum in New York at a convention in Utica in January 1831, Holbrook was then able to call for a national convention of the friends of education in New York City in May for the purpose of finally organizing his national top body, the American Lyceum. At that meeting, a constitution for the national body was voted on, declaring that: "The objects of the Lyceum shall be the advancement of Education especially in common schools, and the general diffusion of knowledge." Questions discussed by the delegates included the following:

What are the greatest desiderata in relation to the improvement of common schools?

What are the most eligible and practical means of advancing and perfecting the science of instruction?

What is the most eligible plan of promoting education, by legislative enactments?

To what extent can the natural sciences be advantageously introduced into common schools?

Among the resolutions voted on by the delegates were the following:

That in the opinion of this Lyceum the weekly meetings of teachers in towns, and the semi-annual Conventions of teachers in counties, under the direction and aid of town and county Lyceums, are eminently calculated to improve the qualifications of teachers, and advance the interests of schools.

That this Lyceum consider the establishment of Seminaries for the education of teachers, a most important part of every system of public instruction.

That we regard the School Teachers of our country (who are now estimated at 50,000) as a body on whom the future character and stability of our institutions chiefly depend; that they are therefore entitled to our highest consideration, and that whatever may be their faults or deficiencies, the remedy for both is in the hands of society at large.

At the convention Holbrook nominated a slate of officers, all of whom were voted in by those assembled. They were as follows: President—Stephen Van Rensselaer (New York); Vice Presidents—Dr. Alexander Proudfit (New York), John Griscom (New York), Roberts Vaux (Penn.), Edward Everett (Mass.), Thomas S. Grimke (S. Carolina); Corresponding Secretaries—Theodore Dwight, Jr., Samuel B. How (President of Dickinson College, Pa.), Prof. A. J. Yates (New York), Josiah Holbrook (Mass.), John Neal (Maine), Oliver A. Shaw (Virginia), Rev. Benjamin O. Peers (Kentucky); Additional Committee—Prof. Olmsted (Yale), Samuel W. Seton (New York), William Forrest (New York), David Russell (New York); Treasurer—Jonathan D. Steele (New York); Recording Secretary—Nathan Sargent (New York).

It was to Holbrook's credit that he was able to recruit such a distinguished group of men for his national body, including some religious conservatives. Two of the men, Grimke and Olmsted, had attended Yale at the same time as Holbrook and had studied under Silliman. Olmsted, a professor of mathematics and physics, had become a true believer in public education early in his career. At the Yale commencement of 1816 he delivered an oration on "The State of Education in Connecticut," advocating stronger support for the common schools. Grimke, who was graduated from Yale in 1807, had become an eminent attorney and state senator in South Carolina. His sisters were to become active feminists, while he espoused the causes of pacifism, temperance, and world peace. In the 1830's, he spoke out eloquently against the disuse of the Bible in the secular common schools, while Greek and Roman mythology were taught in its place. He died prematurely in 1834.

John Griscom, a Quaker and a natural scientist, had founded a private school in New York in 1807 which was reorganized in 1825 as the New York High School for Boys. In 1819, Griscom had made a tour of Europe, during which he visited Robert Owen at New Lanark. Unlike Maclure, Griscom was not converted to Owenism. In fact, his subsequent book, *A Year in Europe,* published in 1823, contained some of the earliest and wisest criticism of Owenism. Griscom wrote:

> We sat up till twelve, engaged in a wordy warfare upon the best means of correcting the abuses of society, and making the whole world a band of brothers. . . .
>
> As it might be imagined, there is very little logic in Owen's reasoning. You may encircle him with the cords of reason and argument, but instead of laboring to untie the knots, he snaps the string, and takes his stand in another position. . . .
>
> It is in vain that his friends have urged to him, that the total destitution of religious faith and principle which marks his scheme, must inevitably, in such a community as this, prevent its adoption; or if adopted as the means of national relief, prevent its success. No argument can dislodge him from his strong hold. . . .
>
> [T]o suppose, as Robert Owen does, that all human enterprise can be circumscribed within his quadrangular villages, and his agricultural colonies; that the vast policy of cities, the energies of commerce, and the powerful rivalship of nations, can be reduced to such mathematical dimensions; or that it would be eventually profitable to the human mind, to have them so reduced, is I cannot but believe, to betray a wonderful deficiency in the knowledge of human nature. . . .
>
> That every attempt to produce a material change in the exterior relations of mankind, upon a system that even admits that the bonds of religious union are useless and unnecessary, must inevitably fail, is my firm persuasion.[6]

There were no overt Owenites among Holbrook's National Lyceum officials, even though, at that very moment in New York, Robert Dale Owen and Frances Wright were publishing *The Free Enquirer* and promoting national education as vigorously as ever. But their equally vigorous promotion of atheism made any association with known Owenites taboo. What was done covertly, we do not know. We assume that the Owenites learned quite early in the game how to operate covertly among groups that opposed them on every other issue but education. The religious struggle was at its height. Not only were the Calvinists combatting the spread of Unitarianism but they were also becoming alarmed over the great increase in Catholic immigration. And conservative Unitarians were now becoming aware of the influx of pantheism from Germany which, toward the end of the decade, would emerge full-blown among radical Unitarians as Transcendentalism.

By 1831, public education was being promoted by the socialists, the Unitarians, and the religious conservatives —each for different reasons. The socialists saw public education as the necessary instrument for the reformation of human character before a socialist society could be brought about. The Unitarians saw public education as the means of perfecting man and eradicating evil. As an intellectual elite, they also viewed public education as the means of exerting social and cultural control over a changing society. And as religionists, they promoted public education as an exercise in the do-goodism and moral activism encouraged by their Unitarian consciences. As for the religious conservatives, they were persuaded to see public education as the means of preserving the American system of government and maintaining the predominantly Protestant Anglo-Saxon culture against the rising tide of Catholic immigration. To them America was a great, divinely inspired experiment in human freedom which only an educated, morally upright electorate could preserve. As William C. Woodbridge put it when he assumed proprietorship of the *American Journal of Education* in August 1830:

[N]o truth is more certain than that the foundation of every free government must be laid in the intelligence and moral principle of the people, which can be produced only by a good education.

It was always easy to appeal to the conservatives by reminding them of what their Calvinist forefathers had done to establish common schools in New England in the early days of the colony. And they were easily and cleverly persuaded by those who wanted their support that public schools would enable them to re-establish conservative religious influence over the younger generation.

But the largest support for public education came, naturally, from the educators themselves, who saw a centralized market for their textbooks, improved schools and better salaries through taxes, and the security and dignity of public employment. Educators were often poor businessmen and inefficient managers, and private schools came and went like the seasons. There were many successful private schools run by competent educator-proprietors who set high academic and moral standards for the profession. But these proprietors were not against public education per se. The main opposition came from parents in towns which had built private academies, from taxpayers, from conservative legislators, and from those opposed to government infringements on individual freedom. But in 1831, there was no thought at all of compulsory school attendance. That idea was still twenty years away.

In July 1832, Holbrook and Samuel R. Hall took another step in organizing the educators of America by forming the American School Agents' Society. Hall, a religious conservative, was an innovative teacher who became interested in the problem of teaching teachers while serving as a minister in Vermont. He created a school for training teachers, and in 1829 published his *Lectures on School Keeping,* which became quite popular among educators and was bought by the Superintendent of Common Schools of New York State for distribution to all the school districts in that state. In 1830, Phillips Academy at Andover engaged Hall to be the director of their new seminary for teachers. The seminary, the first of its kind in America, opened in September 1830.

The purpose of the School Agents' Society was to develop a cadre of paid organizers who would visit different parts of the country, investigate the local schools, organize associations of teachers, and report back their findings. In their report on the objectives of the society, the founders wrote:

> Hundreds of young men may be found, whose talents would entitle them to high hopes of success and usefulness, if they could be brought from their obscurity, and persuaded to devote their lives to the profession of teaching. But pecuniary embarrassments, ignorance of any plan for the systematic education of Teachers, and other discouraging circumstances, will forever exclude them from the ranks of the profession, unless some means be devised to draw them out and train them for the work.[7]

The report also expressed the religious conservative view regarding the need for public education:

> Nothing can preserve our country from despotism on the one hand, and licentiousness on the other, except the universality of public instruction, rendered completely efficacious by an accompanying system of morality, founded on the precepts of the Bible. This bulwark will protect us against the shock of intestine commotion, and secure us against the onset of foreign invasion. May we not then earnestly solicit the co-operation of the patriot, the Christian, and the philanthropist, in our efforts "to promote the cause of Common Education throughout our country?"

By 1832 the religious conservatives had become more alarmed at the invasion of America by the Roman Catholics than by the heresies of the Unitarians. Someone had persuaded the conservatives that public education would be theirs to control once it became universal. And it was this kind of wishful thinking that permitted many conservative educators and ministers to support a cause so completely dominated by the liberals and so quietly manipulated by covert socialists. The simple truth is that by 1832 the Bible had already been excluded from the curriculum of secular public education, with little chance of its reinstatement. The situation had become so critical that in 1830 Thomas S. Grimke, the brilliant South Carolina lawyer, delivered an address before the Phi Beta Kappa Society urging that the Bible be given at least equal time with the pagan classics being taught in the secular schools of America! Grimke warned:

> The negative influences exerted by the present scheme, on the feelings and opinions, and through them on the entire character of youth, are deserving of notice;—for they are often more powerful and durable, because they are silent, secret, and indirect.

Grimke's words had caused enough concern among conservative educators so that a group of them, assembled at a New York Literary Convention in 1830, decided to do a report on the "propriety of studying the Bible as a classic, in the institutions of a Christian country." The report was completed by several religiously conservative educators, and for all practical purposes it was little else than an exercise in futility. The chairman of the group was William Channing Woodbridge, editor of the *Annals of Education*. Woodbridge had purchased the *American Journal of Education* from William Russell in August 1830 and changed its name to the *Annals of Education, and American Journal of Lyceum and Literary Institutions*. As the editor of the nation's only national educational journal, Woodbridge was in a key position to influence American educators. As a religious conservative and an educational liberal, he seemed at times to be on both sides of the fence. He was a cousin of William Ellery Channing and had gone to Yale with Holbrook. He was therefore susceptible to the influences of both men. In 1817, he joined the staff of

Thomas H. Gallaudet's American Asylum for the Deaf and Dumb at Hartford. Gallaudet, too, was an educational innovator whose whole-word, sight-vocabulary method of teaching the deaf to read was to be adapted by him for use with normal children. The new method would have disastrous consequences for American literacy in the twentieth century, long after Gallaudet was dead, but it was Woodbridge's *Annals of Education* which gave Gallaudet's method its first extensive exposure to American educators.[8]

In 1825, Woodbridge went to Europe, visited Hofwyl and got to know Fellenberg. He became a convert to the agricultural school idea. In 1828 and 1829, Woodbridge spent about a year at Hofwyl studying its operations in detail. When he returned to the United States and took over the *Annals of Education*, he published a long series of articles on Hofwyl, Fellenberg's educational philosophy, and the Prussian system of education. For the first two years of its existence, the *Annals of Education* could have been called the Annals of Prussian Education as the virtues of the German state-controlled system were extolled as being far above those of the American private academy. And Hofwyl, of course, was the institution on which Robert Dale Owen had modeled his scheme for national boarding schools. Nowhere in the *Annals of Education* was there any mention of the Owen idea or the fact that the Owen sons had attended Hofwyl. As a religious conservative, Woodbridge had found Fellenberg's religious views quite compatible with his own, and he said as much in an article devoted to religious education at Hofwyl. But Robert Dale Owen took strong issue with Woodbridge in the June 11, 1831 issue of *The Free Enquirer*, accusing Woodbridge of misinterpreting Fellenberg's views. Owen wrote:

All the motives to good conduct which Fellenberg placed before us were of an earthly nature; tangible, comprehensible, present. He spoke to us of the consequences of our conduct.

He spoke to us of the pleasure of virtue, never the joys of paradise; of the miseries of vice, never of the flames of hell. To his parental instructions, in a measure, do I owe it, that my moral principles are based on the rock of demonstration, not on the shifting sands of theology.

There was no response in the *Annals of Education.* Meanwhile, Woodbridge collaborated wholeheartedly with Holbrook in the Lyceum movement, attending its conferences and reporting their deliberations in great detail. But failing health eventually forced Woodbridge to give up his editorship of the *Annals* in 1836.

The American Lyceum continued to grow. A three-day convention was held in New York in May 1833, bringing together more farflung members of the educational community than ever before. In 1834, however, Holbrook decided to leave Boston and move his base of operations to Pennsylvania where the "friends of education" were preparing to push a new public education law through the state legislature. William Russell, former editor of the *American Journal of Education,* was also now living in Philadelphia. Opposition to the new law in Pennsylvania was fierce, and 30,000 signatures were gathered by the opponents to stop it. The opponents were, for the most part, Lutherans who maintained their own private system of parochial schools. Nevertheless, the law was passed, and attempts to repeal it in 1835 failed.

One of the chief activists for public education in Pennsylvania was a New Englander by the name of Walter R. Johnson. Johnson had been a classmate of James G. Carter at both Groton and Harvard, from which he was graduated in 1819. In 1821, he had moved to Germantown, Pennsylvania, to become principal of an academy. While there he published a series of essays on popular education in the Journal of the Franklin Institute and became a founder of the Pennsylvania Society for the Promotion of Public

Schools. His interest in the natural sciences led to his appointment in 1826 as director of the Philadelphia High School established under the Franklin Institute. It was at the Franklin Institute, incidentally, that Robert Owen addressed a Philadelphia audience on June 7, 1827. Johnson became active in the Lyceum movement soon after it was started, and lectured at the American Institute of Instruction conferences. It is said that the Pennsylvania school law of 1834 was largely due to his efforts. Undoubtedly, he and Holbrook worked hard to overcome the opposition. In 1848, Johnson was appointed chemist at the Smithsonian Institution, which had been established by legislation introduced by Robert Dale Owen, who was then a member of Congress from Indiana. Johnson's career and activities suggest that he too may have been a covert Owenite.

With the new Pennsylvania school law passed in 1834, Holbrook spent the following year organizing the teachers of that state into Lyceums and countering attempts to repeal the law. His efforts were successful. At about this time, Holbrook thought of organizing a Universal Lyceum with Lord Brougham, the British liberal Parliamentarian, as president. Lord Brougham had been a friend of Robert Owen's for years, and Holbrook's idea is another of these tell-tale clues that suggest strongly that Holbrook was a covert Owenite. The idea, however, never got off the ground.

In any case, by 1835, largely through the untiring work of Josiah Holbrook, the educators of America had been organized into a solid body of support for public education. In state after state, legislatures began to establish the foundations of tax-supported public educational systems. Maryland had enacted an education law in 1825 providing "for the public instruction of youth in primary schools throughout the state." Its law had been modeled on the New York system. But by 1835, American educators were looking toward Prussia for their model of a perfect state-controlled system. Selling this system to the American people, who were so very satisfied and comfortable with their educational freedom and private institutions, would take another ten years.

8. The Prussian Model

EVER SINCE EVERETT, Ticknor, Bancroft, and Cogswell had studied in Germany, the Harvard Unitarians had acquired a strong taste for German education, scholarship, and philosophy. They admired the German university with its academic freedom, the Prussian public school system with its compulsory attendance laws and teachers' seminaries, and the high status in general that educators enjoyed in German society. Both the *American Journal of Education* and its successor, the *Annals of Education,* ran numerous articles on Prussian education. But it wasn't until Victor Cousin, a French professor of philosophy who was highly regarded by the Harvard liberals, had published his report on the Prussian public school system in 1833, that American educators began to think seriously of using the Prussian system as the model for the national public school system they hoped to establish in America. It had everything the reformers wanted: full state financial support via taxation, compulsory attendance, truant officers, punishments for recalcitrant parents, graded classrooms, uniform curriculum, and teachers trained by the state. True, the Prussian system served the purposes of a despotic state, but it dispensed universal education, and that, it was believed, could only have long-range beneficial effects.

That Victor Cousin should have been the one to write the report was both fitting and appropriate. Cousin had gained considerable notoriety as a great admirer and interpreter of the German transcendentalist philosophers—Fichte, Schelling, and Hegel—and he became the chief channel through which their pantheism and subjective idealism were introduced to French and New England intellectuals. The more liberal of the Harvard Unitarians were particularly susceptible to these seductive ideas, and by 1836 these liberals began to emerge as an articulate American intellectual movement known as Transcendentalism around the figure of Ralph Waldo Emerson, who had resigned his Unitarian ministry in 1834 because he could no longer administer the sacraments with a clear conscience. The Calvinists had warned that Unitarianism was the halfway house to atheism. But they were only partially right. Unitarianism was also the halfway house to pantheism, which some critics thought was far worse than atheism. Why? Because, they said, it elevated man from his corrupt status to a kind of superman—the highest manifestation of God in nature—capable of perfection. In pantheism, God was merely an idea in man's head, a harmless abstraction incapable of showing anger or punishing sinners, the pure creation of a subjective idealism. But in Calvinism, God was an objective reality to be served, feared, and obeyed, respected, revered, and loved. In Calvinism, one could be loyal to God, one could become attached to God. In pantheism, there was no all-powerful objective reality to become loyal to. Instead, one became loyal and attached to the state, the ultimate instrument of *man's* power.

Cousin had become interested in German philosophy after reading Madame de Staël's seminal book on Germany published in 1810, the same work that had introduced the Harvard liberals to the wonders of the German academic world and its feats of scholarship, all of which had persuaded president Kirkland of Harvard to send Everett and Ticknor to study at Göttingen. Cousin, only two years older than Everett, had made his pilgrimage to Germany in 1817 and 1818 at the age of 25. His biographer, Jules Simon, writes:

> He was welcomed everywhere. He stayed for some time with Jacobi. . . . To Hegel he became peculiarly attached. Unrebuffed by Hegel's abrupt ways and his somewhat unsocial character, Cousin boasted of being the first to recognize this philosopher's genius and to foresee his great future. He also entered into continuous relations with Schleiermacher. . . . He saturated himself with German thought, and grew full of enthusiasm for German habits and ideas.[1]

George Bancroft had also fallen under the influence of Schleiermacher at about the same time, and Edward Everett had met Cousin during the latter's visit to Göttingen. But the work that influenced the New England liberal intellectuals the most was Cousin's series of lectures on the history of philosophy published in 1828. An American translation of them was published in Boston in 1832, but many of the Harvard elite had read them in the original French edition, which was reviewed in the July 1832 *North American Review*. The editor of the Review at the time was Alexander Everett, Edward Everett's brother. A brief excerpt from the review will suffice to indicate how favorably Cousin's ideas were received:

> His genius, alike brilliant and profound, has given an attraction to the subject of metaphysics, altogether unprecedented in the annals of philosophy. Since the year 1828,—when he returned to the professorial chair, after a long absence,—his lectures have been attended by crowds not merely of the learning, but the fashion of Paris. We cannot expect a brief

outline of these lectures, to impart an idea of the beauty and eloquence of their style; for this we must refer the reader to the work itself, which will well reward perusal. Those who do not adopt the system of Cousin, or are not prepared to admit, with him, that intellectual philosophy is the culminating point, *'le dernier mot'* of humanity, cannot fail to admire the profoundness of his views, the extent of his learning, his fearless but catholic spirit, his reverence for religion and his just respect for humanity. From a profound analysis of the human mind he has elaborated the thread, which is to conduct him through the labyrinth of systems and schools; while his soaring genius, rising above all the particulars of periods or sects, comprehends in its splendid generalizations, not the actual merely, but the possible, and embraces in one vast idea, God, man and the universe.

With that kind of a sendoff, Cousin was "in" with the Harvard crowd and considered *the* philosopher of the time. Thus, when the translation of his lectures appeared in 1832, they were eagerly read and digested. Emerson read them and two years later quit the Unitarian ministry as a free pantheistic spirit. Concerning the ministry, Emerson wrote, "The profession is antiquated. In an altered age, we worship in the dead forms of our forefathers. Were not a Socratic paganism better than an effete superannuated Christianity?"[2]

The castrated God of the Unitarians had indeed produced an effete, superannuated Christianity devoid of the strong emotional ties which linked Calvin's God with a sinful humanity. Pantheism, on the other hand, elevated humanity to an entirely new and exalted stature. "Yes, man is perfectible," wrote Cousin, "but in a very different sense of the word. Humanity has an aim; and consequently, from the point of its departure, it advances toward it unceasingly and regularly; it advances toward perfection."[3] It was hard for religious liberals to resist such tantalizing notions. In pantheism, man was a part of God because God was everywhere. Cousin had explained it as follows:

> The God of consciousness is not an abstract God, a solitary king, exiled beyond creation to the throne of a silent eternity and of an absolute existence which even resembles the annihilation of existence. It is a God both true and real, both substance and cause, always substance and always cause, being cause only inasmuch as He is substance, and substance only inasmuch as He is cause,—that is, being an absolute cause. He is one and several, eternity and time, space and number, essence and life, individuality and totality; beginning, middle, and end; at the top of the ladder of existence and at the humblest round; infinite and finite both together; a trinity, in fine, being at once God, nature, and humanity.[4]

In this context, God's law ceased to be the Ten Commandments, but became merely the laws of nature. Cousin never once mentioned Calvin (a fellow Frenchman!) in his book, although from beginning to end it was an attack on Calvinism. But he made it quite clear that the Monotheism of Moses was just a passing phase in man's religious development and that the Bible was essentially mythology and of no greater value to mankind than the works of the other religions. Cousin wrote:

> The Mosaic religion is in its developments connected with the history of all the inhabitants of the neighboring countries, of Egypt, of Assyria, of Persia, of Greece, and of Rome; at the same time, that the roots of its origin are entwined with the original roots of the whole human race.[5]

German Biblical scholars had worked overtime to prove that the Bible was not holy scripture, but merely a further development of older mythology. One of the scholars most responsible for downgrading the Bible was Professor Johann Eichhorn of Göttingen, under whom Everett had studied. To Eichhorn, the Old Testament was not to be considered as divine revelation nor the foundation of Christian doctrine. Rather it was to be valued as an ancient source of history liable to all the tests applied to any historical document. Since the entire Calvinist system was based on the unshakable belief in the Word of God as given in the Old Testament, the pantheist intellectuals went to great and scholarly lengths to pull down the whole Biblical structure. Of Eichhorn, the *Biographie Universelle* writes:

> Eichhorn carried as far as possible the consequences of exegesis, that is, this system of interpretation that multiplies the most dangerous paradoxes and tends to shake the foundation on which rests the origin of Christian revelation. He went further than the liberal ideas of his contemporaries, as those had gone further than their predecessors, above all the first reformers whom they left far behind. Some of them who had favored this audacious criticism, saw with pain the excesses of which it had become guilty, and regretted ever having pierced the dike that had held back this devastating torrent.[6]

Thus, while the German scholars worked from one end, Maclure's natural scientists worked from the other. Maclure's aim was atheism; the aim of the German philosophers was pantheism, for pantheism was really the ancient religion of the Teutons, and as Heinrich Heine had said: "man parts not willingly with what has been dear to his fathers." Heine also went on to say, "Germany is at present the fertile soil of Pantheism; that is the religion of all our greatest thinkers, of all our best artists,—and *Deism* is already destroyed there in theory. You do not hear it spoken of,—but everyone knows it. Pantheism is the public secret of Germany. We have, in fact, outgrown Deism. . . . We are free and need no thundering tyrant. We are of age, and need no fatherly care. We are not the hand-work of any great mechanic. Theism is a religion for slaves, for children, for Genevese, for watch-makers."[7]

It was this basic anti-Calvinism which brought the Hegelians and the radical Unitarians together in a new religion, pantheism. The Calvinist critics of religious liberalism found atheism less offensive than pantheism, because at least the atheists did not deify man. The deification of man was seen as the most ominous sign in the new philosophy. The *Princeton Review* wrote in 1840:

> The most offensive aspect of this whole system is, that in deifying man, it deifies the worst passions of our nature. "This," says a writer in Hengstenberg's Journal, "is the true, positive blasphemy of God,—this veiled blasphemy,—this diabolism of the deceitful angel of light,—this speaking of reckless words, with which the man of sin sets himself in the temple of God, showing himself that he is God. The atheist cannot blaspheme with such power as this; his blasphemy is negative; he simply says, There is no God. It is only out of Pantheism that a blasphemy can proceed, so wild, of such inspired mockery, so devoutly godless, so desperate in its love of the world; a blasphemy at once so seductive, and so offensive, that it may call for the destruction of the world."[8]

The warning was quite significant, for in 1840, at the age of 20, Frederick Engels, one of the future leaders of revolutionary communism, was already writing a friend, "The Hegelian idea of God has already become mine, and thus I am joining the ranks of the 'modern Pantheists' . . . knowing well that even the word pantheism arouses such colossal revulsion on the part of pastors who don't think." What particularly dazzled the young revolutionary Germans was "Hegel's principle that humanity and divinity are in essence identical."[9]

With the deification of man went the exaltation of his

institutions, especially the state. The pantheists lay the foundation for the tyrannical total state which was to develop after World War I, usually under the dictatorship of a "great man." Cousin wrote:

> Thus, as nature represents God; and humanity is the summary of nature and of all its laws; and as great men are the summaries of humanity with all its epochs; it follows . . . that the order of things . . . is nothing but the process which gives birth to great men. . . . When nothing great is to be done, the existence of a great man is impossible.[10]

Lest anyone imagine that Cousin was thinking of an Ayn Rand hero like Howard Roark or John Galt, the following should lay that notion to rest:

> A great man, as such, is not an individual; his good fortune is to represent, better than any other man of his time, the ideas of that time, its interests, its wants.[11]

What Cousin meant was that the great man was merely the executive of the collective will, a leader helping humanity on its progressive march toward perfection. In the end, the individual was nothing and humanity was everything. Cousin elaborated:

> In the last lecture I defended victory, I have just been defending power, and it now remains for me to defend glory, in order to have proved humanity to be blameless. We seldom attend to the fact, that if any thing is human, it is humanity that makes it so, even by permitting its existence; to imprecate power, (I mean long and lasting power) is to blaspheme humanity; to bring accusations against glory, is nothing less than to bring accusations against humanity by which it is decreed. What is glory, gentlemen? It is the judgment of humanity upon its members; and humanity is always in the right.[12]

It would take less than a hundred years for the full

implications of that philosophy to flower into the Leninist and Hitlerian states. It was considered daring and sophisticated to promulgate such ideas in the mid-19th century, after a full thousand years of successful human behavior management by the Judeo-Christian system. Neither Judaism, nor Catholicism, nor Calvinism had expected to make men perfect. Certainly according to Calvin, human perfectibility was a contradiction in terms. The best that Calvin had hoped for was to curb the excesses of human evil by devising the most ingenious system of behavior management by spiritual means in history. And the fortunate Christian peoples of Europe and America had, by the 19th century, simply forgotten how evil and corrupt human beings could be. The twentieth century would finally reveal what it was in human nature that made Calvinism work so hard to restrain. And in the twentieth century there would no longer be the excuses of poverty, ignorance, or disease. Nazism, with its human lampshades and gas chambers, would bloom in the most industrialized and cultivated of nation-states, the land of Beethoven and Goethe, of universities and museums, of automobiles and telephones. That Hitler chose to exterminate the elected people of Calvin's God was not only the most vicious expression of anti-Calvinism possible, but also the most logical extension of Hegelian pantheism. It, of course, required elevating the state above religion. Hegel had written that the "state is an institution not consonant with the Judaistic principle, and it is alien to the legislation of Moses." And Cousin had written:

> You must consider, gentlemen, that although religion acts a part in life which is immensely important, and though it holds an elevated station in society, yet there exist other things besides religion. Religion is indeed mingled with all the great transactions of our life; yet it intervenes in them only by its

sanction; it does not constitute their basis. Their immediate and direct basis is the law, it is the state.[13]

Thus, in the Hegelian nation-state, man's law was clearly superior to God's law, for, after all, there was really no such thing as "God's law." At the Nuremburg trials there would be an attempt to demonstrate the existence of some higher laws than those of any particular nation-state. But with the Communists sitting on the same tribunal as liberal Westerners, there would be no possibility of invoking God's law. What would be established is the principle that the laws of the conqueror are superior to the laws of the vanquished.

Runaway total statism, in any case, was the natural political consequence of pantheism, and thus, it was no surprise that Cousin, like Hegel, was a strong advocate of a state-controlled educational system. In 1830, Cousin was sent to Prussia by the French minister of education to find out why the Prussian system was so much better developed than the French. Cousin performed his task with great relish. He knew the Germans better than any of his countrymen, and his admiration for Germany knew no bounds. He was given every assistance by the Prussians in preparing his report, which was completed in June of 1831. It was translated into English by Sarah Austin, a noted liberal Englishwoman, whose husband had been studying law in Germany. Cousin had met the Austins in Bonn in 1827, and from that time on, the Austins and Cousin had become warm friends. Mrs. Austin's translation first appeared in the *Edinburgh Review* in 1833 before it came out in book form in 1834. In December 1833, the *American Annals of Education* reprinted large extracts of the report as printed in the *Edinburgh Review*. It commented: "Such is the account of a system of schools acknowledged to be the best in the world, given by a distinguished philosopher, and adopted by one of the ablest advocates of education. May we not hope, that even its foreign origin will not entirely prevent its influence, in exciting and directing American zeal?'' Meanwhile, Cousin had sent Alexander Everett a copy of the report for review in the *North American Review*.

An American edition of the report was published in New York in 1835, subsidized by James Wadsworth, a wealthy Unitarian landowner from upper New York State who had made public education his special philanthropic interest. A preface to the American edition was written by J. Orville Taylor, one of the young agents recruited by Josiah Holbrook's School Agents' Society. Taylor had distinguished himself by writing a very thorough report on the condition of the common schools in New York State. While the book sold few copies to the general public, it was distributed widely among educators at the taxpayers' expense by order of several state legislatures.

It is appropriate and necessary at this point to quote Cousin's report so that American readers today can see what American educators in 1835 found so admirable about the Prussian system. In his section on primary instruction, and under the title, ''Duty of Parents to Send Their Children to the Primary Schools,'' Professor Cousin wrote:

This duty is so national, so rooted in all the legal and moral habits of the country, that it is expressed by a single word, *Schulpflichtigkeit* (school-duty, or school-obligation.) It corresponds to another word, similarly formed and similarly sanctioned by public opinion, *Dienstpflichtigkeit* (service-obligation, *i.e.*, military service.) These two words are completely characteristic of Prussia: they contain the secret of its originality as a nation, of its power as a state, and the germ of its future condition.—They express, in my opinion, the two bases of true civilization,—knowledge and strength. Military conscription, instead of voluntary enlistment, at first found many adversaries among us; it is now considered as a condition and a means of civilization and public order. I am convinced the time will come when popular education will be equally recognised as a social duty imperative on all for the sake of all.[14]

To acquaint his readers with the "letter and spirit" of the Prussian system, Cousin then went on to quote the full text of the school law of 1819. We shall quote enough of it to give the present reader an idea of the oppressiveness of a system that Cousin and the neo-Hegelians in Boston found to be so admirable:

"Parents or guardians are bound to send their children or wards to the public school; or to provide in some other manner that they receive a competent education. . . .

"Parents and masters who do not send their children, or those entrusted to their care, to a public school, must point out to the municipal authorities or school-committees, whenever they are required, what means they provide for the education of such children.

"Every year after Easter or Michaelmas, the committees and the municipal authorities shall make an inquiry concerning all the families lying within their jurisdiction who have notoriously not provided for their children that private education which they are bound to give them, in default of public education. For this purpose they shall make a census of all the children of age to go to school. The baptismal registers, and those of the civil authorities, shall be open to them at the commencement of every year, and the police must afford them every possible facility and assistance. . . .

"Parents and masters are bound to see that the children under their care regularly follow the school course for the time prescribed by law. . . .

"If, however, parents and masters neglect sending their children punctually to school, the clergymen must first explain to them the heavy responsibility which rests upon them; after that, the school-committee must summon them to appear before it, and address severe remonstrances to them. . . .

"If these remonstrances are not sufficient, coercive measures are then to be resorted to against the parents, guardians, or masters. The children are to be taken to school by an officer of the police, or the parents are to be sentenced to graduated punishments or fines: and in case they are unable to pay, to imprisonment or labour, for the benefit of the parish. These punishments may be successively increased, but are never to exceed the maximum of punishment of correctional police.

"The fines are to be awarded by the school-committee: to be collected, if necessary, with the aid of the police, and paid into the funds of the committee. The execution of the other punishments rests with the police.

"Whenever it shall be necessary to pass sentence of imprisonment, or of forced labour for the benefit of the parish, care shall be taken that the children of the persons so condemned are not neglected while their parents are undergoing the penalty of the law.

"The parents who shall have incurred such sentences may, on the request of the school-committees, and as an augmentation of punishment, be deprived of all participation in the public funds for the relief of the poor. . . .

"If all these punishments are found ineffectual, a guardian shall be appointed specially to watch over the education of the children, or, in case they are wards, a co-guardian.

"Jewish parents, who obstinately refuse obedience to the competent authorities, may be deprived of their civil rights in the provinces in which the edict of the 11th of May, 1812, is in force."[15]

The *American Annals of Education* of April 1835 acknowledged the American publication of Cousin's report with this short notice which summed it all up quite neatly: "Mrs. Austin's translation of this report is republished by Wiley & Long, of New York. It is an account of the best school system in the world, by the first philosopher of the age."

A review would have been superfluous, since the *North American Review* of the same date published a lengthy review of its own. It said:

Whatever may be thought of the tendency and substantial value of Mr. Cousin's metaphysical theories, upon which, as we have intimated, the public opinion is not yet settled, there can be no doubt of the great practical importance of his labors in the cause of education. . . . In England, his writings on this subject, have awakened a strong interest, and probably will give occasion to great practical changes. In this country, they have arrived very opportunely, at a moment when some of the most important states, particularly New York and Massachusetts, are laboring to place their schools on a better footing, and will furnish a body of most valuable information in aid of this purpose. . . . The committee of the legislature have directed the public attention to the Prussian System, by including in their report an outline of its principal features. . . . The committee have also recommended the distribution of Miss Austin's abridgement to all the towns,—a measure which cannot but be attended with the best results.

Thus, by 1835, the Harvard-Unitarian intellectuals had decided that the American system should be modeled after the Prussian. They had no reservations at all regarding the system's oppressive, statist features. If the perfectibility of man required a little coercion, then so be it. Coercion was quite justifiable in this "Crusade against ignorance," as Jefferson had once called it. It was in the light of all this that the promoters of public education saw a great opportunity arise in November 1835 when Edward Everett was elected Governor of Massachusetts.

The publication of Cousin's Report in 1833 in the *Edinburgh Review* was enough to activate the liberals into greater effort in behalf of public education. Holbrook's Lyceum movement was in full swing, teachers' conventions were being organized in many towns, the American Institute of Instruction was preparing for its fourth annual meeting, the School Agents' Society was sending its operatives across the country to awaken slumbering educators in remote districts, and the Cousin report gave the New

England intellectuals the perfect snobbish appeal which added immeasurably to the public school movement's prestige: philosophy's seal of approval as given by the "first philosopher of the age." Yet, while it was easy enough to sell the Prussian model to the American educator and the New England intellectual, the taxpayer and his legislative representative were still to be reached. One man who made considerable efforts to arouse public opinion in favor of the Prussian scheme was Rev. Charles Brooks, a Unitarian minister from Hingham, Massachusetts. Brooks had obtained his Master's degree in theology at Harvard in 1819 and in the following year had become pastor of the Unitarian church at Hingham, some fifteen miles south of Boston.

Brooks had been so impressed with Cousin's account of the Prussian school system that he made his own pilgrimage to Paris to see Cousin in 1834. What impressed him most about the Prussian system, however, was its state normal schools in which teachers were trained. But Brooks was at a loss as to how to persuade Americans that such state-supported teacher-training institutions were needed. On the return trip to the United States, however, he found a way. Brooks explained how it happened:

At a literary soiree in London, August, 1834, I met Dr. H. Julius of Hamburg, then on his way to the United States, having been sent by the King of Prussia to learn the condition of our schools, hospitals, prisons, and other public institutions. He asked to be my room-mate on board ship. I was too happy to accede to that request. A passage of forty-one days from Liverpool to New York gave me time to ask all manner of questions concerning the noble, philosophical and practical system of Prussian elementary education. He explained it like a sound scholar and a pious Christian. If you will allow the phrase, I fell in love with the Prussian system, and it seemed to possess me like a missionary angel. I gave myself to it, and in the Gulf Stream I resolved to *do* something about *State* normal schools. This was its birth in me, and I baptized it my Seaborn School.

After this I looked upon each child as a being who could complain of me before God if I refused to provide for him a better education, after what I had learned.[16]

This was the typical emotional approach to the Prussian system, and whether he knew it or not, Brooks, like Robert Owen, had adopted the Prussian attitude of bypassing and disregarding parental wishes on matters of their children's education. The parental-child relationship was considered subordinate to the child's relationship to the state or educator. The alienation of child from parent was implicit in the whole Prussian system. A child who saw his parents cringe at the authority of state power was bound to have second thoughts about the authority at home. The state as educator became the recipient of the child's loyalty and allegiance. In such a system, political freedom was hardly possible. But the Unitarians were convinced that you could have both coercion and freedom. They never explained how, for the issue of public education by 1835 had become so emotional that rational discussion on the subject was impossible. There was a wide streak of intellectual dishonesty running through the entire popular education movement. Many factors contributed to it. The Unitarians, skating on theologically thin ice, were determined to prove their theory of human nature and thus vindicate their repudiation of Calvinism. The liberal intellectual elite was determined to extend its cultural and social influences through its control of education. They paid lip service to freedom, but their real interest was power. The conservatives were determined to save America from the Catholics. The socialists, forced to work covertly, were determined to create their instrument of radical human reform so that they could overthrow the competitive, capitalist system. And the educators, textbook writers, publishers, and common-school administrators were tantalized by the economic benefits and elevated social status promised by state support and centralized control. There simply was no room for honesty in the movement, because there were too many dishonest motives involved. Opponents of public education were called the "enemies of light and knowledge," and the "friends of education" made it quite clear that if you were opposed to public education, you were opposed not only to education per se but also to the betterment of mankind. And this muddied the waters considerably. But what made all rational argument on public education impossible was the sheer emotionalism of its proponents. They wrote with a sense of urgency that sometimes bordered on the hysterical, as in one article in the October 1835 *Annals of Education* that pleaded with the press to give more coverage to the subject of education which, of course, meant *public* education. The article, written by editor Woodbridge himself, had these paragraphs:

Our brethren will pardon us, therefore, for thus appealing to them as Philanthropists, and Christians, and Patriots, and for urging them, in the language of Jefferson, to engage, with all that talent and zeal which characterize their efforts on other subjects, in this 'Crusade Against Ignorance!' Should it be our last appeal, we would make none more earnest, for the *safety of our country,* as well as for the welfare of future generations. Let the spirit of activity and excitement, which is bursting out in every form of mischief, only be enlisted in this 'Holy War,' and the efforts which are now wasted upon the air, or spent in personal contention, be united against this great source of evil, this *common enemy of every section of our country,* of *every party* which rests its hopes on truth and right, and we may hope to divert the storm which threatens us, if not to prevent its future recurrence.

We often burn with impatience to call forth the ablest in our land to this service. We would speak, if it were possible, in a voice which should reach every legislative hall, every office of state, every study of learning, and every palace of wealth in our land. We have devoted five years past to this contest; we have employed all our means in the circulation of knowledge concerning it; but our powers and our means are small; our sphere of action is limited; our strength is impaired; and with our utmost efforts, we can accomplish little without the co-operation of those who direct the established guides of public opinion,—who reach every village and almost every family in the land. We cordially return our thanks to many who do thus co-operate with us in general efforts, and to those who circulate what we collect; but we appeal to *all*, to engage in the 'CRUSADE AGAINST IGNORANCE!'

With the educators thus worked up into such a lather, no rational argument was possible in opposition to the Prussianization of American education. This was indeed a "holy war," and the activists who waged it had all of the characteristics of fanatics.

The Cousin Report also moved educational activists in Michigan, Ohio, and Virginia. The new state of Michigan adopted the Prussian system at its constitutional convention in Detroit in 1835. The chairman of the Committee on Education was Isaac E. Crary, a 31-year-old New England lawyer who had migrated to Michigan in 1832. He and a friend, Rev. John D. Pierce, had both read the Cousin Report and decided to propose that the state of Michigan establish a school system on the Prussian model. The proposal was accepted by the convention, and thereafter education was made a branch of state government with an officer in charge of the system. Rev. John D. Pierce became Michigan's first Superintendent of Public Instruction.

The University of Michigan was also created by the state in conformity with the Prussian model. The first catalogue of the University of Michigan states: "The State of Michigan has copied from Prussia what is acknowledged to be the most perfect educational system in the world."

Henry Philip Tappan, the first permanent president of the University of Michigan, wrote in 1851: "The Educational System of Germany and particularly in Prussia, is certainly a very noble one. We cannot well be extravagant in its praise. . . . Here is a glorious achievement of an enlightened and energetic despotism. . . . The wisest philosophers and the greatest educators have united in commending this system."

American educators had indeed been bitten by Cousin's statist virus, and they were determined to achieve for themselves the status, privileges, and benefits that were enjoyed by the educators of Prussia.

Religious liberals were not the only ones attracted by the Prussian system. One noted conservative who, in 1836, wrote his own report on the Prussian system was Calvin E. Stowe of the Lane Theological Seminary in Cincinnati, Ohio. Stowe, born in Massachusetts in 1802, had spent three years at the Calvinist Andover Theological Seminary, after which he began his long career as a college instructor. In 1833, Lyman Beecher, the noted orthodox minister, was made president of the Lane Theological Seminary. He offered Stowe the position as professor of Biblical Literature, which Stowe accepted. In 1836, Stowe married Beecher's daughter Harriet who was to achieve fame in her own right as the author of *Uncle Tom's Cabin*. In May of 1836, Stowe was sent to Europe to collect a library for the seminary and to inspect the Prussian schools. Some "friends of education," knowing of Stowe's impending book-buying mission, had asked the Governor of Ohio to appoint Stowe as an agent of the Ohio legislature to examine European schools, especially those of Prussia, and report back his findings. The Governor agreed, and a small payment was voted by the legislature to cover Stowe's expenses. The result was a second Cousin report, but this one written by a religiously conservative American. It was published in 1836 and distributed at state expense to every school district in Ohio and extensively republished and circulated by the legislatures of Pennsylvania, Michigan, Massachusetts, North Carolina, and Virginia.

Stowe had been particularly impressed by the King of Prussia because he was a member of the Calvinist church, even though a majority of his subjects were Lutherans. In 1817, the king had effected a union between the Lutherans and Calvinists in Prussia and created the Evangelical Church. This was in keeping with the Lutheran system, under which the church was governed by an ecclesiastical administration under the supremacy of the territorial prince. It was Luther's close collaboration with the German princes which made the Lutheran church somewhat statist in its political philosophy; while Calvinism, conceived under the persecution of the French king, was definitely distrustful of the state, if not anti-statist. Calvinists were persecuted in France and England, and many of them sought refuge in Geneva, the Calvinist city-state over which no king ruled. There was no city on earth like Geneva, and it was the Calvinist commonwealth which inspired the Puritans who settled in New England, not the princely states of Lutheran Germany. But by 1836 these distinctions were no longer recognized, and Stowe was seduced by German statism. But what impressed Stowe even more was the religious tenor of Prussian education. He wrote:

The *religious* spirit which pervades the whole of the Prussian system, is greatly needed among ourselves.—Without religion—and, indeed, without the religion of the Bible—there can be no efficient school discipline. . . . Religion is an essential element of human nature; and it must be cultivated, or there will be distortion of the intellect and affections. I doubt not it will be conceded that, if any religious instruction is to be given in our schools, the religion of the New Testament is to be preferred to all others; and I have already attempted to show that there is enough of common ground here to unite all the different sects in this great object.[17]

By 1836 the Calvinists had mellowed a good deal. All of American Protestantism had been affected by the liberal trend. The great controversial doctrines of Calvin were now taken far less literally than in previous times. The great issue now confronting the Protestants was the flood of Catholic immigration into the United States. A public school system controlled by the Protestant majority seemed the only way to preserve America's original character. Stowe wrote: "It can be done; for it has been done—it is now done; and it ought to be done. If it can be done in Europe, I believe it can be done in the United States; if it can be done in Prussia, I know it can be done in Ohio."

Both Stowe and Lyman Beecher were especially active in arousing Protestant suspicion of a supposed Catholic threat, particularly in the Ohio Valley. Alarmist books like Samuel F. B. Morse's *A Foreign Conspiracy Against the Liberties of the U.S.*, published in 1834, and Beecher's *A Plea For the West*, published in 1835, exposed what was purported to be a Papal plot to take over the United States. Protestants were urged to abandon their sectarian differences and unite against the "Romish designs."

Other Americans also went to Prussia to write reports. Benjamin Mosby Smith, a Presbyterian clergyman from Virginia, spent two years in Europe, mostly in Prussia, gathering information for a report which he submitted to the Governor of Virginia and the Virginia House of Delegates in 1839. But the Virginians were slow to go the Prussian route and waited until most of the other states had done so first. Another American to write a report on Prussia was Alexander D. Bache, great grandson of Benjamin Franklin, who at the age of 30 had been appointed the first president of Girard College in Philadelphia. The Board of Trustees sent Bache to Europe for two years to study the educational institutions there. On his return, his voluminous report, *Education in Europe,* was published in 1839. Bache then spent three years reorganizing the public schools of Philadelphia. Thus, the Prussian influence on American educators was widespread. It appealed to the liberals as a logical extension of Hegelian statist concepts. It appealed to the conservatives as a means of controlling the Catholic and foreign tide. It appealed to the socialists because it promised the creation of an instrument of central educational policy through which a few could control many. And it appealed to the educators because of its obvious economic and social benefits to themselves. But did it appeal to the American people? They were never asked. The educators had made the decision for them.

9. Enter Horace Mann

EDWARD EVERETT WAS elected Governor of Massachusetts on November 9, 1835, and took office on January 7, 1836. As one of the more influential members of the Harvard-Unitarian elite, he was now in a position to press for the educational reforms that the "friends of education" were demanding in ever more strident terms. Everett had graduated from Harvard with highest honors in 1811 and, upon the urging of Joseph Buckminster, the young Unitarian minister of the Brattle Street Church entered the Harvard Divinity School, where he studied under Kirkland and read the theological works of Johann Eichhorn of Göttingen University. Buckminster, an epileptic, died prematurely in 1812, and in the following year, Everett, at the age of 19, was called to take his place as minister of what was then one of Boston's largest and most affluent Unitarian churches. Everett was in the ministry for only a year, but his sermons reflected the liberal, rational approach to religion characterized by a benevolent God of limited powers.

Unitarianism made salvation dependent on works rather

than grace or election. This was a theology that the affluent merchant class could accept with enthusiasm, for they had the means to buy salvation through philanthropy. One of them, in fact, Samuel Eliot, anonymously donated $20,000 in 1814 to endow a professorship of Greek at Harvard University. Everett was offered the position by Kirkland, and the young, brilliant scholar accepted it, resigning from the ministry. To prepare for the position, Everett was sent to Göttingen with George Ticknor in 1815. At Göttingen, Everett studied under Eichhorn and other noted professors, and in September 1817 was awarded his degree as Doctor of Philosophy. He was, in fact, the first American to become a Ph.D.

Everett spent two more years studying in Europe and returned to the United States in October 1819, whereupon he assumed his duties at Harvard as Eliot Professor of Greek Literature. At about the same time, he also became editor of the *North American Review,* the elite's intellectual mouthpiece. In 1822, Everett married Charlotte Brooks, daughter of Peter Chardon Brooks, one of the wealthiest merchants of Boston. In one fell swoop, Everett not only became a member of a powerful mercantile family, but he acquired also two influential brothers-in-law: the Rev. N. L. Frothingham, a leading Unitarian minister and a Harvard classmate, and Charles Francis Adams, son of John Quincy Adams.

Everett remained at Harvard until 1825, when he ran for Congress and won. He held his seat in the House of Representatives for five terms until he was elected Governor of Massachusetts. Thus, Everett was a member *par excellence* of the Harvard-Unitarian elite, represented their views perfectly and was quite willing to use whatever political power was available to him to extend their cultural, economic, social, and spiritual influences. He was helped, of course, by other members or confederates of the elite in the legislature, in particular, James G. Carter, James Savage, and Horace Mann. Everett had known Carter at Harvard, and James Savage went back to the Anthology Society days and the campaign for public primary schools in Boston. But who was Horace Mann? Today no one remembers Carter, Savage, or Everett, but everyone has heard of Horace Mann, father of American public education. The story of Mann is fascinating in its own right.

Horace Mann was born to a family of farmers in Franklin, Massachusetts, on May 4, 1796. His forebears were among the earliest Puritan settlers in the area, and he was one of five children, all of whom were expected to do their share of farm work. In later years he wrote, "I believe in the rugged nursing of toil, but she nursed me too much." As a result, industry and diligence became his second nature, and he became something of a compulsive worker. But work was not his most serious problem as a youth. What troubled him more than anything was religion, that is, the severe brand of Calvinism to which he was exposed. In later years he wrote in a letter:

More than by toil, or by the privation of any natural taste, was the inward joy of my youth blighted by theological inculcations. The pastor of the church in Franklin was the somewhat celebrated Dr. Emmons, who not only preached to his people, but ruled them for more than fifty years. He was an extra or hyper-Calvinist—a man of pure intellect, whose logic was never softened in its severity by the infusion of any kindliness of sentiment. He expounded all the doctrines of total depravity, election, and reprobation, and not only the eternity but the extremity of hell torments, unflinchingly and in their most terrible significance, while he rarely if ever descanted upon the joys of heaven, and never, to my recollection, upon the essential and necessary happiness of a virtuous life. Going to church on Sunday was a sort of religious ordinance in our family, and during all my boyhood I hardly ever remember staying at home.[1]

In 1808, when Mann was barely twelve, Emmons conducted a revival meeting in order to stem the drift away from religion and to convert those among the young who had not yet demonstrated their faith. It was an emotionally charged affair, and there were more than thirty converts. But Mann was not among them. Instead, he broke with Calvinism. It was a dramatic moment in his life, and years later he was to write: "I remember the day, the hour, the place and the circumstances, as well as though the event had happened but yesterday, when in an agony of despair, I broke the spell that bound me. From that day, I began to construct the theory of Christian ethics and doctrine respecting virtue and vice, rewards and penalties, time and eternity, God and his providence which . . . I still retain."[2]

Thus, Mann, by his own inner resources, repudiated Calvinism much in the same way that the Boston and Harvard Unitarians had done. But Mann's was a personal and emotional act, unaided by the works of suave and sophisticated theologians. One year later, however, his father was dead, and a year after that, his favorite brother Stephen drowned while swimming on the Sabbath. Mann could not help but relate the deaths of his father and brother to his repudiation of Calvinism, and his sense of guilt tormented him. Mann's biographer, Jonathan Messerli, writes:

Not quite sane at night, he wrestled with a personal devil he could neither let go nor subdue. In such mental chaos, it was little wonder that he felt an almost unbearable sense of desolation. One of his childhood associates noted his morbid compulsion, each time he returned to the meetinghouse, to turn to the same page in Watts's hymnal and read over a stanza depicting a solitary soul lost in eternity. The young Horace identified himself with that soul, fully understanding what it meant to be "rudderless and homeless." For him, emancipation had come at a dear price.[3]

As the religious traumas of his youth began to fade more and more into the past, young Horace Mann began to think of the future. Being bookish and introspective, he decided that farm life was not for him and that he would go to college and seek a profession. At the age of 18, with the help of tutors in Latin, Greek, and mathematics, he began his long arduous preparation for Brown University. Brown, located some thirty miles southward in Providence, was the university most Franklin youths chose to attend. It was the door to the greater world. Mann entered Brown as a sophomore in 1816 and graduated in 1819 as class valedictorian. During his senior year he had decided to become a lawyer, and as graduation grew near he made arrangements to serve his legal apprenticeship with a noted attorney in Wrentham, the town adjacent to Franklin. But after a few months in Wrentham, he decided to transfer to Judge Tapping Reeve's renowned law school in Litchfield, Connecticut, which offered a faster, surer road to legal success. But before Mann was ready to leave for Litchfield, he received a letter from Asa Messer, president of Brown, offering him a tutorship. After considerable thought, Mann decided to accept the offer and returned to his alma mater where he taught for two years. Regarding this teaching experience—which was to be Mann's only first-hand experience as an "educator"—Messerli writes:

> Quickly overcoming his initial stage fright as a teacher, Mann cut the more self-centered of his charges down to size, usually with uncharitable sarcasm. Never satisfied with the bare skeleton of a translation, but insisting on a rendering which gave the elegance and full flavor of classical literature, Mann earned the reputation of a demanding teacher. . . . Believing he was unreasonable in what he expected of them one day, they (his students) hissed and hooted him out of class.[4]

Dissatisfied and depressed by the slow pace of his advancement at Brown, Mann resigned in 1821 and enrolled at the law school in Litchfield. It was a good move, for Mann found the studies stimulating, the social life pleasant, and he formed important connections with some of his classmates, one of them being Edward G. Loring, of an elite Boston family.

On leaving Litchfield, Mann decided to begin his law practice in Dedham, Massachusetts, seat of the Court of Common Pleas and the Supreme Judicial Court of Norfolk County. He spent a year "reading" in the law office of a practicing attorney, and in December 1823 was granted the privilege of practicing law in the Norfolk Court of Common Pleas. Two years later he was admitted to practice before the Supreme Judicial Court. Thus, by 1825, his legal apprenticeship was completed. He was almost thirty.

But finally it all began to pay off. Long hours, attention to detail, and a self-interest in winning his clients' cases caused his reputation to spread and his practice to grow. The most important development in his career in this period, however, was the beginning of legal work for merchants and legal firms in Boston. Charles G. Loring, a prominent Boston attorney and cousin of Mann's classmate at Litchfield, sent Mann his Dedham accounts. Mann was finally beginning to make money and he invested some of it in a business partnership with his older brother Stanley.

By 1825, however, Mann had also become interested in politics. He had gained public favor as an eloquent Fourth of July orator, and in 1826 a group of citizens supported him for the state legislature. Mann got enough votes to be elected as the second representative, but the town at that time decided to send only one man to the State House. By 1827 Mann was secretary of the Republican Party of Norfolk County, and in May of that year the voters of Dedham decided to send him to the legislature as their second representative.

No sooner did Mann arrive in Boston than he began to ally himself with the interests of the Boston-Harvard-

Unitarian elite. His friend Edward Loring served as his social and political mentor, introducing him to some of the first social and economic families of the city. Loring himself was allied by marriage and business to the family of Mayor Josiah Quincy, who was to become president of Harvard in 1829, and the family of industrialist Edmund Dwight, who had married a daughter of Samuel Eliot and whose brothers-in-law were George Ticknor and Andrews Norton.

From the very first session in which he took part, Mann voted in the interests of his Boston friends. In the 1827 session he voted against the construction of a bridge over the Charles River that would have competed with a privately owned bridge in which Harvard College and some of his friends owned an interest. In the 1828 session he voted against a measure that would have permitted the orthodox to maintain control over endowments made by orthodox individuals when a parish was later taken over by liberals. Mann's vote was consistent with the controversial Dedham decision of 1820 that permitted Unitarians to take over the property of Congregational churches once they became a majority in the congregation. In support of his position, Mann made a dramatic speech defending religious liberty and invoking the spirit of Roger Williams and Thomas Jefferson. All of this was music to the ears of the Unitarians who now realized that they had a new champion among them. Mann also became the key supporter of railroad-subsidy legislation greatly favored and promoted by Edmund Dwight, Josiah Quincy, and other moneyed friends. In fact, Mann's voting record was so consistently in favor of his Boston friends that some of his constituents in Dedham began to complain. One of the town's patriarchs attacked Mann in a series of articles in the local paper, accusing him of an undisguised desire to gain important financial and political connections in Boston to the detriment of his constituents in Dedham. But Mann survived the attack.

During Mann's first three years in the legislature, he served on a number of House committees covering a wide area of concerns. About the only thing that did not come before him as a committee member were matters pertaining to education. However, as he had adopted his friends' economic concerns, he was now beginning to adopt their social concerns. Their causes were soon to become his.

One of their causes was "temperance," or alcoholism. So Mann, with a group of close friends, formed the Dedham Temperance Society, a voluntary association which would "discountenance the improper use of ardent spirits." The members elected Mann as president. The group was allied in spirit and outlook to the Massachusetts Society for the Suppression of Intemperance, which had been founded in 1813 by a group of predominantly Unitarian ministers, lawyers, and merchants, and reflected William E. Channing's view that alcoholism was not an evidence of sinfulness but rather the result of intolerable pressures generated by society. The solution it offered to the problem was for the rich to set an example to the poor by being temperate, for society to provide adequate recreation and diversion for the poor, and for the distribution of liquor through retail outlets to be curtailed and licensing to be more strictly controlled.

In 1825, however, orthodox minister Lyman Beecher, then preaching in Boston, insisted that intemperance had to be treated as "sin" and that the only cure was a religious one, not a legal one; that excise taxes and stricter control of licenses would not really come to grips with the spiritual problems of the drinker. Only total voluntary abstinence could cure this moral disease. The result was that a group of orthodox ministers and laymen quit the Massachusetts Society and formed a more religiously oriented group, the American Society for Promotion of Temperance, which in 1829 petitioned the legislature for incorporation. Mann's House Judiciary Committee studied the application and issued an adverse report on the grounds that the work of temperance ought to be based on universal, not sectarian, principles. This stunned the orthodox, who bitterly criticized Mann for his stand. Nevertheless, the petition was defeated, which testified to how little influence the orthodox now had among politicians.

Mann then went on to promote his own plan for reform which, as one might suspect, was really Channing's plan. He proposed a stricter enforcement of the licensing laws and restrictions on who could sell liquor. The chief purpose of the law was to close down the many "grog shops" where the poor could get liquor easily, cheaply, and consume it on the spot. Mann's law provided that only innkeepers could sell liquor for consumption on the premises. Those who were not innkeepers were to be classified as retailers who could only sell liquor to be consumed elsewhere. The purpose of the law was to make it more difficult for the poor to buy liquor. It was assumed that the poor would drink less if liquor was less easily accessible. By outlawing the grog shop, Mann had supposedly struck a great blow for temperance.

The Unitarians were jubilant, and Mann's friend Edward Loring reported to him that "the best men in society" had noted his work in the legislature and "desire to trust their cause to you, so Atlas must spread his shoulders." The more he championed the elite's causes, the more he won their approval, and apparently their approval is what Mann was most anxious to have.

But the opposition was not impressed. They gathered their forces and in the session of 1832 pressed for a repeal of Mann's law. They questioned the constitutionality of restraining a man from drinking. Mann had a ready statist answer: the state's power of restraint was necessary "to maintain order and morality and secure the safety of the people." But because there was so much sentiment against intemperance, the most the opponents could get was a revision of the law removing the means for its strict enforcement.

In February 1829, Mann became chairman of a legislative committee to study the condition and treatment of the insane in Massachusetts. Unitarian minister Joseph Tuckerman had made a study of conditions in the Boston jail where he had found fifty female lunatics languishing away. The result was an article by Tuckerman in the *Christian Register,* the Unitarian journal, advocating that the state build a separate hospital for the care and treatment of the insane.

Horace Mann took the matter up during the January 1830 session of the legislature, and he gave the first speech ever made before that body advocating state care for the insane. It was a well-prepared speech, with the facts and figures collected by his committee, an account of how the insane had been treated by society throughout history, and the latest findings of a British doctor claiming that with proper and humane treatment, forty percent of the insane could be cured. He urged that the state erect and operate a hospital for the insane, arguing that by the default of local communities and families, the insane had become wards of the state. In March 1830, Mann's bill authorizing the erection of a Lunatic Hospital was signed by Gov. Levi Lincoln, and Mann was appointed chairman of the commission responsible for building the hospital.

As chairman, Mann went about planning and supervising the building of the hospital at a site in Worcester with his usual thoroughness and diligence, and in January 1833 the nation's first state-owned and operated lunatic asylum was opened.

By 1832, the Unitarian elite realized that in Mann it had found a unique, forceful and articulate legislator who could translate their irrepressible do-goodism into concrete legislative reality. But on August 1, 1832, a personal tragedy befell Mann, which was to temporarily interrupt his legislative career. Charlotte, his beautiful twenty-year-old bride of two years, died of tuberculosis, leaving him in a state of total desolation. Mann, at age 34, had married Charlotte Messer, the youngest daughter of Asa Messer, former president of Brown University, in September 1830. Charlotte, a sickly and frail girl, needed far more attention and care than Mann, who was then pursuing a demanding, time-consuming career, could possibly give. But he realized this only when it was too late.

After Charlotte's death, Edward Loring urged Mann to join him in Boston in a legal partnership. Mann accepted, leaving Dedham for good, thus giving up his seat in the House of Representatives. He took a room in a genteel boardinghouse whose guests included Jared Sparks, then writing his biography of Washington, and the Peabody sisters—Mary and Elizabeth—who ran a small private school in the morning and did editing work in the afternoon. The two sisters took an immediate interest in Mann, and before long Mann confided to Elizabeth the cause of his unhappiness and the new crisis in faith he was undergoing. How could the benevolent God of the Unitarians have permitted his saintly beloved Charlotte to die? Elizabeth, a confidante of William E. Channing, brought Mann to the great Unitarian leader for spiritual help. Messerli describes the therapeutic nature of those visits:

> In the course of his conversations with Channing, Mann pieced together the events of his childhood and dredged up memories long forgotten. He described his early recollections of God as a vengeful ruler. He also recalled that when he later suggested the power of God to elicit love, his mother rejected the idea and insisted that true virtue could only come from a fear of the Almighty. Channing found it hard to believe that throughout Mann's childhood, Christ had never been presented as the great moral teacher. Mann insisted this was so, and that it was only with great effort that he had been able to reject the stern doctrines of his youth. In their place, he had come to

believe that it was the love of God and their fellow men, rather than a fear of retribution for sin, which motivated men to ethical lives. With his rejection of divine retribution for sin, Mann discarded a belief in anything supernatural or miraculous. If laws were broken, God did not step from the clouds to mete out punishment. Rather, in the harmonious order of the universe, punishment was the natural result of a violation of either physical or moral laws. But if this were so, how was Charlotte's death to be explained? As long as he had assumed that the universe was governed by a beneficient sovereign and was a friendly habitation for men, he could also assume that good would eventually triumph. Now he was unable or unwilling to admit that his personal loss was part of a harmonious and reasonable creation. Beneath the sereneness of a natural world, he had experienced an elemental cruelty. Charlotte's death was an undeniable fact which challenged all his sentimental beliefs in a moral universe.[5]

Channing could not solve Mann's spiritual problems, but the two men got to know one another well. In addition to his spiritual and emotional losses, Mann now also faced a sharp economic setback. His brother's business had failed, and Mann was now obliged to pay off some large debts. He left the boarding house, curtailed his social life, and for the next three years lived out of his law office. His friends nevertheless continued to hope for his recovery and return to public life. In the fall of 1834, Mann's banker friends, James K. Mills and Henry Lee, and his industrialist friend, Edmund Dwight, convinced Mann to accept the Whig candidacy for the state Senate. The election on November 7, 1834, turned out to be a great victory for the Whigs, and Horace Mann once more found himself in the state legislature.

During the 1835 session, Mann labored chiefly on a full-scale revision of the laws of Massachusetts, a project which had been started by him and Ira Barton, a Brown classmate, in 1831. The revisions strongly advocated by

Mann included a provision prohibiting the jailing of debtors, a stricter statute limiting Sunday activities, and a stronger law controlling the importation, printing, and distribution of obscene materials. As a religious liberal he did not argue that the Sabbath should be observed as a "holy time," but as an invaluable "social and political institution."

In November 1835, Mann was re-elected to the state Senate. He was also elected president of the Senate after a grueling factional battle and eighteen ballots. During the 1836 session, which was Edward Everett's first term, Mann came to the aid of their mutual friends Edmund Dwight and Josiah Quincy, who needed legislative approval to raise additional private capital for their railroad projects. His vote on this issue encouraged the trend to make the corporation more an instrument of free enterprise than public service, which only demonstrated that Mann's views on public and private domains and functions were not based on any consistent set of economic principles, but merely coincided with those of his Unitarian backers.

In the 1837 session, Mann was once again elected president of the Senate, this time on the first ballot. Again he helped his railroad promoter friends gain legislative permission to raise more capital, and he issued a report which laid a basis for distinguishing between private and public corporations. During the session there were also many petitions for new bank charters as well as requests from existing banks for the right to increase their capital and thus maintain their pre-eminence over the new entrepreneurs. Abandoning any guise of impartiality, Mann repeatedly stepped down from the chair and opposed the would-be *nouveaux riches* in favor of his friends' established institutions on State Street.

When did Mann finally get interested in education? When his backers wanted him to. Although he had an ego proud enough to rebel against the God of Calvin, he seemed totally dependent on his backers for their continued approval. His subservience to their interests was neither groveling nor self-demeaning. On the contrary, he had appreciated their legal business and their recognition of his talents, and he had become ever so willing to put his talents to their use. Poor as he was, he had natural gifts which his friends, with all their money, connections, breeding, and education, did not have. Surrounded by these people, helped by them, consoled and even loved by some of them, he found himself identifying with their ideals, their ambitions, their plans.

In a way, until 1837, Mann was a man without a purpose. True, he had selected his profession and had worked his way to a respected position in the legislature. But he required a higher will to give him a sense of direction. At Brown, as a debater, he had been able to argue both sides of a question quite convincingly. And as a legislator he had become an able instrument of the Harvard-Unitarian elite. Soon they would give him a purpose that would make him the most famous name in American educational history.

Edward Everett's election to the governorship in November of 1835 meant that public education would become an important issue during his administration. This was the opportunity the Unitarians had been waiting for. But probably because of lack of time or preparation, Everett did not propose any educational legislation during his first term in office. However, in his address to the legislature in January 1836, he expressed his basic political philosophy, which reflected the essentially contradictory views of the Unitarians. On the one hand it glorified a libertarian kind of freedom, but on the other it embraced a utilitarianism that would gradually chip away that freedom. Everett said:

> Our system looks to the People not merely as a whole, but as a society composed of individual men, whose happiness is the great design of the association. It consequently recognizes the

greatest good of the greatest number, as the basis of the social compact. . . . Almost the only compulsion exercised toward the citizen, in his private affairs, by the State, is that which compels him to provide the means of educating his children. Left with the least practicable interference from the law, in all other respects, he is obliged to support free schools, by which the elements of useful knowledge are brought within the reach of all, alike those who do and who do not, bear a part of the burden.

Indeed, America of 1836 was something of a libertarian paradise, and the blessings of freedom had their positive economic consequences. Everett painted a very optimistic picture as he said:

It is believed to be the language of sober truth and not of patriotic exaggeration, that there does not exist at this moment, on the face of the earth,—that there never did exist,—a political community as large as the State of Massachusetts, enjoying a greater share of prosperity and happiness, with less suffering and want.

Nor is the remark to be limited to our own Commonwealth; it may be extended generally to our sister states. As one people, the United States present the spectacle never witnessed of a nation, which has entirely liberated itself from a large public debt, by its faithful payment, principal and interest. Our commercial, navigating, manufacturing, and agricultural interests are in general highly prosperous. The past season has, in the aggregate, been one of unusual activity. While in almost every part of the country, industry is amply crowned with its natural rewards, a population increasing without a parallel, and furnished with ample capital for the purpose, is bringing the hitherto unoccupied public domain into the realm of civilization, with a rapidity that seems more like romance than reality.

Considering how ideal conditions seemed in 1836, it is hardly difficult to see why the general public did not share the educators' hysterical urgency for educational reform in the Prussian mold. There was really nothing to get hysterical about. Thus, when Governor Everett put forth his proposals in his address to a rather conservative legislature in 1837, he couched them in very moderate terms in keeping with his own temperament. First, he praised the people of Massachusetts for contributing more money to public education than the total of the state budget.

But to Everett and the educators, that was not enough. He said:

> While nothing can be farther from my purpose than to disparage the common schools as they are, and while a deep sense of personal obligation to them will ever be cherished by me, it must yet be candidly admitted, that they are susceptible of great improvements. The school houses might, in many cases, be rendered more commodious. Provision ought to be made for affording the advantages of education, throughout the whole year, to all of a proper age to receive it. Teachers well qualified to give elementary instruction in all the branches of useful knowledge, should be employed; and small school libraries, maps, globes, and requisite scientific apparatus should be furnished. I submit to the Legislature, whether the creation of a board of commissioners of schools, to serve without salary, with authority to appoint a secretary, on a reasonable compensation, to be paid from the school fund, would not be of great utility.

Then he turned to the matter of the school fund. Under the revised statute it was required that each town raise "one dollar for each person belonging to said town" in order to share in the income from the fund. But this law encouraged the towns to raise only the minimum required and look to the state for the rest. Everett proposed that the law be changed so that the funds would be apportioned to the towns in a direct ratio to the amount they raised by taxing themselves. He explained:

Unquestioned experience elsewhere has taught, that the principle of distribution established by the revised statute, goes far to render a school fund useless. On the contrary, where it is apportioned in the ratio of the sums raised by taxation for the support of the schools (which is the principle adopted by the great and liberal State of New York,) the fund becomes at once the stimulus and the reward of the efforts of the People.

The education lobby went to work in support of Governor Everett's proposals. The directors of the American Institute of Instruction submitted a Memorial to the legislature urging that the state create teachers' seminaries in which future common-school teachers could be trained. This Memorial was followed by a petition drawn up by Rev. Charles Brooks and adopted by a teachers' convention in Plymouth County on January 24, 1837. The petition lauded the Prussian system as described in the Cousin report and suggested that the character of Massachusetts might be greatly improved by imposing this system on itself. It recommended compulsory attendance supervised by local school committees; the establishment of a "Board of Education" in every county; the appointment of a "secretary of public instruction"; and the establishment of a "seminary for the preparation of teachers." It considered the last recommendation of "paramount importance." The petitioners wrote:

Over and over again the Prussians proved, that elementary education cannot be fully attained without purposely-prepared teachers. They deem these seminaries of priceless value; and declare them, in all their reports and laws, to be the fountains of all their success. Out of this fact, in their history, has arisen the maxim, "As is the master so is the school." We are certain that philosophy and experience alike verify this maxim in Massachusetts. We have no wish to say aught against our schoolmasters or mistresses. They are as good as circumstances encourage them to be; as good as the community have demanded; but, we are confident that teachers thoroughly prepared, as they are in Prussia, would put a new face on elementary education, and produce through our State an era of light and of love.

A third Memorial in support of Everett's proposals came from a Bristol County Education Convention held in Taunton and submitted to the legislature in February 1837. It advocated educational statism in no uncertain terms:

> We would call upon the government of our state to exercise a more direct and powerful control over the school; . . . The power of the government is now hardly felt, either to stimulate or direct. The requisitions which it makes upon those upon whom it has placed the care of the schools, are of a nature that renders it of but little importance, as far as the interests of education are concerned, whether they are complied with or not; and all that it does in behalf of the schools which it has established, is, annually to publish the secretary's "Abstract of the Returns;" which answers no other purpose but to show how much the guardianship of an enlightened and powerful supervision is needed to secure that uniformity of method, and that faithfulness in instructors, without which the most lavish expenditure of money will fail to bestow upon our children the invaluable blessing of a good education.

Thus, by 1837, the American educator had been thoroughly won over by Hegelian statism as far as education was concerned. The thrust was for centralized state control and uniformity of curriculum through control of textbook selection and teacher training as advocated by Josiah Holbrook in his Lyceum program. The Prussian system was to serve as the concrete model to imitate. While the Harvard Unitarians in general agreed that Hegelian statism could be applied to the purposes of public education, they were divided on the application of German transcendentalism to religion. Just as the parting of the ways between Calvinists and Unitarians had taken place in 1805 by the Unitarian takeover of Harvard and was confirmed in 1819 by Channing's celebrated Baltimore sermon, a new parting of the ways was to take place between conservative Unitarians who still believed in God as an objective reality in the monotheistic tradition of the Bible, and the Transcendentalists who believed in God either as a pantheistic spirit or a pre-Old Testament deity. Emerson ignited the controversy with his Harvard Divinity School address in July 1838, and Theodore Parker more or less affirmed it with his sermon on "The Transient and Permanent in Christianity" in May 1841.

Thus, it was in the context of such spiritual and cultural controversy that New England intellectuals and educators turned to Hegelian statism as the needed source of moral power over the community. But while the intellectuals were struggling in this spiritual crisis, the ordinary citizens of Massachusetts were still rooted in religious conservatism, even though, by 1837, Calvinism too had undergone doctrinal softening.

In any case, on April 20, 1837, the Massachusetts legislature gave Governor Everett and the educators much of what they wanted. However, the legislators rejected any change in the school fund statute. James G. Carter, chairman of the House Standing Committee on Education, had drafted the legislation, and he was supported by such Unitarian members of the House as Francis C. Gray, Edward G. Loring, Robert Rantoul, Jr. and Oliver W. B. Peabody. Mann, as president of the Senate, was chiefly responsible for its passage there, supported by Josiah Quincy, Jr., chairman of the Senate Committee on Education.

The new law, which was to alter forever the course of American education in the Prussian direction, gave the governor the power to appoint a state "Board of Education" composed of eight persons who, in turn, were empowered to appoint their own paid Secretary. The Secretary's duty was "to collect information of the actual condition and efficiency of the Common schools . . . and to diffuse as widely as possible . . . information of the most approved and successful methods of arranging the studies and conducting the education of the young." This effectively took educational policy out of the hands of the local educators and put it in the hands of a state educational bureaucracy. Both the board and the secretary were required annually "to make a detailed report to the Legislature of all their doings, with such observations as their experience and reflection may suggest, upon the condition and efficiency of our system of popular education and the most practicable means of improving and extending it." The law also gave the board the power "to encourage or provide for the better education of common school teachers of both sexes, in such manner as to them may seem expedient for the promotion of the object."

In all, it was an extremely broad mandate, and the educators now had the opportunity they had been clamoring for to remake the state's public school system in the Prussian image. Now all they needed were the men who could translate possibility and potential into reality. To help Governor Everett find the right men, a "little volunteer council," led by Unitarian industrialist Edmund Dwight, conferred behind the scenes, lending its assistance. Dwight, who had married a daughter of Harvard benefactor Samuel Eliot, was a brother-in-law of Andrews Norton, the Unitarian "Pope" at Harvard, and George Ticknor, who had studied at Göttingen with Everett. Dwight had read the Cousin Report and was thoroughly convinced that America needed the Prussian system. He had known Mann since the latter's days in the House of Representatives, where Mann had worked hard to put through bills helpful to Dwight and others who were promoting the Albany-to-Boston railroad.

With the help of the "volunteer council," Governor

Everett chose his Board of Education. Naturally it would have been impolitic to appoint only Unitarians to the board, but he appointed enough of them to insure control. They included Jared Sparks, Edmund Dwight, James G. Carter, Robert Rantoul, Jr., and Horace Mann. The non-Unitarians were Rev. Emerson Davis, a Congregational minister from Westfield; Edward A. Newton, a prominent Episcopalian banker from Pittsfield; and Rev. Thomas Robbins, a Congregationalist from Rochester. The board was off to a good start. Now all it had to do was appoint a Secretary.

Dwight had let it be known confidentially, even before the Board had been chosen, that he favored Mann as Secretary. But there were other more logical front runners: educator George B. Emerson; activist Unitarian minister Charles Brooks; and the most logical candidate of all, James G. Carter. Carter had been writing about and promoting public education and teacher seminaries since he had left Harvard, he had run his own private school, was a founder of the American Institute of Instruction, and as a legislator had actually drafted the bill creating the Board of Education. It was as if he were being groomed for the part. But Dwight did not want him. Carter lacked the right charisma for the role. What was needed, Dwight believed, was a single-minded, dedicated leader who could both overcome a small hostile minority opposed to the Prussianization of the school system and stir up a large apathetic majority who simply did not care. To Dwight, there was only one man who could perform such an impossible task: Horace Mann. Dwight had seen Mann at work in the Legislature. Mann could get things done despite great opposition. That was his special talent. He had translated a Unitarian dream into reality with the building of the State Lunatic Hospital. In the temperance cause, Mann had shown that he possessed that selfless moral concern that seems to be at the heart of the messianic reformer. Mann had all the right vibrations, and Dwight was able to convince the others on the Board that Mann would make the ideal Secretary. True, Mann had not been an educator and had shown no particular or spontaneous interest in public education as a cause; but he had that special kind of self-sacrificial fervor, and that was more important than his actual educational experience.

Dwight now took upon himself the task of convincing Mann, whose political star in the legislature was rising, to give it all up to become Secretary of the Board of Education. And Mann would respond to the call because his own life had added up to no purpose, and he was emotionally and spiritually ready to be used by others for a great cause. There was also something quite appropriate in the Unitarian choice of a non-educator for such a job. The Unitarians had given up on God's miracles, but they believed in human miracles. For them, Mann was to perform the miracle that would prove that man was indeed perfectible and that evil could be eradicated through education.

10. Toward the Creation of a New Secular Religion

IF HORACE MANN has come down in history as the father of American public education, it is not because he invented the public school. Common schools were in existence in New England for almost two hundred years before Mann became Secretary of the newly created Massachusetts Board of Education. If Mann was the father of anything, it was of centralized, state-controlled public education, governed by a state bureaucracy, and financed by taxes on property. Mann's unique contribution was in changing American education from its libertarian, free-market course to an irreversible statist one. Indeed, if anyone can claim credit for changing America's social, academic and—ultimately—political direction from a libertarian to a statist one, it would be Horace Mann. There were, of course, others—Robert Dale Owen and Josiah Holbrook—who advocated the same policies. But it was Mann who was able to overcome the very considerable opposition to this fundamental change, while others could not.

The key to Mann's success was in his peculiar sense of

184

mission, combined with his practical political experience as a legislator and the strong financial, cultural, and social backing of the Harvard-Unitarian elite. If the American public school movement took on the tone of a religious crusade after Mann became Secretary of the Board of Education, it was because Mann himself saw it as a religious mission. He accepted the position of Secretary not only because of what it would demand of him, but because it would help fulfill the spiritual hopes of his friends. They had faith that Mann could deliver the secular miracle that would vindicate their view of human nature and justify their repudiation of Calvinism. So anxious were they for Mann to accept the position of Secretary, that Edmund Dwight, for the next twelve years, gladly added a large sum of his own personal funds to Mann's yearly salary, and Mann's banker friend James K. Mills lent him the money with which to clear up the debts incurred through the failure of his brother's business. After living for three years in his law office in a depressing state of austerity, he was now liberated from financial worry by his benefactors in order to be free to turn Unitarian dreams into legislated reality.

That Mann knew what was expected of him is made clear through his journal entries. On May 18, 1837, a month before he accepted the position, Mann wrote:

> Whoever shall undertake that task must encounter privation, labor, and an infinite annoyance from an infinite number of schemers. He must condense the steam of enthusiasts, and soften the rock of the incredulous. What toil in arriving at a true system himself! What toil in infusing that system into the minds of others! . . . What a spirit of perseverence would be needed to sustain him all the way between the inception and the accomplishment of his objects! But should he succeed; should be bring forth the germs of greatness and of happiness which Nature has scattered abroad, and expand them into maturity, and enrich them with fruit; should he be able to teach, to even a few of this generation, how mind is god over matter; how, in

arranging objects of desire, a subordination of the less valuable to the more is the great secret of individual happiness; how the whole of life depends upon the scale which we form of its relative values,—could he do this, what diffusion, what intensity, what perpetuity of blessings he would confer! How would his beneficial influence upon mankind widen and deepen as it descended forever![1]

And on May 27, the day the Board's members were named, Mann revealed his own statist views in these words:

It is the first great movement towards an organized system of common education, which shall at once be thorough and universal. Every civilized State is as imperfectly organized, without a minister or secretary of instruction, as it would be without ministers or secretaries of State, Finance, War, or the Navy. Every child should be educated: if not educated by its own father, the State should appoint a father to it. I would much sooner surrender a portion of the territory of the Commonwealth to an ambitious and aggressive neighbor than I would surrender the minds of its children to the dominion of ignorance.[2]

Like so many of the reformers, Mann believed that the minds of other people's children were his to educate, or surrender, or protect. On June 14, in anticipation of the appointment, Mann wrote:

I cannot think of that station, as regards myself, without feeling both hopes and fears, desires and apprehensions, multiplying in my mind,—so glorious a sphere, should it be crowned with success; so heavy with disappointment and humiliation, should it fail through any avoidable misfortune. What a thought, to have the future minds of such multitudes dependent in any perceptible degree upon one's own exertions! It is such a thought as must mightily energize or totally overpower any mind that can adequately comprehend it.[3]

Then, on June 28, on the eve of being offered the position by the Board, Mann wrote:

> I tremble, however, at the idea of the task that possibly now lies before me. Yet I can now conscientiously say that here stands my purpose, ready to undergo the hardships and privations to which I must be subjected, and to encounter the jealousy, misrepresentation, and the prejudice almost certain to arise; here stands my mind, ready to meet them in the spirit of a martyr.[4]

Thus, even before his appointment, Mann was thoroughly convinced that anyone who would oppose centralized, state-controlled education would be prejudiced, jealous, and untruthful. The following day, after he had received the offer, Mann was overwhelmed by a sense of altruism:

> I have received the offer. The path of usefulness is opened before me. My present purpose is to enter into it. . . .
> God grant me an annihilation of selfishness, a mind of wisdom, a heart of benevolence! How many men I shall meet who are accessible only through a single motive, or who are incased in prejudice and jealousy, and need, not to be subdued, but to be remodelled! how many who will vociferate their devotion to the public, but whose thoughts will be intent on themselves! There is but one spirit in which these impediments can be met with success: it is the spirit of self-abandonment, the spirit of martyrdom.[5]

Whatever qualities Mann's rivals for the job might have had, they did not have his sense of martyrdom. After conveying his acceptance to the Board, Mann wrote:

> Henceforth, so long as I hold this office, I devote myself to the supremest welfare of mankind upon earth. . . . *Faith* is the

only sustainer. I have faith in the improvability of the race,—in their accelerating improvability.[6]

But if he still had any doubts about giving up his law practice and promising political career for what seemed to many a vastly inferior position, they were dispelled by a letter from William E. Channing himself:

> My Dear Sir:—I understand that you have given yourself to the cause of education in our Commonwealth. I rejoice in it. Nothing could give me greater pleasure. I have long desired that one uniting all your qualifications should devote himself to this work. You could not find a nobler station. Government has no nobler one to give. You must allow me to labor under you according to my opportunities. If at any time I can aid you, you must let me know, and I shall be glad to converse with you always about your operations. . . .
>
> If we can but turn the wonderful energy of this people into a right channel, what a new heaven and earth must be realized among us! And I do not despair. Your willingness to consecrate yourself to the work is a happy omen. You do not stand alone, or form a rare exception to the times. There must be many to be touched by the same truths which are stirring you.[7]

The key sentence in Channing's letter not only expressed the grand Unitarian dream, but in the same breath also summed up its delusions: "If we can but turn the wonderful energy of this people into the right channel, what a new heaven and earth must be realized among us!" It wasn't enough that the American people, as individuals, now had the freedom to channel their own energies in the directions of their own choices. A morally superior elite, self-appointed and certain of its altruist mission, had decided that they alone knew which direction an entire people should be turned in. Never for a moment did this elite ever entertain the idea that they might possibly be wrong. In fact, what was particularly characteristic of them was their conviction that they possessed the one and only truth. Their intellectual intolerance when confronted with any opposing views became the hallmark of their reformist activism. Those who were for the public school movement were the "enlightened"; and those who opposed it or suggested alternatives were the "powers of darkness."

The first thing Mann did on assuming his new position was give himself a crash course in education by reading everything he could get hold of on the subject. He read Cousin's Report and all of the back issues of the *Journal of Education* and the *Annals of Education*.

In August 1837, Mann made preparations for his first circuit or tour of county conventions and school inspections in order to find out first-hand the state and condition of the public schools in the local communities. Circulars were sent to school committee members in every town, informing them of the time and place of the meeting to be held in their county. Mann then bought a horse and saddle and set forth on his historic mission. His first stop was Worcester, site of that year's American Institute of Instruction convention, at which he took part in a panel discussion, and following which his first educational gathering would be held.

The Institute convention was a good place for Mann to start playing his new role, for it permitted such public school activists as Rev. Charles Brooks, James G. Carter, George B. Emerson, and others, to hear Mann speak and get used to the idea that he was their new leader, even though each one of them knew far more about education than he did. But despite his initial nervousness, Mann proved himself equal to the occasion and not only won the confidence of this important body of educators, but was pledged their cooperation in helping him carry out his new duties as Secretary. As a tribute, the convention voted by acclamation to add Mann's name to its list of vice-presidents.

The Worcester County Convention then followed. James B. Carter was elected its president, and Mann gave an address. In a state where the Common School was in decline and the private academy on the rise, Mann's task was not only to justify the continued existence of the Common School and to inspire renewed public support for it, but to argue in favor of improving it, extending it, and making it the dominant if not the sole educational institution for the nation's children. It was basically a selling job, and Mann proved himself to be as good a salesman as he was a politician, for by the time the convention was over, its participants had formed a Worcester County Association for the Improvement of Common Schools with James G. Carter as its president.

Mann then returned to Boston to prepare for the next leg of his state tour. He had mapped out an itinerary for September that would take him through the remote western part of the state where interest in public education was weakest. Nevertheless, the audience that came out to hear him in Springfield was good, thanks to some advance preparation by Edmund Dwight. But the audience in Pittsfield was sparse. Pittsfield was the home of Edward Newton, the Episcopalian member of the Board of Education, who did not share the Unitarian brand of enthusiasm for public education and was somewhat suspicious of Unitarian motives. In Greenfield, however, Mann found Congregational minister Board member, Rev. Emerson Davis, who was very much in favor of the cause and provided a full house to hear the new Secretary.

Mann completed his western tour in a little more than three weeks, returned to Boston, and then headed south. Channing, who had promised his support, spoke at the Taunton convention, thereby drawing newspaper interest. From Taunton, Mann headed toward the offshore islands. At Edgartown, on Martha's Vineyard, Mann had a good audience but offended the local orthodox clergy by visiting an Indian village on Sunday instead of attending one of the churches. Since there was no Unitarian church in town,

Mann had decided to attend none. On Nantucket, however, Mann was greeted by Rev. Cyrus Peirce, a Unitarian clergyman-educator whom he had met at the American Institute convention in Worcester. Peirce, a graduate of the Harvard Divinity School, had taught in a private school on Nantucket until his Unitarian conscience persuaded him to devote his efforts to improving the public schools. Mann was greatly impressed by Peirce's accomplishments on the island. In addition, a good audience turned out to hear him speak.

Back on the mainland, Mann spoke to a meeting at Barnstable and then to one at Plymouth at which Rev. Charles Brooks also spoke. By the last week in October, Mann was back in Boston. A final convention in Salem on November 7 concluded his first complete circuit of the state. The tour had been most useful. He had been able to identify and confer with the leading supporters of the cause in their local communities. He was able to size up the extent of public apathy and opposition, and he was now in a much better position to plan future strategy and suggest legislative action to bring about a new centralized educational policy.

On January 1, 1838, Mann delivered his First Annual Report to the Board of Education. The report concentrated on four major areas of concern: 1. *The physical condition of the schools.* Mann gave his views on how these schools could be turned into beautiful temples of learning. 2. *The deficient manner in which the school committees performed their duties.* Mann was critical of their slipshod methods in selecting teachers, their neglect of the law requiring uniformity of school books, which were to be furnished to the students at town expense when parents failed to furnish them. He was critical of their nonenforcement of attendance, regularity, and punctuality, and their infrequent visits to the schools. Mann attributed this negligence to the fact that the committeemen were unpaid and tended to do only what the townspeople wanted them to do. 3. *Community apathy to the public schools*. Mann identified two types of such apathy: that coming from the indifferent and ignorant and that coming from parents who preferred the academies and private schools. Mann elucidated on why public education had to become the dominant form of education, and he listed his objections to private schools as the means of popular education. 4. *Teacher competency*. Mann attributed poor teacher quality to low compensation, low standards of attainment, and the fact that many teachers entered the profession only temporarily.

The report was, in reality, an agenda for legislative and governmental action on each of the topics covered. Towns had to be encouraged to appropriate more tax money for the building of new and the improvement of old public schools. If these were to be government institutions, they had to reflect the power and benevolence of the state in their outward appearance. Mann had written in his report:

> And what citizen of Massachusetts would not feel an ingenuous and honorable pride, if, in whatever direction he should have occasion to travel through the State, he could go upon no highway, nor towards any point of the compass, without seeing, after every interval of three or four miles, a beautiful temple, planned according to some tasteful model in architecture, dedicated to the noble purpose of improving the rising generation, and bearing evidence, in all its outward aspects and circumstances, of fulfilling the sacred object of its erection?[8]

The public school, in short, was to become a government "temple" of learning, nonsectarian, of course, but quasi-religious in its purpose. Everyone in those days believed that the underpinning of a useful education was moral instruction, and it was assumed by all of the promoters of public education, Unitarian and orthodox alike, that the government schools would dispense moral education. They also agreed that the teachings of no one religious sect could be used in the public schools. A law had been passed in 1826 prohibiting the use of any textbooks in schools "calculated to favor any particular religious sect or tenet." The original public schools of Puritan times had been religious institutions. But the modern public school was to be devoid of religious teaching. That was, of course, what the Owenite socialists wanted: secular, if not atheistic, state schools. But no respectable promoter of public education in 1837 would have openly come out in favor of the Owenite idea. But for all their talk of a need for moral instruction in the public schools, no one was quite sure how to teach morality without teaching religion. The problem, never solved by Mann or anyone else, became a permanent dilemma of public education and a source of continuing conflict between schools and parents, schools and religions.

The second topic Mann had taken up, that of the school committeemen, was a crucial one. Under the then existing system, the school committee represented the townspeople and supervised the public schools to the extent that the townspeople wanted them supervised. The committeemen were unpaid citizens whose duty it was to see that the town complied with the state's school laws which, until 1838, were minimal. But with the new Board of Education, Mann realized that the local school committeemen should become local agents of the Board of Education, carrying out the legislated directives of the state rather than merely serving the wishes of their fellow townsmen. Central policy could only be translated into local policy if the school committeemen were responsive to the directives of the Board of Education and took their duties seriously. That was why Mann recommended that the state pay the committeemen and require them to submit an annual report to the Board. In that way the committeemen would become agents of the state rather than representatives of the townspeople who chose them.

Topic three, community apathy, required a campaign against the private schools and a campaign to propagate the great social and spiritual values and purposes of the public school. Here it would be a matter of selling educational statism to the people by assuring them that universal public education would cure all of the ills of society and bring about the millenium—heaven on earth. As for topic four, the competency of teachers, state-controlled teacher training would be offered as the only solution.

No sooner was Mann's report read and accepted by the Board of Education, than Mann got busy organizing his own lobby in the legislature to enact his recommendations into law. This was not a terribly difficult task since Mann knew the legislature inside out and was assured the help of such key legislators as James Savage, on the House Education Committee, and James G. Carter, on the Senate Education Committee. On January 18, 1838, Mann and the Rev. Charles Brooks addressed the House of Representatives on education. Brooks expounded the virtues of the Prussian system and strongly urged the lawmakers to support the creation of teachers' seminaries for the proper training of public school teachers. But the legislators were reluctant to vote tax money for the training of teachers when private academies were doing the job at no cost to the taxpayer.

Impatient to get their teacher training experiment off the ground, despite legislative resistance, Mann and his Unitarian backers decided to try another approach. Mann was to be informed that Edmund Dwight would place ten thousand dollars at the disposal of the Board of Education to be expended for "qualifying teachers," on the condition that the Legislature would place in the hands of the Board an equal sum, to be spent for the same purpose. A letter from Dwight describing this offer, dated March 12, 1838, was delivered to Mann, and Mann communicated the offer to the Legislature through the education committee. Ten days later, James Savage, chairman of the committee, reported in favor of the offer to the Legislature. On April 19, the Dwight proposal was approved by both the Legislature and Governor Everett, thus giving the educational statists the means with which to create a state-sponsored teachers' seminary, or Normal School, as it was to be called. Also, in April, acting on Mann's recommendations, the Massachusetts Legislature passed bills authorizing payment to school committeemen, the consolidation of small school districts, new procedures to help the Board of Education gather information from the towns, and a $500 raise in pay for the Secretary. Despite the raise, Dwight continued to subsidize Mann's salary for all of his years in office.

At this point, one must marvel at how this small clique was able to accomplish so much in such a short period of time. There was something almost conspiratorial in the way they managed to manipulate the legislature to achieve their ends. The Unitarians and their allies saw nothing wrong in using private money and private planning to create changes in the state's educational system which most of its citizens were not in favor of. Mann, with his confederates in the Legislature, aided by the educational network centered at Harvard, and financially supported by several wealthy Unitarians, was able to use the levers of state power to their greatest advantage. But with the Prussian ideal well in mind, the "friends of education" knew that this was only the beginning of a long process. Men like James Savage had started laboring for public education as far back as 1819. But what is significant is that men like Savage worked as members of a group, doing their part to advance the cause in whatever position they happened to be. In fact, it seemed as if the sole purpose of being elected to the Legislature was to advance the cause rather than oneself.

Some of the orthodox, of course, were suspicious that the Unitarians were up to no good, and it wasn't long before Mann found himself involved in his first real battle with the opposition. It all started in March 1838, when orthodox minister, Rev. Frederick A. Packard, recording secretary of the American Sunday School Union, sent a letter to Mann asking him if a particular book, John S. Abbott's *Child at Home,* would be suitable for the common school library Mann and the Board of Education were planning to assemble. The idea of getting the Legislature to appropriate money to each common school for the establishment of a library was part of the Board's general plan to upgrade the public schools and get some of its own cherished ideas into the heads of the pupils. The Board, mainly through the efforts of Jared Sparks, then decided to select a group of books which it would recommend that the new libraries purchase. In addition, authors were to be commissioned by Sparks to write a series of inspirational biographies for the young, and arrangements were to be made with a friendly publisher to bring out all of these books in special inexpensive editions for the libraries. When the books were finally ready, the Board took pains to point out that its only power was to recommend the books, not to force the common schools to buy them. Thus, even at that early stage of centralized state control of education, the inevitability of a conflict of interest arising between state educational officials and commercial arrangements made by them was already apparent.

At the time Packard had written Mann, the Board was looking for suitable books. While it was obvious that the recommended selections would include many by Unitarian authors, Packard wanted to see how biased the Board would be. It didn't take him long to find out. Mann rejected the Abbott book on the grounds that it was too sectarian in content and that the law of 1827 forbade the use of sectarian books "favoring any particular religious tenet" in the public schools. Packard replied that the law also required that the common schools teach the "principles of piety," and he asked Mann how these "principles of piety" could be taught "without favoring some particular religious tenet."

It was a dilemma that would remain an inherent part of secular state education right up to the present. But, back in 1838, Mann insisted that the Abbott book, as well as all of the other books issued by the American Sunday School Union, were unsuitable for the common school libraries. For Mann, it was important to consolidate secularism's capture of public education. There could be no compromise on this issue.

Packard then brought up the matter before a meeting of the General Association of Massachusetts, the state's largest organization of orthodox ministers, charging Mann with a sectarian bias of his own—in favor of Unitarianism. But the Association itself decided not to enter the controversy. For the next three months, Packard and Mann privately exchanged letters, each arguing his position. Packard then decided to take the controversy to the press and published his views in two articles in the *New York Observer*. The first article, entitled "Triumph of Infidelity," appeared in August 1838, and the second, directed in the form of an open letter to Dr. Heman Humphrey, orthodox president of Amherst College, appeared in October. The title of the first article was not without significance, for on July 15, 1838, Ralph Waldo Emerson had delivered his controversial Divinity School Address at Harvard, shocking even conservative Unitarians with its pantheism. To the orthodox, the liberal trend toward atheism was unmistakable.

By addressing his second article to Dr. Humphrey in an open letter, Packard had hoped to enlist on his side one of the most respected and influential orthodox ministers in New England. The last thing the Board of Education wanted was to get into an argument with Dr. Humphrey. The controversy had already persuaded the Board's one Episcopalian member, Edward Newton, to resign. While the Unitarians were not at all unhappy to see him go, they realized that there was a great danger to the movement in alienating the orthodox. So William B. Calhoun and Emerson Davis came to Mann's rescue by writing letters to Humphrey and persuading him to remain silent. Davis also wrote to the editor of the *Observer*, urging him to cut short Packard's series of open letters to Dr. Humphrey. Meanwhile, Mann wrote in his journal, "They (the orthodox) shall not unclinch me from my labors for mankind."

Undaunted, Packard then published a pamphlet entitled *The Question, Will the Christian Religion Be Recognized as the Basis of the System of Public Instruction in Massachusetts?* The pamphlet was then reviewed favorably in the Boston *Recorder* by Rev. Richard Storrs, orthodox minister of Braintree, who was convinced that the Board of Education had committed itself to "faults and fatal principles that the Common Schools can flourish and accomplish the end they aim at without the aids of Christianity." Again, the Board persuaded Mann not to be drawn into an open controversy with the orthodox. So Mann wrote to Storrs privately, explaining his sincere intent to function within the limits of the School Law of 1827 which forbade the use of sectarian textbooks in the public schools. Storrs replied that he believed Mann to be sincere but nevertheless guilty of a "fundamental error" if he thought that "the intellectual and moral improvement" of the young was possible without religion. Storrs also questioned the alleged religious impartiality of a Board where all but three members belonged to "that denomination which has done all in its power to crush orthodoxy throughout the Commonwealth."

While Mann maintained a public silence, his friends were able to defend his point of view in the press. Nor did all of the orthodox come out against Mann. Many, in fact, supported his position. The orthodox Protestant sects weren't nearly as united in their views as were the liberal "friends of education." Calvin Stowe's laudatory report on the Prussian system had been reprinted by the Massachusetts Legislature in 1838. As an orthodox minister, his views helped persuade many of the orthodox to accept the Prussianization of American education.

The argument, made by Stowe, that a common ground could be found in the New Testament teachings to unite all of the different sects in the public schools on the matter of moral instruction was the notion that permitted most of the orthodox to go along with Mann and the new Board of Education. In addition, there was a liberalization trend within some of the orthodox sects. In Connecticut, for example, Rev. Horace Bushnell, influenced by the same German theologians and philosophers who had influenced the Unitarians, was discovering that he could unite Trinitarian doctrine with German idealism and religious intuition. It was quite possible to reject Calvinist logic in favor of German intuition and still call oneself a Congregationalist. But only diehard Calvinists would know what was going on; but by then, they were a somewhat small minority. The truth is that, by 1838, Protestant theology was in a state of chaos, running the gamut from orthodox Calvinism to Emersonian pantheism. The intellectuals tended to be among the more extreme religious liberals, and socialism was the new doctrine attracting the interest of the enlightened. Mann, himself, was a believer in natural religion. In his journal he wrote on May 8, 1837:

> Have read to-day the first article in the 130th number of the "Edinburgh Review," upon Lord Brougham's "Discourse on Natural Theology:" a most deeply interesting paper,—elevated, tolerant, philosophical. I know it is thought by many, perhaps by most professing Christians, to be a fatal heresy, and worthy of being purged by fire; but, for myself, natural religion stands as pre-eminent over revealed religion as the deepest experience over the lightest hearsay. The power of natural religion is scarcely begun to be understood or appreciated. The force and cogency of the evidence, the intensity and irresistibleness of its power, are not known, because its elements are not developed and explained. It gives us more than an intellec-

tual conviction,—it gives us a feeling of truth; and however much the lights of revealed religion may have guided the generations of men amid this darkness of mortality, yet I believe that the time is coming when the light of natural religion will be to that of revealed as the rising sun to the day-star that preceded it.[9]

The appeal of natural religion was that it did away with the notions of sin and innate depravity. A man suffered the consequences of his behavior when that behavior violated natural law. It was only necessary to know natural law and to live in harmony with it in order to lead a virtuous life. The only problem was in determining "natural law." In the physical sphere, the laws of nature were pretty obvious, but in the social sphere, what was natural and what was unnatural were matters of conjecture and debate.

Despite the religious controversy, Mann, in the fall of 1838, continued to do his work, making the rounds of the county conventions. On October 8, he was introduced to George Combe, the Phrenologist, whose book, *The Constitution of Man*, Mann had read with the greatest interest. Combe had come to the United States from Edinburgh with his collection of skulls to lecture on Phrenology, the new "science" of human nature. Phrenology had been developed by a German physician, Franz Joseph Gall, who in the course of his work with the insane became convinced that the brain was the organic seat of what we now call personality development. It was the first attempt by science—or rather, pseudoscience—to explain the origin of abnormal and criminal behavior other than as a manifestation of innate depravity or original sin. It was the secular world's first venture into the study of human behavior which would in time evolve into something called "psychiatry." Robert Owen contended that evil was caused by the social environment and miseducation at the hands of religionists. But Gall contended that there was an organic cause to evil behavior. By observing the coincidence between the unusual prominence of particular parts of the cranium, and the existence in more than usual strength of particular feelings or talents, Gall had arrived at the conclusion that different parts of the brain were the organic seats of different aspects of behavior. By dissecting and examining hundreds of skulls and brains, he had worked out a map of the brain in which, he was convinced, he could identify the specific organic locations of such personality traits as "combativeness, destructiveness, love of approbation, benevolence, conscientiousness," etc. He identified several dozen such traits, which were then called "propensities, faculties, temperaments, and talents." Thus, if a person became a compulsive murderer it was because that part of the brain which was the seat of destructiveness was unduly larger than the part devoted to benevolence. The harmonious personality was one in which all of the parts of the brain were of such proportions as to work harmoniously together.

It was impossible for Gall to prove his theory by showing exact cause and effect, and therefore few if any true scientists accepted it. But because it offered such a reasonably credible nonreligious explanation for the origin of evil, Phrenology found many adherents among American Unitarians who were anxious to counter the Calvinist doctrine of innate depravity with something scientific.

As early as 1807 news of Dr. Gall's work had spread from the Continent to England, and in 1815 Gall's associate, Dr. John Gaspar Spurzheim, a French physician, journeyed to Edinburgh, the science capital of Great Britain, where Phrenology had been dismissed as unscientific nonsense. Spurzheim lectured, made friends, and converted to Phrenology one George Combe, a young lawyer, and his medical-student brother, Andrew. The result was the creation of the Edinburgh Phrenological Society and Combe's lifelong association with the new "science," of which he eventually became chief spokesman after the death of Spurzheim in 1832.

There was a third Combe brother, Abram, two years older than George, who was converted to Owenism in 1820 after visiting New Lanark and meeting Robert Owen. Abram Combe became so much of a true believer that he established an Owenite colony at Orbiston, Scotland, at about the same time that Owen was busy with New Harmony. Equally important, Abram Combe formulated a religious creed to go with Owenism. Because Owen had alienated all of the established religions by his denunciation of them as the root cause of man's misery, Combe endeavored to show that Owenism was not against religion per se, but only against those religions based on unnatural revelation and irrational superstition. Combe published his views in 1824 in a book entitled *The Religious Creed of the New System*. Combe, who had been raised in an Orthodox environment, attributed his new religious views to Robert Owen. He wrote:

> As Mr. Owen has been prevented, by what he must have considered, more pressing avocations, from giving to the public his ideas on religion, I have ventured, in the mean time, to submit the following pages, for their perusal. To *say* that a production, which Mr. Owen has neither seen nor heard of, *contains his sentiments on the subject of religion*, might justly be considered presumptive; but I can aver with sincerity, that the following pages contain a candid statement of the religious impressions, which an attentive perusal of his writings has made upon my mind.[10]

According to Abram Combe, the laws of nature were the laws of God, and the "dictates of Reason" were the "voice of Deity." Thus, it was possible to establish a rational, natural religion as opposed to the irrational, unnatural religions already established. Combe wrote:

All the evils that afflict humanity have proceeded from the blindness of Man, in following the imaginary notions of his deluded fellow-creatures, in opposition to the *words of Deity*, as expressed in the undisputed Revelation of Nature, supported by Reason, and confirmed by Experience. . . .

The names of Hume, Paine, Palmer, and Carlile, have been loaded with the most opprobrious epithets; while, as far as I can judge, the utmost exertions of these individuals have only tended to prove, that the Laws of Nature are the Laws of God, and that the Works of Nature are the best Revelation from God to Man. . . . All the doctrines and precepts which produce misery in the world, and about which mankind continually dispute, and quarrel, and fight, are, without exception, "unnatural and irrational."[11]

Combe also showed how this natural and rational religion led to a collectivist, altruist morality:

True religion points out Nature as the first and only undisputed revelation from God to Man, and recommends Reason as a guide which never leads any one astray. . . . Thus, when True Religion enters the mind, it induces the individual to follow Nature and Reason—these shew him that no individual forms his own character—that it is his true interest to unite with his fellow-creatures—and that by opposing *their* happiness he takes the most effectual way to injure his own. Thus—union being affected—envy, towards his superiors in wisdom and experience is turned into affection and esteem, and anger and hatred, towards his inferiors, into pity and forbearance.[12]

Combe summarized it all by stating: "Everything which, in its ultimate effects, tends to increase the happiness of the community is good, and everything which has an opposite tendency is evil." Abram Combe died in 1827 at the age of 42. Three years later, Robert Owen himself delivered two lectures on "The New Religion," which he described as a "religion founded on the immutable laws of the universe, contrasted with all Religions founded on human testimony.'' In his view, the supernatural religions were the cause of all evil, and "natural religion" could be the foundation of heaven on earth. Owen wrote:

> Now, when the effects of religion, as it has been hitherto taught, and impressed upon the human race, shall be followed through all their ramifications, it will be discovered that the religion of the world is the sole cause of all the disunion, hatred, uncharitableness, and crime, which pervade the population of the earth; and that, as long as this ignorant and worldly religion shall be taught to mankind, it will be utterly impracticable to train men to love one another, or to have common charity for each other. And all who reflect, know, that until practical measures shall be devised to make them love each other in reality, and to have pure and genuine charity, without any unkindness in their dispositions for the whole family of mankind, there will be no hope on which to rest for the general permanent amelioration of the condition of our species. No: the happiness of man never can be secured, until he shall be trained from infancy in a knowledge of true religion, derived from the everlasting and unchanging laws of nature, undefiled by any errors opposed to those laws, which, when understood, and honestly acted upon, will be sure to produce universal love, charity, and harmony throughout the population of the world.[13]

Only a secular educational system would be able to destroy or cancel out the evil influences of unnatural religion, for, according to Owen, "no effectual permanent improvement can be made in the condition of the people of this country, so long as they shall be forced to receive, from childhood, the unnatural doctrines of the religion of the world, which, heretofore, all children have been compelled to receive; to the almost entire destruction of their rational faculties and moral feelings."

By preaching "natural religion," both Abram Combe and Robert Owen endeavored to prove that Owenism was not completely devoid of spiritual content. Owenite socialism was not based on the pure materialism that was to characterize Marxian socialism some years later. Meanwhile, Abram Combe's Phrenologist brother, George, combined the doctrines of natural religion with Phrenology, and came up with his own approach to human nature, which he expounded in a book entitled *The Constitution of Man*, published in 1829. Combe felt that only a scientific study of the nature of man could reveal what kind of a social system suited him best. It was all well and good for the Owenites to talk of natural law. It was something else to identify all of these laws with which one was supposed to live in accordance. Human nature, Combe contended, was also ruled by natural laws, and Phrenology, he argued, explained these laws.

Horace Mann attended all of Combe's lecture series, which attracted a large Unitarian audience. It was not difficult to understand why. Combe had shared the common revulsion against Calvinism. In fact, the story of his own religious struggle was very similar to Mann's. In 1845, Combe wrote:

I was educated in rigid Calvinism, and sincerely embraced it, so far as my nature was capable of doing so. In boyhood, it appeared to me to embody into a system not only sound interpretations of scripture, but the undeniable facts of nature. The human mind seemed to me then to be fundamentally vicious in its desires and perverted in its powers, and all nature seemed to labour under the malediction of the Divine Being. These opinions, however, while they appeared to me to be true, were never congenial to my nature, and caused me great uneasiness. I felt an internal revulsion against them, which I ascribed to the corruption of my own nature. The doctrine of Election, and the pre-ordained damnation of countless millions of my fellow creatures, shocked my Benevolence and Conscientiousness; while the converse idea that certain individuals were chosen from all eternity to inherit everlasting felicity, seemed necessarily to imply favouritism and partiality in the

Deity. My sense of justice never permitted me to place myself among the elect: on the contrary, my consciousness that I was no better than my fellow men, joined with the belief that few will be saved, led me to place myself among those who are destined to be condemned. The doctrine of vicarious punishment gave me no relief, although intellectually believed. It appeared in its very conception to involve injustice, and never removed the difficulties attending the predestined rejection of particular individuals. My own rejection was an abiding conviction, and often did I wish that I had never been born. I envied the horses and the sheep that had no souls, and wished that I could cease to exist when I ceased to breathe. Death was then very terrible in my eyes, as the grand step from sin and sorrow here into indescribable misery hereafter. After I became acquainted with the great facts in regard to the extent and constitution of the universe, and the uniformity of the laws by which its phenomena are regulated, as these are disclosed by the sciences of Astronomy, Geology, Chemistry, Anatomy, and Physiology, the cloud of superstition under which I had been educated gradually dissolved, and Phrenology, by unfolding the sources of many of the errors of Calvinism which appear like truth, aided the process of emancipation. The same deep interest in religious sentiments continue, but now the dictates of my moral faculties harmonise with those of my intellect, and I am convinced that this world and the human mind have been constituted on the principles of benevolence and justice, and that a far more direct and beneficient government is exercised by the Divine mind over them both by means of natural laws than is generally believed.[14]

Combe offered his listeners a vision of a rational, just world without sin in which the criminal was simply one in whom the organs of the propensities were large, and the organs of the moral and intellectual faculties were deficient. Education to some extent was capable of correcting minor imbalances, but the criminal had major imbalances. "I stated it to be my conviction," he wrote, "founded on observation, that such individuals are incapable of resisting the temptations to crime presented by ordinary society, that they are moral patients, and should not be punished, but restrained, and employed in useful labour during life, with as much liberty, as they can enjoy without abusing it."[15]

While Combe was a little sceptical about the perfectibility of man, he was naive enough to believe that "knowledge" could conquer evil. Thus, he strongly believed in the idea of moral progress. "If the physical history of the globe," he wrote, "clearly indicates progression in an advancing series of changes, the civil history of man equally proclaims the march, although often vacillating and slow, of moral and intellectual improvement."[16] Phrenology, in contrast to Calvinism, was a progressive philosophy. Combe wrote:

> In our own country two views of the constitution of the world and of human nature have long been prevalent. . . . The one is, that the world, including both the physical and moral departments, contain within itself the elements of improvement . . . it having been constituted by the Creator on the principle of a progressive system, like the acorn in reference to the oak. . . .
>
> The other hypothesis is, that the world was perfect at first, but fell into derangement, continues in disorder, and does not contain within itself the elements of its own rectification. . . .
>
> The theologians who condemned the natural world, lived in an age when there was no sound philosophy, and almost no knowledge of physical science; they were unavoidably ignorant of the elementary qualities of human nature, and of the influences of organization on the mental powers. . . . It has never been with them a practical principle, that human nature itself may be vastly improved in its moral and intellectual capacities, by those means which Physiology and Phrenology have recently opened up to us.[17]

Combe, like Mann, realized that sectarian religion would have to be overcome before a secular national educational system, dedicated to the improvement of human nature, could become a reality. "The real difficulty," he wrote, "which liberal men experience in endeavoring to found education on a right basis lies in the different views which each opponent in his own mind entertains of human nature."[18] It is a difficulty which persists to this day.

George Combe is important to this history, not only because he himself actively promoted the idea of public education and became Horace Mann's intellectual mentor and closest friend, but because he affirmed the Unitarian position on human nature with an attractive "scientific" explanation. Spurzheim had blazed the Phrenological trail with a visit to Boston in 1832. When Spurzheim suddenly died in November of that year, a Boston Phrenological Society was created by his Unitarian followers. Combe's visit solidified the Unitarian-Phrenological connection still further. During his lecture tour in 1839, Combe was a houseguest in Genesco, New York, of one particularly distinguished and wealthy Unitarian, James Wadsworth, who had subsidized the publication of the American edition of Victor Cousin's report on the Prussian schools. During the visit, Wadsworth told Combe: "Are you aware that in the 'Constitution of Man' you have given a new religion to the world? . . . The views of the Divine government there unfolded will in time subvert all other religions and become a religion themselves."[19] Today, the religion that most closely resembles what Wadsworth called "Combeism" is Secular Humanism, with its central focus on human behavior, its study and control.

Channing also happened to be visiting Wadsworth at the same time as Combe, and the latter recorded this interesting discussion in his diary on June 24, 1839:

> This morning Dr. Channing asked me whether I thought that something like Owen's ideas might not be realized on a modified scale, and with a more highly improved population? He could not conceive that the present state of toil and feverish pursuit of wealth, carrying suffering to so large a portion of the

people, was to be eternal, and he did not see any obstacle in human nature that was insurmountable to their adopting a co-operative system for supplying their physical wants, and seeking their chief pleasures in moral and intellectual inter-course. I told him that these were precisely my views. I had opposed Owenism on account of the choice of the worst brains to fulfill the highest moral functions. I told him that the high political rank of the people in America, with a high universal education, might increase the difficulties of finding domestic servants so much as to force the higher classes into something like co-operation; but that I regarded this as still very distant.[20]

Neither Channing nor Combe could foresee the radical technological transformation that capitalism would bring to pass. Nor could they envisage the unparalleled creation of wealth by the capitalist system, which would alter the material conditions of man. But it was logical for them to see in the competitive, capitalist system the causes of evil and suffering, and expect that a co-operative society would eliminate them. But the experience of the twentieth century has shown that the socialist co-operative society causes far more evil and suffering than capitalism. It is one of the most important lessons the twentieth century has taught man, with its Gulag Archipelagos, Berlin Walls, and suppression of human liberty. Owen, Channing, and Combe were wrong, yet their ideas, in one guise or another, are more prevalent today than they were in their own day.

Mann was deeply influenced by Channing and Combe and became a convert to Phrenology. He also proceeded to convert others. In March 1839, Mann wrote Combe, who was then lecturing in Philadelphia:

There have been some striking conversions, since you were here, to the religious truths contained in your "Constitution of Man." Some of these have happened under my own ministry. A young graduate of one of our colleges wrote me, a few months since, to inquire in what manner he could best qualify himself for teaching. He had then been employed in teaching for two years, after having received a degree. I told him, that, in the absence of Normal schools, I thought he had better take up his residence in this city, visit the schools, make himself acquainted with all the various processes which various individuals adopt to accomplish the same thing, and read all the best books that can be found on the subject. He accordingly came: and, when he applied to me for a list of books, I, of course, named your "Constitution" as the first in the series. After about a fortnight he called on me, and said he had read it through with great pleasure, but did not think he had mastered the whole philosophy. A few days after, he came again, not a little disturbed: he had read it again, comparing it with his former notions (for he was highly orthodox), and found that the glorious world of laws which you describe was inconsistent with the miserable world of expedients in which he had been accustomed to dwell. I spent an entire evening with him, and endeavored to explain to him that your system contained all there is of truth in orthodoxy: that the animal nature of man is first developed: that, if it continues to be the active and the only guiding power *through life*, it causes depravity enough to satisfy any one: but if the moral nature, in due time, puts forth its energies, obtains ascendancy, and controls and administers all the actions of life in obedience to the highest laws, there will be righteousness enough to satisfy any one: that, if he chose, he might call the point, where the sentiments prevailed over the propensities, the hour of regeneration: nor was the phrase—a second birth—too strong to express the change: that this change might be wrought on the hearing of a sermon, or when suffering bereavement, or in the silence and secrecy of meditation, or on reading Mr. Combe's "Constitution of Man:" and, as God operates upon our mental organization through means, these might be the means of sanctifying us. He adopted my views on the subject, and is now, I believe, a convert beyond the danger of apostasy. . . .[21]

Is any of this relevant today? Only insofar as it enables us to understand the messianic motivations of men like Mann and Channing who rejected Calvinism, believed in moral progress, and were determined to create an educational system that would make that progress possible. Combe wrote: "By teaching Phrenology in our secular school, I am laying a natural foundation of religion and morals, in the minds of our children, and I see that they are drinking the views presented to them eagerly in. . . . This instruction will prove the bulwark of social order when the supernatural falls into decay, and posterity will thank us as sincerely as our opponents now abuse us for our present course of action."[22]

Horace Mann echoed the same sentiments when he wrote in the *Common School Journal* (Volume 3, Number 1):

The common school is the institution which can receive and train up children in the elements of all good knowledge and of virtue before they are subjected to the alienating competitions of life. This institution is the greatest discovery ever made by man: we repeat it, *the common school is the greatest discovery ever made by man.* In two grand, characteristic attributes, it is supereminent over all others: first, in its universality, for it is capacious enough to receive and cherish in its parental bosom every child that comes into the world; and, second, in the timeliness of the aid it proffers,—its early, seasonable supplies of counsel and guidance making security antedate danger. Other social organizations are curative and remedial: this is a preventive and an antidote. They come to heal diseases and wounds: this, to make the physical and moral frame invulnerable to them. Let the common school be expanded to its capabilities, let it be worked with the efficiency of which it is susceptible, and nine-tenths of the crimes in the penal code would become obsolete: the long catalogue of human ills would be abridged: men would walk more safely by day: every pillow would be more inviolable by night: property, life, and character held by a stronger tenure: all rational hopes respecting the future brightened.[23]

It was a glorious vision, founded on a grand illusion: the idea of moral progress. Man's knowledge has expanded, his wealth has increased, his technology has advanced at an explosive rate. But one night's viewing of television in the 1980's would convince anyone that human nature has not changed at all since the beginning of recorded history. The capacity for evil among men remains constant. The only thing that seems to change is the nature of the restraints placed on man by other men or by moral convictions derived from religion or philosophy.

11. The Transition to Educational Statism

BY NOVEMBER 1838, Horace Mann had completed his second annual circuit of county conventions. Attendance was off at most of the conventions, indicating that popular interest in public education was less than enthusiastic. There was no great clamor for a centralized system of education that was going to increase taxes and usurp local control. The vast majority of citizens were quite satisfied with the public and private educational facilities already in existence, and they were not at all impressed with what the Prussians had. But to the promoters of public education, the Prussian model was to be imitated at all levels. The Normal School—a seminary for training common school teachers—was considered the most important component of the system, and Mann spent much of 1838 and '39 organizing the Normal Schools that the Legislature had approved by matching state funds with Edmund Dwight's contribution. In Plymouth County, where a group of citizens had proposed to locate one of the Normal Schools, the convention was enlivened by the presence of both Daniel

213

Webster and John Quincy Adams, who spoke forcefully in favor of public education. Adams told the audience:

> We see monarchies expending vast sums, establishing Normal Schools through their realms, and sparing no pains to convey knowledge and efficiency to all the children of their poorest subjects. Shall we be outdone by Kings? Shall monarchies steal a march on republics in the patronage of that education on which a republic is based? On this great and glorious cause let us expend freely, yes, more freely than on any other.[1]

Despite Adams's eloquent plea, the people of Plymouth county were unwilling to make the financial contribution that would have enabled Mann to open the state's first Normal School in that area. Instead, the honor went to the town of Lexington where the first American Normal School opened on July 3, 1839, under the direction of Cyrus Peirce. A second Normal School was opened at Barre, in Worcester county, in September 1839, and a third at Bridgewater in September 1840. The Legislature had voted to support each school for a trial period of three years, after which the experiment was to be reconsidered before further support would be given.

The creation of the first Normal School at Lexington was the culmination of an effort begun in 1825 with the publication of James G. Carter's "Outline of an Institution for the Education of Teachers." In it, Carter envisaged the future state-controlled teachers' college as "an engine to sway the public sentiment, the public morals, and the public religion, more powerful than any other in the possession of government."[2] Clearly, then, statism was the guiding philosophy behind the public school movement, and it was largely through that movement that statism began to change the American philosophy of government. The man-made institution of the state could now be trusted because men were rational, progressive, enlightened, benevolent, and scientific. The Calvinist distrust of human nature was no longer considered appropriate. On this subject, Horace Mann made his own views known in 1847 when he wrote in the *Common School Journal:*

Let us settle the question, in the first place, what our theory of government is. Are its functions penal and retributive merely, or are they also directory and preventive? Is not our theory of government too enlarged to permit us to regard rulers as men culled out and set up only to punish evil-doers? If this be all, then where is the honor of being elected to the office of legislator? If the end and aim of the lawgiver be no higher than to define and to denounce trespasses, knaveries, batteries, counterfeits, arsons, and treasons, then the office is detestable, and one would suppose, beforehand, that there could not be found, in a decent community, a sufficient number of decent people who would consent to fill it. . . .

But the ruler of the present day has nobler prerogatives. . . . His duty is to counsel, rather than to chastise: to multiply, and make more conspicuous and attractive, all possible inducements to good, rather than to terrify and frighten with denunciations against evil. He is to devise profound and far-reaching plans; he is to establish institutions and create systems which will work positive good, and thus secure to the world the immense advantages which prevention has over remedy. . . .

The true lawgiver,—he who makes laws that will endure the test of time,—never prescribes a penalty for the commission of a crime, without seeking, at the same time, for some antidote against its repetition. He never builds a jail or prison for the punishment or confinement of offenders, without founding or fortifying some institution to prevent offences. . . . He never votes supplies for pauperism or destitution, without laying some plan of wise and preventive benevolence, which shall spread abroad competence and comfort. In fine, his statute-book will be more deeply imbued with the spirit of reward and encouragement for well-doing, than with threatenings and terrors against doing evil.[3]

For all practical purposes, Mann had defined the liberal-Unitarian-Phrenologist-Owenite philosophy of government, which saw the lawgiver as the messianic reformer who would devise "profound and far-reaching plans" and "establish institutions and create systems which will work positive good." Every future statist dictator would easily see himself in that role.

Because of its proximity to Boston and Cambridge, the Normal School at Lexington quickly became the model school for teacher training, attracting visitors and public school enthusiasts. Mann could not have chosen a better man for director than Cyrus Peirce (whose name is sometimes spelled Pierce in the literature), a graduate of the Harvard Divinity School, a Unitarian minister, an educator, and a believer in Phrenology. It is therefore not surprising to discover that the required course of studies included an intensive reading of George Combe's *Constitution of Man.* Phrenology was the Normal School's first venture into what we now call "educational psychology." It was also public education's first venture into educational quackery.

Also attached to the Normal School was a model elementary school in which the teacher trainees could practice what they were learning. One of the teaching innovations they practiced was a new technique for teaching reading: the whole-word method. The new method, developed to circumvent the difficulties of the English alphabetic system, had been invented by Thomas H. Gallaudet, director of the Hartford Asylum for the Deaf and Dumb. Because the deaf could not hear, they could not be taught to read by learning alphabet sounds. Instead, they were taught to read by associating whole words with pictures. Gallaudet thought that this method could be adapted for use by normal children and he described it, for the first time, in a letter in the August 1830 issue of the *American Annals of Education,* whose editor, William Channing

Woodbridge, had taught at Gallaudet's Asylum from 1817 to 1821. In 1835, Gallaudet published his *Mother's Primer,* the first whole-word, or sight-vocabulary, primer ever to be published. Its first line has a surprisingly familiar ring: "Frank had a dog; his name was Spot." Because it was thought that Gallaudet's new method would save children the trouble of having to learn the alphabet and letter sounds, the Boston Primary School Committee decided to adopt the primer on an experimental basis in August 1836. The teachers using it were asked to give the committee their opinion of the new method's effectiveness within a year. This they did, and on the basis of that opinion, the committee issued a favorable report in November 1837, recommending the Primer's adoption in Boston's primary schools.

Mann became Secretary of the Board of Education in June 1837, several months before the primary school teachers issued their favorable report on Gallaudet's whole-word method. No sooner had Mann become an "expert" in education than he endorsed the new method and extolled it in his Second Annual Report issued in 1838. Cyrus Peirce shared Mann's enthusiasm for the new method, and it, along with Phrenology, became part of the Normal School's instructional training. Thus, the Normal School at its inception became the immediate vehicle for pedagogical innovation and quackery. It was only natural that teacher training as a state enterprise would suffer immediate distortion of purpose and in time become a shelter for incompetence posing as "innovation" and "progress."

In November 1838, Mann also brought forth the first issue of the *Common School Journal,* of which he would serve as editor for as long as he was Secretary. The Journal would serve as a vehicle for advancing the cause of public education in general and Mann's views in particular. It would give the movement coherence and direction—a "party line," so to speak—and also serve as a record of its progress.

One of the thorniest problems Mann and his friends faced was getting the middle and professional classes to give up private schools and lend their full and active support to public education. Mann decided to take the bull by the horns and in 1839 launched a series of articles in the *Common School Journal* "Addressed to the Professional Men of Massachusetts," urging them, in the strongest emotional rhetoric, to withdraw their children from the private schools and put them in public ones. It was the first time in American history that educators called on parents to sacrifice their children's academic and moral well-being for the sake of a social experiment. It is indeed significant that the very institution of state education required that initial sacrifice on the part of concerned parents who were urged to give up palpable individual benefits for the sake of a theoretical collective good.

By the mid-1830's the growing middle and professional classes had all but abandoned the common schools, leaving the latter for the poorest and least literary elements of the community. The private schools not only offered better instruction, but had also become status symbols for an upward-moving middle class. In addition, the private schools offered special programs for students preparing for a variety of careers. Education was purchased for its practical academic and instructional benefits. To parents, education was not seen as the means of reforming the character of man or creating a new society free of competition. Its primary purpose was the development of a student's intellectual skills. Its secondary purpose was to provide a congenial moral and social atmosphere for the growing youngster.

But it was difficult to escape in the press and lecture hall the heavy messianic barrage of the "friends of education" who saw in the common school the very hope of mankind. A conservative, practical middle class was to be given the hard sell. First, the reformers reminded the middle class of the common school's sacred origins. It was, they argued, the purpose of their pious ancestors to establish free schools in order to foster equality. The *Common School Journal* put forth its own peculiar version of Puritan history:

> Our fathers encountered the perils of the ocean, and endured the privations of a wilderness, nay, they suffered and died, for the great cause of equality. They established institutions for the express purpose of sustaining the poor, of guarding the defenceless; or, rather, they established institutions calculated to destroy the distinction between the rich and the poor, and to place men upon one common level.[4]

It was very bad history. The Puritans had created town schools to insure the continuance of the Biblical commonwealth by rearing a literate community. The notion of equality was farthest from their minds, since they believed in the Calvinist doctrine of election which recognized inequality as a fact of existence. Biblical literacy was necessary because Biblical authority ruled the community. And that is why Hebrew, Greek, and Latin were studied in the New England wilderness, not in order to foster equality, but to enhance the community's understanding of the sacred Scripture. That the "friends of education" could get away with such bad history meant that by 1830 the Puritan past was only dimly known by the population as a whole. And thus it was all that much easier to intimidate the middle class. The *Common School Journal* argued:

> Any thing which tends to lessen the value of our free schools is hostile to the designs of our pious ancestors. Any man, who through pride or parsimony permits these schools to decline, can hardly be regarded as a friend to this country. I speak with

plainness, for I am pleading the cause of humanity and of God. And I say that any man who designs the destruction of our free schools is a traitor to the cause of liberty and equality, and would, if it were in his power, reduce us to a state of vassalage.[5]

Thus, bad history was combined with moral blackmail to make the middle class feel that by sending their children to private schools they were betraying everything their ancestors held sacred. After accusing the middle and professional classes of trying to create social divisiveness and establishing the principles of an aristocratic society, the writer then asked:

Why do you take your children from the district school, and put them to the private school? . . . You contend, that town schools are corrupting in their influence; that some of the scholars are addicted to profanity and obscenity, or, are rude and vulgar in their manners; and that you take your children from them lest their manners and morals should be corrupted. . . . Suppose the town schools are as corrupt as is represented—what is your duty under these circumstances? to abandon them altogether, and let them sink deeper and deeper in corruption? No; it is your duty, as public men, to reform them. . . . If your children are placed in the town schools, you will have a greater motive to attempt their improvement. To reform the community, you must come down to a level with them, and thereby show, that you have an interest in their welfare. . . .

I know you may say that, as parents, you ought not to expose your children to temptation; and that, while these schools are corrupt, you are exposing your children, by sending them where they will be in danger of being corrupted. This plea is plausible, and deserves grave consideration. But after all the reflection I have been able to bestow upon it, I am persuaded that it is the dictate of wisdom, and it is your duty, to put your children into the district school. Your children must associate with the children of the poor and vicious at some period or other; and in my estimation the sooner the better, so far as it is done by sending them to the same school.[6]

These same arguments would be used 130 years later to persuade parents of their moral duty to put their children on buses for the sake of racial integration. The fact is that the public school was seen in the 1830's by its promoters as primarily a social instrument and only secondarily as an academic one. All of the arguments that were used to persuade the middle and professional classes to send their children to the public schools were social in nature, since it was readily admitted that the public schools were academically inferior.

Implicit in the public school philosophy was the idea that a parent's duty toward the community was more important than his duty to his own children, that love of community was more important than love of one's own children. This was indeed a move toward statism in stages. Once one accepted the notion that other people's children—those of the community—were more important than one's own, then one was well on the way toward statism. A hypothetical higher goal was held out as the reward for one's sacrifice. That it meant the closing of many private schools was understood. The *Common School Journal* minced no words:

> Our academies and high schools are, at the present day, by far too numerous; and in this, principally, lies the evil. If three fourths of them were annihilated, and the money, expended upon them, put into our Common Schools, and the best teachers transferred from the former to the latter, a great point would be gained for the cause of Education.[7]

Thus, the thrust of the public school movement was not aimed at providing educational opportunities for the poor or increasing literacy, for the complaint was that there were *too many* private schools in existence. The aim of the movement was merely to shift education from private control to government control because government now had a higher unifying social purpose than was originally conceived by the Founding Fathers.

The early statists in America, those of the 1830's and 40's, visualized the state in benign parental terms. All men were brothers in one family, and the state was the parent, a richer, better, and more just parent than one's own. Such were the sentiments expressed by one Rev. Stetson of Medford at a Common School Convention in 1839, when he said:

> I want to see the children of the rich and the poor sit down side by side on equal terms, as members of one family—a great brotherhood—deeming no one distinguished above the rest but the best scholar and the best boy—giving free and natural play to their affections, at a time of life when lasting friendships are often formed, and worldliness and pride and envy have not yet alienated heart from heart.[8]

The Rev. Horace Bushnell, the liberal Congregationalist minister from Connecticut, was even more explicit in his characterization of the state as parent. Mann quoted him in the *Common School Journal* of February 15, 1840, as a supporter of nonsectarian public education. Bushnell said:

> The great point with all Christians must be, to secure the Bible in its proper place. To this as a sacred duty all sectarian aims must be sacrificed. Nothing is more certain, than that no such thing as a sectarian religion is to find a place in our schools. It must be enough to find a place for the Bible as a book of principles, as containing the true standards of character, and the best motives and aids to virtue. If any Christian desires more, he must teach it himself, at home. To insist that the State shall teach the rival opinions of sects, and risk the loss of all instruction for that, would be folly and wickedness together.

. . . Connecticut has ever been a good mother; and a good mother is about the first of earthly beings. Let her be so still. Let her be regarded as the nursery of education, and of good men.

Bushnell was the new liberal breed of Trinitarian minister whose intuitive approach to religion was far closer to Transcendentalism than Calvinism. It was therefore natural that he would lend his support to the public school movement, for he himself felt ill at ease in the strict sectarian confines of Calvinist Congregationalism. However, instead of leaving Congregationalism, as did the Unitarians, he preferred to stay within the Trinitarian tradition and work for its liberalization.

Although Mann spent a pleasant summer holiday with the Combes in Maine in August 1839, he considered that year the most painful he'd ever lived, apart from the year in which he had lost his young wife. Ill health and continued opposition to the "sacred cause" plagued him. And, in November, Governor Edward Everett and the Whigs went down to defeat because they had pushed through an unpopular law restricting the sale of liquor. The new Governor, Marcus Morton, made it clear that he intended to abolish all "supernumerary officers, or agencies, or commissions not immediately necessary for the public good," and this included the Board of Education and its Secretary. Morton opposed the trend toward centralized state control of public education which Mann was leading. He believed, as many still did, that the responsibility and management of the common schools should remain where they had been for two hundred years, in the hands of the townspeople who supported them.

Thus, in March 1840, a Bill was introduced in the Massachusetts House of Representatives abolishing the Board of Education and the Normal Schools. In presenting the Bill, the House Committee on Education also submitted a

Report outlining its reasons for advocating the Board's abolition. First, the committee made it clear that it was not against the Common School system as it had existed for two centuries. It was against the Board, because the latter "has a tendency, and a strong tendency, to engross to itself the entire regulation of our Common Schools, and practically to convert the Legislature into a mere instrument for carrying its plans into execution." The Report rejected in no uncertain terms the European idea of centralization:

The true way to judge of the practical operations of the Board of Education is not merely to consult the statutes by which the Board is established, but also to examine its own reports. . . . A very cursory examination of these documents will suffice to show, that, so far from continuing our system of public instruction, upon the plan upon which it was founded, and according to which it has been so long and so successfully carried on, the aim of the Board appears to be, to remodel it altogether after the example of the French and Prussian systems. . . .

After all that has been said about the French and Prussian systems, they appear to your Committee to be admirable, as a means of political influence, and of strengthening the hands of the government, than as a mere means for the diffusion of knowledge. For the latter purpose, the system of public Common Schools, under the control of persons most interested in their flourishing condition, who pay taxes to support them, appears to your Committee much superior. The establishment of the Board of Education seems to be the commencement of a system of centralization and of monopoly of power in a few hands, contrary, in every respect, to the true spirit of our democratical institutions; and which, unless speedily checked, may lead to unlooked-for and dangerous results. . . .

Your Committee have already stated, that the French and Prussian system of public schools appears to have been devised, more for the purpose of modifying the sentiments and opinions of the rising generations, according to a certain government standard, than as a mere means of diffusing elementary knowledge. Undoubtedly, Common Schools may be used as a potent means of engrafting into the minds of children, political, religious, and moral opinions;—but, in a country like this, where such diversity of sentiments exists, especially upon theological subjects, and where morality is considered a part of religion, and is, to some extent, modified by sectarian views, the difficulty and danger of attempting to introduce these subjects into our schools, according to one fixed and settled plan, to be devised by a central Board, must be obvious. The right to mould the political, moral, and religious, opinions of his children, is a right exclusively and jealously reserved by our laws to every parent; and for the government to attempt, directly or indirectly, as to these matters, to stand in the parent's place, is an undertaking of very questionable policy.[9]

The Committee was also critical of the Board's school library project that had led to the dispute between Mann and Packard. While the Report mentioned no names, it questioned the premise that it was possible to choose books that had no sectarian or political points of view. "Books, which confine themselves to the mere statement of undisputed propositions, whether in politics, religion, or morals, must be meager, indeed," the Report stated. It continued: "A book, upon politics, morals, or religion, containing no party or sectarian views, will be apt to contain no distinct views of any kind and will be likely to leave the mind in a state of doubt and skepticism, much more to be deplored than any party or sectarian bias."[10]

The Committee was also opposed to the Board's tendency to impose a central authority over the teaching profession, particularly in Massachusetts where the profession was already so highly developed. The Report stated, "But, among us, with so many accomplished teachers, a public Board, established for the benefit of the profession of teaching, seems as little needed as a public Board for the benefit of divinity, medicine, or the law. Undoubtedly, in all these professions, great improvements might be made; but it is better to leave them to private industry and free competition, than for the Legislature to put them under the superintendence of an official Board."

The proposed Bill also called for the abolition of the Normal Schools created by Mann and the Board. Citing them as another Prussian import, the Committee saw no reason why the State should get into the teacher-training business when the private sector was already adequately filling the need at no expense to the taxpayer. The Report's own words stated the free-market principle clearly:

> Comparing the two Normal Schools already established with the academies and high schools of the Commonwealth, they do not appear to your Committee to present any peculiar or distinguishing advantages.
>
> Academies and high schools cost the Commonwealth nothing; and they are fully adequate, in the opinion of your Committee, to furnish a competent supply of teachers. In years past, they have not only supplied our own schools with competent teachers, but have annually furnished hundreds to the West and the South. There is a high degree of competition existing between these academies, which is the best guaranty for excellence. . . .
>
> If it be true, that the teachers of any of our district schools are insufficiently qualified for the task, the difficulty originates, as it appears to your Committee, not in any deficiency of the means of obtaining ample qualifications, but in insufficiency of compensation. Those districts, which are inclined to pay competent wages, can at all times be supplied with competent teachers.[11]

The Committee had argued against the Board and the Normal Schools on sound economic grounds. They wanted education and educators to be subject to the same free-market forces that the rest of the economy was subject to. They saw no reason to elevate the field of education to some higher social or messianic function of the state. This, the Committee made clear, was quite alien to the American purpose. The Report summed up these sentiments in a strong and prophetic statement:

> In conclusion, the idea of the State controlling Education, whether by establishing a central Board, by allowing the Board to sanction a particular library, or by organizing Normal Schools, seems to your Committee a great departure from the uniform spirit of our institutions,—a dangerous precedent, and an interference with a matter more properly belonging to those hands, to which our ancestors wisely intrusted it. It is greatly to be feared, that any attempt, to force all our schools and all our teachers upon one model, would destroy all competition, all emulation, and even the spirit of improvement itself.[12]

The liberals had been prepared for the attack and, as soon as the Committee's Report was released, the liberals responded quickly with a Minority Report that accused their opponents of paranoia:

> They seem to be in great fear of *imaginary* evils; but are not able to produce a single fact, to justify their apprehensions. It is the alleged tendencies of the Board, to which they object. There is a possibility, they think, of its doing wrong; of its usurping powers which would endanger freedom of thought.
>
> If every institution is to be abolished, which it is possible to pervert to some evil purpose, we beg leave to ask, what one would be left? In all human affairs, the possibility to do wrong goes with the power to do right. Take away the power of doing wrong, and the power of doing right will be destroyed, at the same time.[13]

As for the argument that the Prussian system was in opposition to the American way, the liberals had a ready answer:

> In the Revolutionary War, our fathers had no hesitation in borrowing their system of military tactics from Prussia; but to take any instruction from the same quarter, when searching for

the best modes of advancing public education, some persons seem to think is fraught with danger. The State of Ohio, a few years since, with an enlightened liberality, commissioned the Rev. Dr. Stowe to examine, while in Prussia, its school system. On his return, he made a report to the Legislature of that State, which was afterwards republished by our own Legislature. Let anyone examine that report, and he will have no further fears on this subject.[14]

For all practical purposes, it was Stowe's endorsement of the non-sectarian principle of public education that swung enough of the orthodox to the Board's side so that it could survive. The Unitarians knew how to neutralize the orthodox Protestant opposition by using Stowe's arguments instead of Mann's. Besides, by 1840, American Protestantism was quite fragmented by its sectarian differences. The only force that tended to unify them was fear of a growing Catholic population. In Boston, where Irish Catholic immigration was reaching new heights, some of the Protestants saw in centralized public education a means of protecting American culture against Catholic influences. Thus, when the vote was finally taken on March 20, 1840, 182 of the legislators voted to abolish the Board, but 245 voted to maintain it. It was a great triumph for the cause of centralized public education and the beginning of the end of American educational freedom and pluralism as it had existed since Colonial times. The majority of Protestants had indeed accepted the idea of public education as an instrument of social and cultural control. But for the Protestants, the price of public education would be paid in an erosion of sectarian and theological differences. Ironically, it was not Mann, but Stowe who made sectarianism almost a sin when he wrote in his report to the Ohio Legislature:

I pity the poor bigot or the narrow-souled unbeliever, who can form no idea of religious principle, except as a sectarian thing; who is himself so utterly unsusceptible of ennobling emotions, that he cannot even conceive it possible that any man should have a principle of virtue and piety superior to all external forms, and untrammelled by metaphysical systems. From the aid of such men we have nothing to hope, in the cause of sound education; and their hostility we may as well encounter in one form as another, provided we make sure of the ground on which we stand, and hold up the right principles in the right shape.[15]

On the day the voting took place in the Massachusetts Legislature, Horace Mann was in New York delivering a lecture. When he received word of the Board's victory, he wrote in his journal: "Heard yesterday from Boston that the bigots and vandals had been signally defeated in their wicked attempts to destroy the Board of Education." The truth is that without their implicit anti-Catholic bigotry, a crucial number of Protestants would not have backed the Board. Indeed, virtually all of the arguments advocating abolition of the Board in the Committee's Report were libertarian and free-market in substance. Statism was the enemy of the Board's opponents, not any particular religion or sect. A vote for the Board was simply a vote for statism.

Mann spent the next six weeks touring the country with the Combes, traveling as far West as Cincinnati. When he got back to Boston in May, he found "all things had subsided into accustomed quiet or torpor in relation to the Board of Education." In January 1841, Mann issued his Fourth Annual Report. All of his recommendations were calculated to increase centralized control: the consolidation of small school districts into single larger districts; the necessity for strict uniformity in school books; and the use of registers to enforce regular and punctual attendance. It was still too early to recommend compulsory attendance laws, but every means short of such laws were to be taken to encourage regular, punctual attendance.

In February 1841, another attempt was made in the Massachusetts House of Representatives to abolish the Board of Education by having its power and duties transferred to the Governor, his Council and the Secretary of State. But that too was defeated by a vote of 131 to 114. The Board of Education had weathered its last real legislative test. By September 1841, Mann's benefactor, Edmund Dwight, was so convinced that Mann had done his work, that he urged Mann to re-enter political life. But Mann thought otherwise, believing that his sacred mission in education was far from completed.

In his Fifth Annual Report, Mann again stressed the importance of adequate teacher training and screening and criticized two Shaker societies for refusing to allow their teachers to be examined or their schools visited. The Report was helpful in getting Mann's allies in the Legislature to push through a bill approving an appropriation for the Normal Schools that would extend the experiment for another three years. This time, the chairman of the House Committee on Education was John Palfrey, one of Mann's Harvard-Unitarian backers and editor of the *North American Review*. Mann was particularly elated by that legislative victory, for it assured the future of the Normal Schools. He wrote in his journal: "Language cannot express the joy that pervades my soul at this vast accession of power to that machinery which is to carry the cause of education forward, not only more rapidly than it has ever moved, but to places which it has never yet reached."[16]

In May 1842, Mann was the principal speaker at the New York State Convention of School Superintendents at Utica. The convention was attended by such luminaries in the public school movement as Joseph Henry, Alonzo Potter, John Griscom, George B. Emerson, and Thomas H. Gallaudet, father of the whole-word method of reading instruction. The main theme running through the convention was that the non-sectarian common school was replacing the church as the instructor in morality. For Mann, Phrenology held the key to a new morality based on natural religion. In October 1841, Mann had written to Combe:

> I perceive, with unbounded pleasure, that the "Constitution of Man" has had a sale wholly unprecedented in the history of scientific works. As demonstrating a spirit of inquiry on this class of subjects, and the adoption of the best means to gratify it, this fact is most cheering to those who wait for the coming of the intellectual Messiah. . . . Its views must be penetrating the whole mass of mind as silently and latently indeed as the heat, but as powerfully as that for productiveness and renovation. What constitutes a broader and deeper channel for the diffusion of these truths is that they are reproducing themselves in the minds of liberal clergymen, and hence are welling out from the pulpit, and overflowing the more barren portions of society. A Unitarian clergyman told me last week that he had just preached a sermon drawn from your "Moral Philosophy," and had been complimented for it by his parishoners. If once the doctrine of the natural laws can get possession of the minds of men, then causality will become a mighty ally in the contest for their deliverance from sin as well as from error. As yet, in the history of man, causality has been almost a supernumerary faculty: the idea of special providences or interventions, the idea that all the events of life, whether of individuals or of nations, have been directly produced by an arbitrary, capricious, whimsical Deity, alternating between arrogant displays of superiority on the one hand, and a doting, foolish fondness on the other, has left no scope for the exercise of that noble faculty. What a throng of calamities and follies it will banish from the world, as soon as it can be brought into exercise![17]

Not surprisingly, Mann's Sixth Annual Report, issued in January 1843, was a virtual dissertation on Phrenology as applied to the study of physiology. To Mann, it meant that the laws of health had to be integrated in the common school curriculum. "The hastiest glance at the condition in which we are placed in this life," he wrote, "will demonstrate not merely the utility but the necessity of Physical

Education, as a department of knowledge to be universally cultivated. . . . Thousands of the more advanced scholars in our schools are engaged in studying geometry and algebra, rhetoric and declaration, Latin and Greek, while this *life-knowledge* is neglected.'' Slowly but surely, the scope of the common school was being enlarged to include far more than its original basic instruction. As the instrument of human reform, the common school curriculum would have to reflect its new and greater purpose.

12. The Conservatives' Last Stand

IN 1843, MANN made his famous tour of Europe during which he visited the Prussian schools he had read and heard so much about. But before sailing in May, he married Mary Peabody. The tour, part honeymoon and part visit with the Combes, took him through England, Ireland, Scotland, Prussia, Saxony, Holland, Belgium, and France. By November, he was back in Boston ready to put down in great detail in his Seventh Annual Report all that he had seen and learned, particularly in Prussia. The Report, issued in January 1844, was to provoke the most heated controversy of his career as Secretary. Rather than repeat what Cousin and Stowe had written in their reports, which concentrated largely on the organization and maintenance of the Prussian schools, Mann had decided to focus his attention on their teaching methods. The result was a glowing report on Prussian teachers and methods which reflected disparagingly on their counterparts in Boston.

To the Association of Boston Masters, this was the last straw. For seven years they had silently endured Mann's nonstop criticism of the Common Schools and their teachers. Such criticism was unavoidable in Mann's eyes, for how else was he to convince the public and the legislature that central control was necessary, that methods of instruction had to be changed, that Normal Schools for teachers were needed? But all of this had undermined and eroded public confidence in Massachusetts teachers. And so, the Boston Masters, who took considerable pride in their schools, decided to issue a full-scale critique of Mann's report. They knew that continued silence on their part would be taken by the public as an admission that Mann was right and that his criticism of them was justified. This was the genesis of that remarkable document known as *Remarks on the Seventh Annual Report.*

In reality, this was the first formal, organized attack on "progressive" education ever to be made by traditionalist American educators. Henceforth, it would polarize American educators into two distinct groups with opposing philosophies of education: the "progressives," who viewed public education primarily as a tool for social and cultural reform to be achieved through the remaking of human nature; and the traditionalists, who viewed education, public or private, primarily as a development of an individual's intellectual skills in combination with moral instruction based on Judeo-Christian ideals.

Mann also used the Seventh Annual Report to promote the idea of an American public educational system patterned after the Prussian model. There were still many Americans who resisted the idea, because they saw it as a threat to freedom. But Mann tried to convince them otherwise. He wrote:

> If Prussia can pervert the benign influences of education to the support of arbitrary power, we surely can employ them for the support and perpetuation of republican institutions. A national spirit of liberty can be cultivated more easily than a national spirit of bondage; and if it may be made one of the great prerogatives of education to perform the unnatural and

unholy work of making slaves, then surely it must be one of the noblest instrumentalities for rearing a nation of freemen. If a moral power over the understandings and affections of the people may be turned to evil, may it not also be employed for good?[1]

It was the argument that the end justified the means, that centralized education could promote the idea of freedom, when in reality it would promote the idea of national conformity. On the matter of compulsory attendance, which was also a part of the Prussian system, Mann wrote:

A very erroneous idea prevails with us, that the enforcement of school attendance is the prerogative of despotism alone. I believe it is generally supposed here, that such compulsion is not merely incompatible with, but impossible in, a free or elective government. This is a great error.[2]

Mann argued, in essence, that if you voluntarily voted away your freedom, you were still free! He even believed that the highly centralized, compulsory Prussian system would promote freedom in Prussia itself. Looking into the future, he wrote:

No one who witnesses that quiet, noiseless development of mind which is now going forward, in Prussia, through the agency of its educational institutions, can hesitate to predict, that the time is not far distant when the people will assert their right to a participation in their own government.[3]

Of course, history proved Mann quite wrong. The Prussian state, dominated by Hegelian statism and pantheism, became, successively, Bismarck's nationalist Germany, Kaiser Wilhelm's warfare state, the weak Weimar Republic, and finally, Hitler's totalitarian nightmare with its pre-Christian Teutonic symbolism, demented racism, and unparalleled barbarism. And through it all, the German public schools served no other purpose than to be the prime instrumentality of whoever controlled the state.

It ought to be noted at this point that the motivation of Mann, Combe, and the liberals in general on this issue was more religious than political. They had rejected Calvinism, its unjust God and unjustified view of man. They were willing to put their faith in man, his secular state, his sense of justice, provided he was educated along phrenological principles. Thus, if you set men free from the behavioral constraints of Calvinism, you had to create a centralized educational system whereby you could impose the rational constraints of natural religion. The rational secular state, run by enlightened statesmen and bureaucrats, would solve all of man's problems and eliminate poverty, ignorance, and social injustice.

But to the Boston Masters, who spent their days in the schools trying to educate real human beings, Mann's vision not only seemed unrealistic but downright dangerous. They wanted to bring Mann and the public he was arousing back down to earth, and their *Remarks on the Seventh Annual Report* was calculated to do just that. First they criticized the "literary and moral amateurs" who seemed to repudiate the idea that "experience is the best schoolmaster." They stated that there had been little opposition to the formation of the Board of Education because it was expected that the Board would work for improvement of the Common Schools. "The desire was for *improvement,* and not for *revolution,*" they stated. But revolution was what they were getting, and they described the effects of that revolution on their profession:

> Little was it expected that, by means of experiments in new doctrines and theories, much reproach would be directly or indirectly thrown upon one class of individuals, who had so long borne the burdens in the great work, for the aggrandizement of another class, who are less modest in their pretensions.

But the new measures have become matters of history. A sacrilegious hand was laid upon every thing mental, literary, and moral, that did not conform to the new light of the day. Fulminations of sarcasm and ridicule, from the lecture-room and the press, in essays and speeches, were the forebodings of the new era in the history of common schools, and in the experience of teachers. . . . All exaggerated accounts of cases in the school discipline of some teachers, and the supposed disqualifications of many others, seemed to be set forth to lessen the authority, influence, and usefulness of teachers, and give a new direction to public sentiment.[4]

The fact that the public was easily seduced by these new theories and methods made the work of the day-to-day teacher that much more difficult. The Masters were quite critical of the public's readiness to succumb to any new educational fad:

In matters of education, how vain and worthless have been spasmodic efforts and hot-bed theories, in which the projectors have disregarded experience and observation! Of such vagaries, in the first place, may be mentioned the *infant school system,* which, for a while, was the lion of its day. The fond parent, the philosopher, and the philanthropist, were equally captivated by the scintillations of infantile genius. . . .

Next came Phrenology with all of its organs and propensities, rejecting all fear, emulation, and punishments: but in this country its great champions and advocates, who required brick without giving straw, proved to be unworthy disciples of Combe and Spurzheim. They had hardly told the fame and wonders of this new science before they all fell, as in one night, into a mesmeric sleep. There have sprung up, at different times, a great variety of *monitorial* school systems, promising much, but effecting little. . . . The monitorialists proposed to give, for any number of pupils on one day, as many teachers in the next. Next, the antipodes to the monitorialist, came the *Normalist,* who thinks there will not be good schools in Massachusetts, till all the teachers shall be trained, for a course of years, in some seminary for teachers. . . . All the principals of the Normal schools, though in a high rank of scholars, were comparatively inexperienced in public school-keeping, when they entered upon their arduous work. They might easily comprehend theories and systems of instruction, and they might explain them to their pupils; but that "practice which makes perfect" can only be acquired by experience and observation amidst the responsible duties of teaching under a variety of circumstances, that can never be really understood in a model school of thirty very young children. . . .

It is believed no little injustice has been done to the general character of teachers, by those who have been over-anxious for the reputation and success of the Normal schools.[5]

The Boston Masters were not at all pleased with what was going on in the Normal schools, and they quoted from the writings of several Normal school principals, commenting: "It is hard to conceive of any thing more *radical* and less *conservative*, than such views, when considered in connection with the administration of all the institutions of New England, during the last two centuries. Nothing can be more at war with approved principles."

And because the Normal schools were state institutions, they were even more dangerous, according to the Boston Masters:

The State seal gives these new doctrines an importance and consideration with some persons, which otherwise they might not possess. The public mind has been so far poisoned, that great distrust is felt in all teachers of the *old* school. . . .

By visionary notions of untried theories, and hearsay and false testimony respecting the general conservative practices of two hundred years, and by an esprit du corps characteristic of all violent reforms, much mischief has been effected, and much good prevented.[6]

The *Remarks* were quite specific in their criticism of Mann's Report. One section analyzed in detail the "Prussian Modes of Instruction'' as reported and praised by Mann; another section, entitled "Modes of Teaching Children to Read," was a thorough critique of the new wholeword method of beginning reading instruction being promoted by Mann, Cyrus Peirce, and others in the Normal schools; and a final section was devoted to the controversial subject of School Discipline. The Boston Masters, aware of the seriousness of their attack, had overlooked nothing and covered all bases. As heralding a conservative counteroffensive, it was indeed a solid piece of work, summing up quite neatly for the future historian the conservative academic position of the time. But would it be enough to change the course of things?

In a letter to George Combe, dated December 1, 1844, Mann described the affair:

My Report caused a great stir among the Boston teachers: I mean those of the grammar-schools. The very things in the Report which made it acceptable to others made it hateful to them. The general reader was delighted with the idea of intelligent, gentlemanly teachers; of a mind-expanding education; of children governed by moral means. The leading men among the Boston grammar-school masters saw their own condemnation in this description of their European contemporaries, and resolved, as a matter of self-preservation, to keep out the infection of so fatal an example as was afforded by the Prussian schools. The better members dissuaded, remonstrated, resisted; but they are combined together, and feel that in union is their only strength. The evil spirit prevailed. A committee was appointed to consider my Report. A part of the labor fell into the worst hands. After working on the task all summer, they sent forth, on the 1st of September, a pamphlet of a hundred and forty-four pages, which I send you, and leave you to judge of its character. I was then just finishing my Annual Abstract, a copy of which I send you, and which I commend to your attention for its extraordinary merits. As soon as the preparation of the Abstract was complete, which was my *recreation* during the hot days of summer, I wrote a "Reply to the Boston

Masters.'' In this Reply, you will see of how much service your letter and others have been to me. . . .

I think the Reply is doing something in Boston. All except the ultra-orthodox papers are earnest, I may almost say vehement, against the masters. I ought to have said that one of the masters, William J. Adams, Esq., came out in the newspapers with a public retraction, and disavowal of his signature.[7]

Mann's *Reply to the Remarks* was a masterful blend of wounded indignation and savage sarcasm. He condemned the *Remarks* as an outrage and accused ''the Thirty-One,'' as he labeled them, of misrepresenting him, quoting him out of context, and insulting his intelligence. And for a while it looked as if the Reply would make short shrift of the conservative counteroffensive. But the Boston Masters were not to be so easily quashed. Despite divided public opinion and the tremendous prestige of Mann and his highly placed backers, who came quickly to his rescue, the Masters knew that they had no choice but to defend sound educational principles based on long practice and experience, or else go down in history exactly as Mann had characterized them. And so they put together a *Rejoinder to the Reply* of some 215 pages, and proved by exhaustive and accurate documentation that they had indeed not misrepresented Mann. The Masters also sought to arouse public sympathy by describing the difficulty of their task in attempting to counter Mann's flowery eloquence and polemical cleverness with their bare facts. They wrote:

. . . They feel that theirs is an ungrateful task. They are called on to speak in their dull tones, to those whose ears have listened to the sweet voice of music; to hold up the graceless and naked forms of facts, to those whose eyes have feasted on visions of fairy splendor. From sentiments which have been sent forth glowing with the beauty of the Secretary's peculiar eloquence, they must strip off their fair attire, and present them once more in the uninteresting aspect of sober reality. They must pluck away the graceful flowers of rhetoric whenever they are not woven around the brow of truth, and bare the deformity which their charms concealed. These are some of the difficulties which must attend their labors.[8]

The *Rejoinder* was published in March 1845. It, too, required a response from Mann who then wrote an *Answer to the Rejoinder* of 124 pages. In it Mann ridiculed the Masters mercilessly, calling the *Rejoinder* "solid pages of defamation and vindictiveness!" He also reported, with great delight, that the *Remarks* had backfired on its authors. The Harvard-Unitarian elite had been so repelled by the philosophy of education expressed by the Boston Masters that they organized a fund whereby two more Normal Schools might be built with matching funds from the state. In addition, by 1845, the Board of Education was composed of more Trinitarian Protestants than Unitarians, and they viewed a centralized public education system as the only means of neutralizing the growing Catholic influx. Edward G. Loring, Mann's old school friend who now served on the Boston School Committee, reported in 1846 "that it is a matter of daily remark, that immigration is constantly countervailing the Puritan leaven of our people, and reducing the scale of public morality and public intelligence." Only the public schools could save Protestant society.

The Stowe-Mann alliance between liberal Trinitarians and liberal Unitarians had left the uncompromising orthodox out in the cold. Thus, after the publication of Mann's *Answer to the Rejoinder*, the Boston Masters found themselves quite isolated, with virtually no public support other than that of a few orthodox publications. But they were a tenacious lot and fired one last salvo with a title that reflected their own wry humor and independent spirit in defeat: *Penitential Tears; or A Cry From the Dust, by "The Thirty-One," Prostrated and Pulverized by the Hand of Horace Mann.* Its fifty-nine pages carried one of the most eloquent and impassioned defenses of traditional or conservative educational principles ever written. The opening paragraph summed up the results of the controversy:

The castigation which Mr. Mann, with equal candor and truth, has inflicted upon us, shall not be without its salutary effects. It is good for us to be afflicted; if in the insolence of prosperity, we have ventured to question the infallibility of one who seems born to dictate, and whose sacred authority may overbear, when it cannot enlighten, we shall, in our affliction, take a wiser course. We are conquered; we are prostrate; we confess it. For if we measure the degree of our humiliation by the motives of our conqueror, we know not that we shall ever be able to rise again. Yet the wretched privilege is allowed to the most abject beings, to complain; and we have the Honorable Secretary's own authority, for believing that he is a man of such philanthropy, such meekness, such generosity, his heart so leaps into his mouth, at the very suggestion of a plan of benevolence, or the prospect of doing good, that his placability will, no doubt, pardon us, when he sees us subdued, and weeping—prostrate at this feet;—*at least all of us but one.*[9]

Then they asked:

What is our offense? . . . The truth is, that we have ventured, very respectfully, to question the wisdom of certain innovations, which, in any other age than the present, would have been discarded as too absurd even for thought or deliberation. . . . It should be remembered too, that the innovations were exceedingly radical: they went to change the foundations of our system. All coercive authority was to be expelled from our schools; emulation was to be discarded; text books were undervalued; solitary study was to give place to almost perpetual recitation; the innocence of human nature was assumed; and all children, good, bad, and indifferent, were to be led along by cords of love; a religion was to be taught definite enough for a child to understand it; and yet neither Jewish, Pagan, Mahometan, or Christian; or if the name of Christianity was admitted, it was to consist of no definite truths, (for these had all been disputed and were therefore sectarian,) but it was to be a *general* Christianity, so weakened and diluted, that infidels might believe, and sensualists applaud it. . . .

In Mr. Mann's benevolence, education ceases to be a task to the pupil; all the burden is put upon the teacher; no hill of difficulty is to meet the young pilgrim; he is to be surrounded with clouds of incense, and to tread on softness and flowers; the innate love of knowledge is to be his sole stimulus, sufficient to arm him against all difficulties, and to incite him to all the industry he needs.[10]

Again, the Masters appealed for public understanding:

The public need not to be told that the duties of a practical schoolmaster are exceedingly onerous. It is all a long dreary march up hill. Let schemers say what they will, the task of putting true knowledge into the early mind, is slow, toilsome, unostentatious and discouraging. . . .

In these unappreciated duties, in which, as Johnson says, "every man that has ever undertaken the task, can tell what slow advances he has been able to make, and how much patience it requires to recall vagrant inattention, to stimulate sluggish indifference, and to rectify absurd misapprehension," in these duties a man needs all the sympathy of an enlightened community. He certainly does not wish to see them infected with false theories, and taught to indulge in impossible expectations. What can be more calculated to move a poor schoolmaster's indignation, when he is toiling alone to row his frail canoe against wind and tide—few to visit and none to pity him—than to hear of an itinerant philosopher, going from Dan to Beersheba to teach the people to make demands that none can gratify, and to form hopes that must be disappointed. The merchant hates the pedler, and the physician the quack, and all men *ought* to hate popular delusion. In the meantime, while our task is increased by enormous exaggeration, our accustomed implements are taken from our hands. We must burn our rods; we must use no emulation; we must discard our text books; we must interest the dull, the thoughtless and the lazy; we must make labor as light as recreation. We must throw away the alphabet, and then teach children the power of letters; we must work impossible wonders; and all this to prove that education is an advancing science, and that seven annual reports have not been made in vain.[11]

The Masters then offered some ageless advice:

. . . These soft and silken reformers who wish to smooth the passes to knowledge, and make a world for the young which God has never made, would only spoil the rising generation, supposing they could carry their plans into execution. A wise man devoutly thanks God that the price of knowledge is labor, and that when we buy the truth, we must pay the price. If you wish to enjoy the prospect at the mountain's summit, you must climb its rugged sides. . . .

Perhaps the place where Mr. Mann's theories are best carried out is among the Indians. There we can easily imagine, that the instinctive love of such knowledge as they teach is adequate to all the purposes of education. They never whip their children, (any more than they do at the Lexington Normal School,) never stimulate their emulation by setting before them the high prizes of life; never mortify their vanity, and never teach them the alphabet; they are taught *things* not *words;* how to entrap the deer; how to cast the tomahawk; and, we have no doubt, the process of education is all smooth and delightful.

But, pray, is this facility owing to their superior wisdom, or a deplorable want of conceptions of the high objects after which an immortal and intellectual being should strive? . . .

. . . The effect of the modern schemes must be to dwarf the intellect; if it is always delightful for a boy to learn, he will of course only learn what is delightful.[12]

The Masters also reviewed the wisdom of centralized power in education, and referred back to the attempt in 1840 to abolish the Board of Education:

There was an able report made in the Legislature, written by

Hon. Allen W. Dodge, in which the claims of the board were powerfully contested, and some strong arguments used to prove it was positively pernicious. His view, if we recollect aright, was, that the character of New England had always been to lean on no central power; the diffusion of her intelligence was the foundation of her strength. When Great Britain took away the charter of Massachusetts in the commencement of the Revolution, the reason why she did not fall into anarchy was, the little republics, called towns, were every where diffused; an organization existed, strongly fixed and widely spread, which saved us from the horrors our enemies designed for us; that on these towns, and on their officers, rested and must rest mainly the great responsibility in improving education; they were near; a central power would be remote; and however we might select an agent to design and invent for us, the toil and care, the detail and conflict, must be with the school committee and instructers; that even if not so, the very habit of looking to some concentrated point would be pernicious; it would relax our vigilance and impair our strength, just as a limb, swathed in bandages and suspended in a sling, becomes impaired in its vigor by remitting its activity.[13]

The Masters preferred the republic of self-governing communities to the centralized state power that Mann was creating in the name of educational reform. Let it not be said that American resistance to centralized public education was not profoundly philosophical, realistic, spirited, and prophetic. And let it not be said that the opponents of centralized education were opposed to sound education. On the contrary. The Masters made that clear when they wrote:

Education is a great concern; it has often been tampered with by vain theorists; it has suffered much from the stupid folly and the delusive wisdom of its treacherous friends; and we hardly know which have injured it most. Our conviction is, that it has much more to hope from the collected wisdom and common prudence of the community, than from the suggestions of the individual. Locke injured it by his theories, and so did Rousseau, and so did Milton. All their plans were too splendid to be true. It is to be advanced by conceptions, neither soaring above the clouds, nor grovelling on the earth,—but by those plain, gradual, productive, common-sense improvements, which use may encourage and experience suggest. We are in favor of advancement, provided it be towards usefulness. . . .

We have uttered our testimony—we have spoken in earnest but not in anger. We love the Secretary, but we hate his theories. They stand in the way of all substantial education. It is impossible for a sound mind not to hate them. Every good man will hate them, in proportion as he reverences truth and loves mankind. We hope to see them laid as low in the dust *as we are*.[14]

Despite all of the arguments and eloquence of the Masters, the cause of educational statism was now stronger than ever. In March 1845, the Massachusetts Legislature voted to appropriate $5,000 in matching funds to the $5,000 raised by Mann's Harvard-Unitarian friends to build two additional Normal Schools, one at Westfield and one at Bridgewater. Mann's friends had proposed that liberal Unitarians Ralph Waldo Emerson and Theodore Parker be the speakers at the dedicatory ceremonies in September 1846, but Mann vetoed the idea, knowing that this would needlessly provoke the orthodox. Instead, he chose Rev. Heman Humphrey, the most influential orthodox member of the Board of Education, to do the honors. Only by dividing the opposition could Mann insure the future of the Board of Education.

In describing the dedication ceremony in the October 1, 1846, issue of the *Common School Journal*, Mann emphasized the importance of the state grants that made these schools possible. Then he wrote:

But what constituted the crowning circumstance of the whole was, that the Legislature, in making the grant, changed the title or designation of the schools. In all previous reports, laws, and resolves, they had been called "Normal Schools." But by the resolves for the erection of the new houses, it was provided that these schools should thereafter be known and designated as *State* Normal Schools,—the State thus giving to them a paternal name, as the sign of adoption, and the pledge of its affection.

To Mann, who believed the Normal School to be "a new instrumentality in the advancement of the race," the linking of state power to teacher education was indeed a crowning circumstance, creating what James G. Carter had described in 1825 as a powerful "engine to sway the public sentiment, the public morals, and the public religion, more powerful than any other in the possession of government." And once a nation's teachers' colleges become the primary vehicle through which the philosophy of statism is advanced, this philosophy will very soon infect every other quarter of society, for the most potent and significant expression of statism is a state educational system. Without it, statism is impossible. With it, the state can and has become everything.

Postscript

AFTER MORE THAN a hundred years of universal public education, we can say that it nowhere resembles the utopian vision that drove its proponents to create it. It has not produced the morally improved human being the Unitarians insisted it would, nor has it changed human nature in the way the Owenites predicted. (Ironically, one of the public school's biggest problems today is the physical safety of its teachers!) It has turned education into a quagmire of conflicting interests, ideologies, and purposes, and created a bureaucracy that permits virtually no real learning to take place. Nonsectarian education has become secular humanist indoctrination, as biased in its worldview against religion as Calvinism was in its favor. The Catholics were aware enough to see what it would all lead to and bolted the public school rather than accept the destruction of their faith. As for the Normal Schools, they have blossomed into state teachers' colleges that cannot produce competent instructors in basic academic skills. The whole experiment has been a colossal failure.

As for Hegelian statism, which was to prove how good and just man could be once liberated from the restraints of outmoded religion, it has, instead, produced statist tyrannies and rivalries the likes of which the human race has never seen and brought humanity to the brink of its own self-annihilation.

The only bright spot in the whole picture is the technological wonder that capitalism has brought to mankind through the very individual, competitive system that Owen railed against and Channing deplored. Neither liberal altruism, nor universal public education, nor socialism lifted the poor from their lower depths. Capitalism did.

Is public education necessary? The answer is obvious: it was not needed then, and it is certainly not needed today. Schools are necessary, but they can be created by free enterprise today as they were before the public school movement achieved its fraudulent state monopoly in education. Subject education to the same competitive market forces that other goods and services are subjected to, and we shall see far better education at much lower overall cost. Instead of a "crusade against ignorance" to reform the world, we shall have schools capable of performing the limited and practical functions that schools were originally created to perform.

The failure of public education is the failure of statism as a political philosophy. It has been tried. It has been found sorely wanting. Having learned from our mistakes, would it not be better to return to the basic principles upon which this nation was founded? Education was not seen then as the cure-all for mankind's moral diseases. But it was on that premise that the reformers built the present system. They were wrong. The system cannot work because in a free society government has no more place in education than it has in religion. Once Americans grasp the full significance of this idea, they will understand why the return of educational freedom is essential to the preservation and expansion of American freedom in general.

Notes

CHAPTER ONE

1. Source for these statistics is the National Center for Educational Statistics, U. S. Department of Health, Education & Welfare as published in *The World Almanac and Book of Facts 1980* (New York: Newspaper Enterprise Association, Inc., 1980). In 1980 Public School enrollment was 40,984,093, number of teachers was 2,183,500, and total expenditures was $95,961,561,000.

CHAPTER TWO

1. Williston Walker, *John Calvin* (New York: Shocken Books, Inc., 1969), p. 270.
2. John Calvin, *Institutes of the Christian Religion*, Vol. 2 (Grand Rapids: Wm. B. Eerdmans Publishing Co., 1972), pp. 652-3.
3. *Ibid.*, p. 457.
4. *Ibid.*, p. 675.
5. Urian Oakes quoted in Thomas J. Wertenbaker, *The Puritan Oligarchy* (New York: Charles A. Scribner's Sons), p. 218.
6. John Calvin, *op. cit.*, p. 453.
7. Perry Miller and Thomas H. Johnson, editors, *The Puritans: A Sourcebook of Their Writings* (New York: Harper & Row, 1938).

8. Lawrence A. Cremin, *American Education: The Colonial Experience 1607-1783* (New York: Harper & Row, 1970), p. 544.
9. *North American Review,* July 1848, p. 241.

CHAPTER THREE

1. John Calvin, *Concerning the Eternal Predestination of God* (London: 1961), p. 155.
2. Arthur W. Brown, *William Ellery Channing* (New York: Twayne Publishers, Inc., 1961), p. 27.
3. *Ibid,* p. 23.
4. Jack Mendelsohn, *Channing: The Reluctant Radical* (Boston: Little, Brown, 1971), pp. 42–43.
5. Russel B. Nye, *George Bancroft: Brahmin Rebel* (New York: A. A. Knopf, 1944), p. 18.
6. David B. Tyack, *George Ticknor and the Boston Brahmins* (Cambridge: Harvard University Press, 1967), p. 85.
7. Hugh Pollard, *Pioneers of Popular Education 1760–1850* (Cambridge: Harvard University Press, 1957).
8. Robert Owen, *The Life of Robert Owen Written by Himself* (London: 1857), p. 16.
9. *Ibid,* p. 57.
10. *Ibid,* pp. 59–60.
11. *Ibid,* pp. 139–40.
12. Robert Owen, *A New View of Society or Essays on the Formation of the Human Character* (London: 1816; Clifton, N.J.: Augustus M. Kelley Publishers, 1972), pp. 149–50.
13. Robert Owen, *The Life of Robert Owen Written by Himself, op. cit.,* p. 134.
14. *Ibid,* pp. 110-11.
15. A detailed account of the campaign to establish primary public schools in Boston is given in Stanley K. Schultz, *The Culture Factory* (New York: Oxford University Press, 1973), pp. 30–43.
16. *American Journal of Education,* 1826, p.494.

CHAPTER FOUR

1. Jack Mendelsohn, *op. cit.,* p.158
2. William Ellery Channing, "Unitarian Christianity, A Dis-

course on Some of the Distinguishing Opinions of Unitarianism" in *Three Prophets of Religious Liberalism* (Boston: Beacon Press, 1961).

3. Edward A. Dowey, Jr., *The Knowledge of God in Calvin's Theology* (New York: Columbia University Press, 1952), p. 37.
4. John Calvin, *Concerning the Eternal Predestination of God* (London: 1961), p. 123.
5. *Ibid*, p. 14.
6. *Ibid*, p. 58.
7. *Ibid*, p. 63.
8. *Ibid*, pp. 68–69.
9. Jack Mendelsohn, *op. cit.*, p. 168.
10. *Ibid*, p.186–187
11. *North American Review*, April 1824, p. 285.
12. *North American Review*, January 1824, p. 159.
13. Samuel Eliot Morison, *Three Centuries of Harvard* (Cambridge: Harvard University Press, 1936), p. 244.
14. James G. Carter, *Letters to the Hon. William Prescott, LLD. on The Free Schools of New England with remarks upon the principles of instruction* (Boston: 1824), p. 51.
15. *Ibid*, p. 34.
16. James G. Carter quoted in *Memoirs of Teachers, Educators, and Promoters and Benefactors of Education, Literature, and Science*, Vol. 1, Edited by Henry Barnard, LL.D. (New York: F. C. Brownell, 1859), p. 189.
17. James G. Carter, "Outline of an Institution for the Education of Teachers," *Essays on Popular Education* (Boston, 1826), pp. 47–51. Reprinted in *Education in the United States, A Documentary History*, Vol. 3, Edited by Sol Cohen (New York: Random House, 1974), pp. 1304–5.
18. "Improvement of Common Schools," *North American Review*, January 1827. Although the article is unsigned, Ticknor's authorship is affirmed in *Memoirs of Teachers, Educators, etc.* (see note 16), p. 188.
19. "Improvement of Common Schools," Article X, *North American Review*, January 1827, pp. 156–57.
20. *Ibid*, pp. 161, 166.
21. *Ibid*, p. 169.

CHAPTER FIVE

1. Robert Dale Owen, *Threading My Way* (New York: Carleton & Co., 1874; New York: A. M. Kelley, 1967).
2. *The New-Harmony Gazette,* April 23, 1828.
3. John R. Commons and others, editors, *A Documentary History of American Industrial Society* (Cleveland: A. H. Clark Co., 1910–11).
4. Orestes A. Brownson, *The Convert* in *The Works of Orestes A. Brownson,* collected and arranged by Henry F. Brownson (New York: AMS Press Inc., 1966), Vol. V, p. 63.
5. *The Free Enquirer,* December 5, 1829.
6. Frances Wright, *Popular Tracts by Robert Dale Owen and Others: to which is Added: Fables by Frances Wright* (New York: 1854), pp. 9–10.
7. Robert Owen, *The Life of Robert Owen, op. cit.,* p. 207.
8. *Ibid,* p. 210.
9. John R. Commons, *op. cit.,* Vol. V, p. 95.
10. *Ibid,* p. 160.
11. *Ibid,* p. 108.
12. *Ibid,* p. 109.
13. *Ibid,* p. 112.
14. *Ibid.*

CHAPTER SIX

1. Orestes A. Brownson in *The Works of Orestes A. Brownson, op. cit.,* Vol. XIX, pp. 442–43.
2. *William Barton Rogers, Life and Letters* (Boston: Houghton, Mifflin, 1896) Vol. 1, p. 69.
3. Robert Owen, *The Book of the New Moral World* (London: 1836), pp. iv, 2, 35, 42, 43, 50, 60, 61.

CHAPTER SEVEN

1. Orestes A. Brownson, *The Convert, op. cit.,* p. 62.
2. George Browning Lockwood, *The New Harmony Com-*

munities (Marion, Ind.: 1902). Lockwood writes: "Maclure put $150,000 into the New Harmony experiment. The avowed intention of Maclure was to make New Harmony the center of American education."

3. Robert Dale Owen, *Threading My Way*, op. cit., p. 267.
4. William Lucas Sargant, *Robert Owen and His Social Philosophy* (London: 1860), p. 203.
5. George P. Fisher, *Life of Benjamin Silliman* (New York: Scribner & Co., 1866).
6. John Griscom, *A Year in Europe* (New York: 1823), pp. 379, 386, 392.
7. *American Annals of Education*, September 1, 1832, p. 443.
8. For a detailed account of the origin and significance of Gallaudet's whole-word method of reading instruction, see Samuel L. Blumenfeld, *The New Illiterates* (New Rochelle: Arlington House, Inc., 1973).

CHAPTER EIGHT

1. Jules Simon, *Victor Cousin*, translated by M. B. Anderson and E. P. Anderson (Chicago: 1888).
2. Ralph L. Rusk, *The Life of Ralph Waldo Emerson* (New York: Columbia University Press, 1949), p. 160.
3. Victor Cousin, *Introduction to the History of Philosophy*, translated from the French by Henning Gotfried Linberg (Boston: 1832), p. 189.
4. Jules Simon, *op. cit.*, p. 49.
5. Victor Cousin, *op. cit.*, p. 339.
6. Article on Johann Eichhorn (1752–1827) in J. Fr. Michaud, *Biographie Universelle, Ancienne et Moderne* (Graz: Akademische Druck-u. Verlagsanstalt, 1967), Vol. XII, pp. 321–22.
7. "Transcendentalism," *Princeton Review*, January 1839, p. 66; "The Latest Form of Infidelity," *Princeton Review*, 1840, p. 79.
8. *Ibid*, p. 90.
9. Karl Marx, Frederick Engels, *Collected Works*, Vol. 2 (New York: International Publishers, 1975), pp. 489–90.

10. Victor Cousin, *op. cit.*, p. 303.
11. *Ibid*, p. 307.
12. *Ibid*, p. 308.
13. *Ibid*, p. 343.
14. Victor Cousin, *Report on the State of Public Instruction in Prussia* (New York: 1835), pp. 23, 24.
15. *Ibid*, pp. 25–29.
16. John Albree, *Charles Brooks and his work for Normal Schools* (Medford: 1907), pp. 16–17.
17. Calvin Stowe, *The Prussian System of Public Instruction and its Applicability to the United States* (Cincinnati: 1836).

CHAPTER NINE

1. Mary Tyler Peabody Mann, *Life of Horace Mann* (Boston: 1888), p. 13.
2. Jonathan Messerli, *Horace Mann* (New York: A. A. Knopf, 1972), p. 20.
3. *Ibid*, p. 23.
4. *Ibid*, pp. 58–59.
5. *Ibid*, p. 171.

CHAPTER TEN

1. Mary Mann, *Life of Horace Mann*, *op. cit.*, p. 70.
2. *Ibid*, p. 72.
3. *Ibid*, p. 75.
4. *Ibid*, p. 78.
5. *Ibid*, p. 80.
6. *Ibid*.
7. *Memoir of William Ellery Channing with Extracts from his Correspondence and Manuscripts* (Boston: 1848), III, p. 89.
8. *First Annual Report of the Secretary of the Board of Education, Common School Journal*, Vol. 1, Nos. 16 and 17.
9. Mary Mann, *op. cit.*, pp. 67–68.
10. Abram Combe, *The Religious Creed of the New System* (Edinburgh: 1824).

11. *Ibid.*, pp. 30, 38.
12. *Ibid*, p. 20.
13. Robert Owen, *The New Religion; or, Religion founded on the immutable Laws of the Universe, contrasted with all Religions founded on Human Testimony* (London: 1830), p. 9.
14. Charles Gibbon, *Life of George Combe* (London: Macmillan & Co., 1878), pp. 379–80.
15. *Ibid*, p. 60.
16. George Combe, *The Constitution of Man* (Boston: 1835), p. 10.
17. *Ibid*, p. 13.
18. Charles Gibbon, *op. cit.*, p. 308.
19. *Ibid*, p. 356.
20. *Ibid*, p. 65.
21. Mary Mann, *op. cit.*, pp. 112–13.
22. Charles Gibbon, *op. cit.*, p. 283.
23. *Common School Journal*, Vol. 3, No. 1, January 1841, p. 15.

CHAPTER ELEVEN

1. *Common School Journal*, Vol. 1, No. 13, July 1, 1839, p. 193.
2. James Carter, "Outline of an Institution for the Education of Teachers," reprinted in *The First State Normal School in America*, With an Introduction by Arthur O. Norton (Cambridge: Harvard University Press, 1926).
3. *Common School Journal*, Vol. IX, No. 1, January 1, 1847, p. 4.
4. *Common School Journal*, Vol. 1, No. 9, May 1, 1839, p. 144.
5. *Ibid.*
6. *Common School Journal*, July 1, 1839, p. 198.
7. *Common School Journal*, Vol. 1, No. 14, July 15, 1839, p. 216.
8. *Common School Journal*, Vol. 1, No. 4, February 15, 1839, p. 56.
9. Remarks in the House of Representatives by Allen W. Dodge, March 18, 1840, *Common School Journal*, Vol. 2, No. 15, August 1, 1840, pp. 226–27.
10. *Ibid*, p. 228.
11. *Ibid*, pp. 228–29.

12. *Ibid.*
13. Minority Report by John A. Shaw and Thomas A. Greene, *Common School Journal*, Vol. 2, No. 15, August 1, 1840, p. 230.
14. *Ibid*, p. 232.
15. Calvin Stowe, *op. cit.*
16. Mary Mann, *op. cit.*, p. 161.
17. *Ibid*, p. 155.

CHAPTER TWELVE

1. Horace Mann, *Seventh Annual Report of the Secretary of the Massachusetts Board of Education* (Boston: 1844), p. 23.
2. *Ibid*, p. 148.
3. *Ibid*, p. 159.
4. Association of the Masters of the Public Schools, *Remarks on the Seventh Annual Report of the Hon. Horace Mann, Secretary of the Massachusetts Board of Education* (Boston: Charles C. Little and James Brown, 1844), pp. 6–7. The section of the *Remarks* devoted to the reading-instruction dispute is reprinted in full in Samuel L. Blumenfeld, *The New Illiterates* (New Rochelle: Arlington House, 1973), pp. 315–351.
5. *Ibid*, pp. 8–9.
6. *Ibid*, p. 17.
7. Mary Mann, *op. cit.*, pp. 231–32.
8. Association of the Masters of the Public Schools, *Rejoinder to the "Reply" of the Hon. Horace Mann . . . to the "Remarks" of the Association of Boston Masters upon his Seventh Annual Report* (Boston: 1845).
9. Association of Boston Masters, *Penitential Tears; or A Cry From the Dust, By "The Thirty-One," Prostrated and Pulverized By The Hand Of Horace Mann, Secretary, Etc.* (Boston: C. Stimpson, 1845), p. 2.
10. *Ibid*, pp. 7–8.
11. *Ibid*, pp. 11–12.
12. *Ibid*, pp. 17, 23, 24.
13. *Ibid*, p. 51.
14. *Ibid*, pp. 56–57.

Index

Is Public Education Necessary?
by Samuel L. Blumenfeld

"brilliant revisionist history" Fortune Magazine
September 1983

ORDER NOW! — CALL (208) 322-4440

SEND ME:

BOOKS By Samuel L. Blumenfeld:

☐ **How to Tutor** $11.95
(You need to know how to in today's world)

☐ **Is Public Education Necessary?** $9.95
(Learn the answer to this vital question)

☐ **NEA: Trojan Horse in American Education** $9.95
(The first full length expose of the N.E.A.)

☐ **Alpha Phonics: A Primer for Beginning Readers** $21.95
(You can easily teach your own children good reading & writing the proper way)

☐ **The Blumenfeld Education Letter** .... (quarterly) $9.00
(a monthly newsletter which assists parents in tutoring their children, evaluating their schools, texts, and curricula, and generally assuring that their children actually become educated)

☐ **Guilty of Love** by Ed and Sharon Pangelinan $9.95
(Parents jailed 132 days for love of God, their children and country)

Copies of these books may be ordered by simply filling out the form below and returning to The Paradigm Co., Box 45161, Boise, ID 83711.

Add $1.50 Delivery. For larger quantity discounts please inquire at (208) 322-4440.

Please send me: The books checked above.

Mailing Address (Please Print)

Name _____

Street _____

City _____ State _____ Zip _____

Phone No. _____

ORDER NOW!

Checks may be made payable to
The Paradigm Co.
P.O. Box 45161— Boise, Idaho 83711

Enclosed is my check for $_____
Charge my: VISA ☐   Master Card ☐
Credit Card Number (all digits)

Exp. Date _____

FOR FASTER SERVICE...MASTERCARD OR VISA HOLDERS
CALL (208) 322-4440
24 HOURS — 7 DAYS

Is Public Education Necessary?
by Samuel L. Blumenfeld

"brilliant revisionist history" Fortune Magazine
September 1983

ORDER NOW! — CALL (208) 322-4440

SEND ME:

BOOKS By Samuel L. Blumenfeld:

☐ **How to Tutor**.. $11.95
(You need to know how to in today's world)
☐ **Is Public Education Necessary?**.. $9.95
(Learn the answer to this vital question)
☐ **NEA: Trojan Horse in American Education**.. $9.95
(The first full length expose of the N.E.A.)
☐ **Alpha Phonics: A Primer for Beginning Readers**.. $21.95
(You can easily teach your own children good reading & writing the proper way)
☐ **The Blumenfeld Education Letter** .... (quarterly) $9.00
(a monthly newsletter which assists parents in tutoring their children, evaluating their schools, texts,
and curricula, and generally assuring that their children actually become educated)

☐ **Guilty of Love** by Ed and Sharon Pangelinan... $9.95
(Parents jailed 132 days for love of God, their children and country)

Copies of these books may be ordered by simply filling out the form below and returning to The Paradigm Co.,
Box 45161, Boise, ID 83711.

Add $1.50 Delivery. For larger quantity discounts please inquire at (208) 322-4440.

Please send me: The books checked above.

Mailing Address (Please Print)

Name _____

Street _____

City _____ State _____ Zip _____

Phone No. _____

ORDER NOW!

Checks may be made payable to
The Paradigm Co.
P.O. Box 45161— Boise, Idaho 83711

Enclosed is my check for $_____
Charge my: VISA ☐ Master Card ☐
Credit Card Number (all digits)

Exp. Date _____

FOR FASTER SERVICE...MASTERCARD OR VISA HOLDERS
CALL (208) 322-4440
24 HOURS — 7 DAYS

Is Public Education Necessary?
by Samuel L. Blumenfeld

"brilliant revisionist history" Fortune Magazine September 1983

ORDER NOW! — CALL (208) 322-4440

SEND ME:

BOOKS By Samuel L. Blumenfeld:

☐ **How to Tutor**.. $11.95
(You need to know how to in today's world)

☐ **Is Public Education Necessary?**... $9.95
(Learn the answer to this vital question)

☐ **NEA: Trojan Horse in American Education**... $9.95
(The first full length expose of the N.E.A.)

☐ **Alpha Phonics: A Primer for Beginning Readers**...................................... $21.95
(You can easily teach your own children good reading & writing the proper way)

☐ **The Blumenfeld Education Letter** ....(quarterly) $9.00
(a monthly newsletter which assists parents in tutoring their children, evaluating their schools, texts, and curricula, and generally assuring that their children actually become educated)

☐ **Guilty of Love** by Ed and Sharon Pangelinan.. $9.95
(Parents jailed 132 days for love of God, their children and country)

Copies of these books may be ordered by simply filling out the form below and returning to The Paradigm Co., Box 45161, Boise, ID 83711.

Add $1.50 Delivery. For larger quantity discounts please inquire at (208) 322-4440.

Please send me: The books checked above.

Mailing Address (Please Print)

Name _____

Street _____

City _____ State _____ Zip _____

Phone No. _____

ORDER NOW!

Checks may be made payable to
The Paradigm Co.
P.O. Box 45161— Boise, Idaho 83711

Enclosed is my check for $_____
Charge my: VISA ☐ Master Card ☐
Credit Card Number (all digits)

Exp. Date _____

FOR FASTER SERVICE...MASTERCARD OR VISA HOLDERS
☎ CALL (208) 322-4440
24 HOURS — 7 DAYS